Global justice networks

Manchester University Press

PERSPECTIVES ON DEMOCRATIC PRACTICE

Series editors: SHIRIN M. RAI and WYN GRANT

With the ebbing away of the 'third wave' of democratisation, democratic practice is unfolding and consolidating in different ways. While state based representative democracy remains central to our understanding of the concept, we are also conscious of the importance of social movements, non-governmental organisations and governance institutions. New mechanisms of accountability are being developed, together with new political vocabularies to address these elements in democratic practice. The books published in this series focus on three aspects of democratic practice: analytical and normative democratic theory, including processes by which democratic practice can be explained and achieved; new social and protest movements, especially work with a comparative and international focus; and institution-building and practice, including transformations in democratic institutions in response to social and democratic forces. Their importance arises from the fact that they are concerned with key questions about how power can be more fairly distributed and how people can be empowered to have a greater influence on decisions that affect their lives.

This series takes forward the intellectual project of the earlier MUP series, *Perspectives on Democratization.*

Already published

Global justice networks
Geographies of transnational solidarity

Paul Routledge and Andrew Cumbers

Manchester University Press

Manchester and New York

Distributed exclusively in the United States exclusively
by Palgrave Macmillan

Published by Manchester University Press
Oxford Road, Manchester M13 9NR, UK
and Room 400, 175 Fifth Avenue, New York, NY 10010, USA
www.manchesteruniversitypress.co.uk

Distributed in the United States exclusively by
Palgrave, 175 Fifth Avenue, New York,
NY 10010, USA

Distributed exclusively in Canada by
UBC Press, University of British Columbia, 2029 West Mall,
Vancouver, BC, Canada V6T 1Z2

British Library Cataloguing-in-Publication Data
A catalogue record for this book is available from
the British Library

Library of Congress Cataloging-in-Publication Data applied for

ISBN 978 0 7190 7685 5 *hardback*

First published 2009

18 17 16 15 14 13 12 11 10 09   10 9 8 7 6 5 4 3 2 1

Typeset
by Florence Production Ltd, Stoodleigh, Devon
Printed by the MPG Books Group
in the UK

Contents

List of tables

List of abbreviations

AFC	African Federation of Labour OMIT
ANPA	All Nepal Peasants Association
ANT	actor-network theory
ANWA	All Nepal Women's Association
AoP	Assembly of the Poor
APVVU	Andhra Pradesh Vyarasaya Vruthidarula Union
ATTAC	Association for the Taxation of Financial Transactions for the Aid of Citizens
BKF	Bangladesh Krishok Federation
BKU	Bharatiya Kisan Union
CLOG	Congress of Rural Organisations
CONIC	Continental Coordinating Commission of Indigenous Nations and Organisations
CPN-UML	Communist Party of Nepal (Unified Marxist-Laininst)
ESRC	Economic and Social Research Council
EZLN	Ejercito Zapatista de Liberacion Nacional (Zapatistas)
FSPI	Federation of Indonesian Peasant Union
FTAA	Free Trade Area of the Americas
GATS	General Agreement on Trade in Services
GCN	Global Company Network
GFA	Global Frame Agreement
GJM	Global Justice Movement
GJN	Global Justice Network
GUF	Global Union Federation
IC	International Council
ICEF	International Chemical and Energy Federation
ICEM	International Federation of Chemical, Energy, Mining and General Workers

ICFTU	International Confederation of Free Trade Unions
IGO	International governmental organisation
IFG	International Forum on Globalisation
IG-BCE	Industriegewerkschaft Bergbau, Chemie, Energie
IMC	Independent media centre
IMF	International Metalworkers Federation OMIT
IMF	International Mining Federation OMIT
IMF	International Monetary Fund
IMO	International Mining Organisation OMIT
INGO	International nongovernmental organisation
ITF	International Transport Workers Federation OMIT
IUF	International Union of Food and Agricultural Workers
KRRS	Karnataka Rajya Raitha Sangha
MAI	Multi-lateral Agreement on Investment
MIRA	Mississippi Immigrants Rights Association OMIT
MNC	multinational corporation
MONLAR	Movement for National Land and Agricultural Reform
MST	Morimento des Trabalhadores Rurais Sem Terra (Landless Workers' Movement)
NAFTA	North American Free Trade Agreement
NBA	Narmada Bachao Andolan (Save the Narmada Movement)
NKIF	Norwegian Chemical Workers Union
NOPEF	Norsk Olje og Petrokjemisk Fagforbund
NUM	National Union of Miners
OC	Organising Committee
OECD	Organisation for Economic Cooperation and Development
PAICE	Paper and Allied Industries, Chemical and Energy Union
PGA	People's Global Action
PT	Partido dos Trabalhaderes (Workers Party)
RMT	Rail Maritime and Transport Union
SAP	Structural Adjustment Programme
SECC	Soweto Electricity Crisis Committee
SWP	Socialist Workers Party

TGWU	Transport and General Workers Union
TNC	transnational corporation
USAS	United Students Against Sweatshops
USWA	United Steelworkers of America
WB	World Bank
WEF	World Economic Forum
WSF	World Social Forum
WTO	World Trade Organisation

Acknowledgements

We wish to thank Corinne Nativel, who was our research assistant during the fieldwork and initial writing-up of the results, for her considerable contribution to this research. We would also like to thank Prue Elletson, for research assistance at the European Social Forum in London, 2004, and Shirin Rai and Jeffery Juris for comments on an earlier draft of this book. This research was made possible through the generous support of the Economic and Social Research Council (ESRC) who funded the original research project that led to the writing of this book (RES-000–23–0528).

1
Neoliberalism and its discontents

A new global 'movement' has arisen over the past decade
to confront global capitalism. The emergence of what has
been termed the global justice movement (GJM) is the
most significant development in counter-systemic politics
(Wallerstein, 2002) since the end of the Cold War. In the
wake of the 'End of History' pronouncements (Fukuyama,
1992), celebrating the collapse of the Soviet Union and the
perceived victory of liberal democracy and market capitalism, the upsurge in global protest in response to the continuing realities of global uneven development served as a rude
awakening to capitalist elites (Tormey, 2004a). Moreover,
the genuine translocal and transnational connections that
characterise the GJM, and their global scope, are more
significant for international oppositional movements than
the Socialist Internationals of the nineteenth and twentieth
centuries or the new social movements and anti-war
movements of the 1960s. In contrast to the more sporadic
nature of past forms of transnational mobilisation, more
sustained global networks of solidarity have been established
that link up hitherto disparate local struggles to broader
movements and agendas.

The movement – according to your political standpoint –
has been variously described as: heralding the creation of
a global civil society capable of correcting a perceived democratic deficit in the new world order; posing a revolutionary
challenge to global capitalism; and constructing alternative
social and political spaces that reject the consumerism and
militarism of mainstream society (St Clair, 1999; Brecher
et al., 2000; Gill, 2000; Klein, 2000, 2002; Starr, 2000;
Bircham and Charlton, 2001; Callinicos, 2003; Kaldor, 2003;

Drainville, 2004; Tormey, 2004a). However, there remains considerable conceptual fuzziness and wishful-thinking about the GJM. In particular, there has been a lack of detailed scrutiny about its component parts, its operational networks and their dynamics, strategies and practices (but see Juris, 2004a for an exception).

Our purpose, in this book, is to argue that a single, coherent, global movement does not (yet) exist and indeed, is unlikely to exist in the form that some would envisage. Whilst the constituent parts of this 'movement' can agree on what they are against – a rapacious form of development driven by an unregulated market ethos that has come to be known as 'neoliberalism' – there are many fissures and fault-lines that divide it. A central element of this book is that these are both political and geographical. The existence of different political perspectives are important in understanding the 'movement', as is an understanding of the role of space, place and scale in shaping its operational dynamics. Indeed, we argue that the emergence of new globally-connected forms of collective action against neoliberalism are indicative of a range of variously place-specific forms of political agency that coalesce across space at particular times, in specific places in a variety of ways. To signify this, we use the term 'global justice networks' (GJNs) to characterise these emergent new forms of transnational political agency. Seeking to go beyond wishful thinking about the potentialities of these GJNs, we ground our conceptual arguments in detailed empirical investigation of three critical strands of the 'movement': a grassroots peasants' network; an international trade union network; and the Social Forum process.

In this introductory chapter, we wish to outline the contours of this phenomenon before addressing the character of GJNs in more detail in subsequent chapters. Hence, this chapter firstly considers the rise of neoliberalism as a global economic project. Second, the chapter traces the genesis of the international resistance against this project including some of the key events, for example, the 1994 declaration of the Zapatistas against the North American Free Trade Agreement (NAFTA), the global days of action against international institutions such as the World Trade Organisation (WTO), and the subsequent emergence of European and

World Social Forums. Third, the chapter considers some of the broad characteristics of this resistance. The chapter ends with an outline of subsequent chapters.

Neoliberalism as a global economic project

Neoliberalism is a theory of political economic practices that proposes the maximisation of entrepreneurial freedoms within an institutional framework characterised by private property rights, individual liberty, free markets and free trade that are essential for the advancement of human well-being. The role of the state is to establish those military, defence, police and judicial functions required to secure private property rights and to support freely functioning markets. Where markets do not exist, such as in education, health care, social security or environmental pollution, then they must be created, by state action if necessary (Harvey, 2006a). Neoliberalism privileges lean government, privatisation and deregulation, while undermining or foreclosing alternative development models based upon social redistribution, economic rights or public investment (Peck and Tickell, 2002).

On a global scale, neoliberalism is synonymous with the term 'Washington Consensus', coined in the 1990s to describe a relatively specific set of macro-economic policy prescriptions that were considered to constitute a 'standard' reform package promoted for crisis-wracked countries by Washington-based institutions such as the International Monetary Fund (IMF), World Bank (WB) and US Treasury Department. Nevertheless, neoliberal globalisation is neither monolithic nor omnipresent, taking hybrid or composite forms around the world (Larner, 2000).

David Harvey (2006a) argues that the neoliberal turn in the global economy emerged from a crisis of capital accumulation in the 1970s precipitated by the global economic recession of 1973 (that was exacerbated by the rise in oil prices in the wake of the Arab-Israeli war). This was accompanied by rising unemployment and inflation, and widespread discontent. The latter was manifested particularly in militant trade union activity in Western Europe, the United States and elsewhere, and communist and socialist party electoral gains across Western Europe. Such conditions, Harvey argues, represented both an economic and a political threat to ruling classes everywhere. Hence neoliberalism should be considered a project to re-establish the conditions for capital accumulation and the restoration of class power. This is an important point. Neoliberalism is first and foremost a political strategy for class rule. Where necessary, this means ignoring the nostrums of free market thinking if they do not deliver for ruling class interests (Harvey, 2006a). Thus, for example, states and international institutions, such as the IMF and WB, will intervene in economic crises to protect the interests of global financial centres such as Wall Street or the City of London (*ibid*).

Indeed Harvey (2003) emphasises 'accumulation by dispossession' as being at the heart of the neoliberal project. Accumulation by dispossession is characterised by four main elements: privatisation, opening up new areas for capital accumulation (e.g. public utilities, public institutions, seeds, genetic material); financialisation, through the deregulation of the global financial system (e.g. speculation, predation, corporate fraud, raiding of pension funds, asset stripping though mergers and acquisitions); management and manipulation of financial crises (e.g. the debt trap, structural adjustment programmes, currency devaluations); and state redistributions (e.g. privatisation of social housing, health and education, reduction of state expenditures on social welfare, revisions of the tax code to benefit returns on investment rather than incomes and wages).

One of the principal means for instituting accumulation by dispossession was through Structural Adjustment Programmes (SAPs), imposed upon the developing economies of countries in the Global South by the IMF and the WB. Commencing in 1980, SAPs institutionalised a shift from what had been termed 'development' practices, systematically imposing foreign control over law and economic policy on post-colonial countries. SAPs dismantled many of the accomplishments of post-colonial regimes, reversing the nationalisation of industries, cutting anti-poverty programmes, downgrading civil services and revoking land reforms.

As such policies have been implemented by countries throughout the Global South: they have been characterised by the commodification and privatisation of land and the forceful expulsion of peasant populations; conversion of various forms of property rights (e.g. common, collective, state) into exclusive private property rights; suppression of rights to the commons; commodification of labour power and the suppression of alternative (indigenous) forms of production and consumption; colonial, neo-colonial and imperial processes of appropriation of assets (including natural resources); monetisation of exchange and taxation, particularly of land; the slave trade (especially within the sex industry); and the use of the credit system as a means of capital accumulation (Harvey, 2006a).

Of course, economies in the Global North were not exempt from these policies either – early examples of the adoption of neoliberal economic policies were 'Reaganomics' in the United States (associated with the Presidency of Ronald Reagan) and 'Thatcherism' in the United Kingdom (associated with the Prime Ministership of Margaret Thatcher) during the 1980s. Peck and Tickell (2002) argue that neoliberalism has seen a shift from 'roll-back neoliberalism' during the 1980s – which entailed a pattern of deregulation and dismantlement (e.g. of state-financed welfare, education, and health services and environmental protection) to an emergent phase of 'roll-out neoliberalism'. This emergent phase is witnessing an aggressive intervention by governments around issues such as crime, policing, welfare reform and urban surveillance, with the purpose of disciplining and containing those marginalised or dispossessed by the neoliberalisation of the 1980s.

The imposition of neoliberal policies has been particularly pernicious in the labour market where states have, to varying degrees, introduced anti-union legislation as a means of restoring capital's 'right to manage'. Furthermore, the deregulation and flexibilisation of employment has provided corporations with greater room for manoeuvre with regard to hiring, firing and the use of labour. With the greater mobility of capital, facilitated by financial deregulation, unions have seen their power bases in the industrialised North weakened through job losses and plant closure, with a global shift (Dicken, 2006) of operations to non-unionised workplaces in the Global South.

Overall, neoliberalism has entailed the centralisation of control of the world economy in the hands of transnational corporations and their allies in key government agencies (particularly those of the United States and other members of the Group of Eight Nations [G8][1]), large international banks, and international institutions such as the IMF, the WB and the WTO. These institutions enforce the doctrine of neoliberalism enabling unrestricted access of transnational corporations (TNCs) to a wide range of markets (including public services), while potentially more progressive institutions and agreements (such as the International Labour Organisation and the Kyoto Protocols) are allowed to wither (Peck and Tickell, 2002). Neoliberal policies have resulted in the pauperisation and marginalisation of indigenous peoples, women, peasant farmers and industrial workers, and a reduction in labour, social and environmental conditions on a global basis – what Brecher and Costello (1994) term 'the race to the bottom' or 'global pillage'. In response to this, new forms of trans-local political solidarity and consciousness have begun to emerge, associated with the partial globalisation of networks of resistance, as we discuss below.

Michael Hardt and Antonio Negri (2000) term the emerging global economic system 'Empire' and characterise it as 'a decentered, detteritorialising apparatus of imperial control' (xii). Characterised by an absence of boundaries, they argue that there is no *place* of power – constituted by networks, it is both everywhere and nowhere, a *non-place*. However, geopolitical and geoeconomic power does get territorialised in certain places. For example, the United States – as the world's only superpower – wields an immense influence on international relations and, through its control of the IMF and WB, the global economy (Blum, 2000; Mertes, 2002).

Hardt and Negri (2000) and Hardt (2002) also argue that resistance to 'Empire' constitutes a counter-Empire, not limited to local autonomy, but one that thinks and acts globally, effecting a politics of association, rather than a series of discrete local actions. In short, resistance must create a 'non-place' – everywhere and nowhere – from where alternatives to Empire are posed (Hardt and Negri, 2000: 205–218). The problem with this formulation is that it ignores the geographical contexts and contingencies of political action. It seems to pose resistance as practising a reactive politics that mirrors 'Empire', rather than articulating a different kind of politics in different places. Rather than constituting a 'non-place' of resistance, GJNs resisting neoliberalism have forged an associational politics that constitute a diverse, contested coalition of place-specific social movements, which prosecute conflict on a variety of multi-scalar terrains that include both material places and virtual spaces.

Emergence: the irresistible rise of resistance to neoliberalism

> This intercontinental network of resistance, recognising differences and acknowledging similarities, will search to find itself with other resistances around the world. This intercontinental network of resistance is not an organising structure; it doesn't have a central head or decision maker; it has no central command or hierarchies. We are the network, all of us who resist. (Subcommandante Marcos 2003: 37)

The emergence over the past decade of what the media has (erroneously) termed the 'anti-globalisation movement' has excited much attention in political and academic circles. In particular, there has been considerable commentary and analysis of: the Zapatista rebellion in Chiapas, Mexico against the North American Free Trade Agreement (NAFTA) (Cecena, 2004; Baschet, 2005; Olesen, 2005); global days of action in Seattle, Genoa, Gleneagles and elsewhere against neoliberal institutions and governments (St Clair, 1999; Gill, 2000; Juris, 2004a; Klein, 2002; Notes from Nowhere, 2003; Routledge, 2005); initiatives against transnational corporations (Gunnell and Timms, 2000; Klein, 2000; Starr, 2000); the transnationalisation of trades unions (Moody, 1997; Waterman, 1998); and the establishment of the World Social Forum and various regional forums (Böhm, Sullivan, and Reyes, 2005; Sen et al., 2004; Sparke et al., 2005). Indeed, place-based, but not necessarily place-restricted, resistance to neoliberal globalisation and its bastard twin-armed neo-liberalisation (see Retort, 2005) continues across the planet.

When seeking to trace the origins and genesis of this resistance, it is crucial to underline the sequence of smaller steps, the periods of latency (Melucci, 1996) that preceded the momentum of their 'emergence' and visibility to the public via street mobilisations (Agrikolianski et al., 2005;

della Porta, 2007). To many, Seattle (1999) – a highly mediated event – represented the key turning point. But it was
prefigured by a growing tide of resistance in the 1980s and
1990s (Juris, 2004a), particularly in the Global South (WDM,
2000) to which we now turn.

Antecedents of global resistance

Before outlining some of the prefiguring events in the
emergence of GJNs, it is important to acknowledge that, for
indigenous peoples around the world, colonialism never
ended. Theirs has been an uninterrupted struggle against
genocide, displacement and cultural invasion for at least five
hundred years. All that has changed is that their struggles
now resonate with those of people elsewhere in the Global
South, and in the Global North, trying to maintain control
of their land, labour, livelihood, environment and culture.
To an extent all local struggles are now resisting a global
process of 'accumulation by dispossession'. Hence, while
resistance can be recognised throughout many centuries, it
has entered a new phase forging international solidarity.
Drawing significantly upon two key activist texts (Notes
from Nowhere, 2003; Starr, 2005; see also Juris, 2004a), we
have decided to begin our archaeology of the present in the
1980s; the decade that saw the implementation of SAPs
in the Global South which were greeted by 'IMF riots' or
'bread riots' – insurrections including general strikes and
massive street protests (WDM, 2000). These, we would
argue, represent the first stirrings of a broader resistance to
a global neoliberal agenda.

Responding to the devastation being caused by SAPs, in
1990 the African Council of Churches called for the year
of the Old Testament Jubilee (i.e. 2000) to be the deadline
by which international lenders were to forgive African debt.
British debt campaigners took up this challenge and started
to work with this idea. Similar to liberation theology, the
Jubilee 2000 movement linked radical political economy
with a theologically-founded culture of resistance and
demanded debt relief for countries in the Global South
(Starr, 2005). Meanwhile, in Europe, the 1980s saw the emergence of grassroots movements constructing autonomous
institutions to meet a variety of needs threatened by growing

commodification and privatisation. These projects included the creation of infoshops, social centres and squatted settlements (e.g. in Italy, Germany, the UK and Holland), as well as street blockades and property crime against corporations. For example, in 1986 the German autonomist movement (*Autonomen*), helped to organise an 80,000 people-strong protest against an IMF meeting in Berlin, and explicitly linked IMF policies with the cutting of social welfare in Europe and with the processes of militarism and imperialism (see Gerhards and Rucht, 1992).

In 1985, the struggle against the mega-dam project along the Narmada River, India emerged and drew together groups which had been fighting dam-related problems in India since the 1970s. The *Narmada Bachao Andolan* (NBA, or Save the Narmada Movement) became one of the first grassroots movements to attempt to internationalise its struggle, forging solidarity links with groups and organisations across the world (Routledge, 2003b). Also in 1985 the Brazilian *Movimento dos Trabalhadores Rurais Sem Terra* (MST), or Landless Workers' Movement, formalised the practice of large-scale land occupations which had been taking place in Brazil since 1978. Within ten years or so the MST used a process of militant occupation and then legalisation of settlements to resettle more than 350,000 families in 23 of the 27 Brazilian states. In 1999 alone, 25,099 families occupied land. They also built 60 food cooperatives, independent education programmes, etc. Meanwhile, in 1985, Greenpeace London prefigured the global day of action tactic by launching the International Day of Action Against McDonald's, which has been held on 16 October ever since (Notes from Nowhere, 2003).

The following year, in 1986, the *Coordination Paysanne Europêenne* was formed in Europe, a network affirming common interests in family farming, sustainability and solidarity with all farmers rather than competition between them. In 1990, a first Continental Encounter of Indigenous Peoples was organised in Quito, Ecuador. Delegates from over 200 indigenous nations launched a movement to achieve continental unity. To sustain the process of international networking, a Continental Coordinating Commission of Indigenous Nations and Organisations (CONIC) was formed at a subsequent meeting in Panama in 1991. A second

Continental Encounter was organised in October 1993 at Temoaya, Mexico (Starr, 2005).

In 1991, the agitation in India's Narmada Valley led to an unprecedented WB review of the Sardar Sarovar dam – the largest of the dams being constructed on the Narmada River, financed by a WB loan of US$ 450 million. The review, which condemned the project on a variety of social and environmental grounds, resulted in the withdrawal of WB financial support for the project in 1993. Meanwhile, in India, the NBA was one of the movements behind the establishment of the National Alliance of People's Movements, a network to struggle against neoliberal modernisation within the country (Routledge, 2003b). In 1992, the indigenous U'wa people in Colombia decided they would not permit Occidental Petroleum to drill in their homeland, and began a struggle that, ten years later, would force the withdrawal of Occidental Petroleum. This took place in the context of an emerging international critique of the behaviour of transnational corporations (cf. Juris, 2004a). Also in 1992, European and Latin American farmers created an international farmers' organisation, *La Via Campesina*, which included small- and medium-sized producers, agricultural workers, rural women and indigenous peoples, to collectively resist the effects of neoliberal economic policies on their livelihoods (Notes from Nowhere, 2003).

New Year's Day, 1994, in Mexico, on the day of implementation of the NAFTA, saw the emergence of the *Ejercito Zapatista de Liberacion Nacional* (EZLN), or Zapatistas. This media-savvy guerrilla movement articulated a radical and poetic resistance against neoliberalism, established autonomous zones in their home state of Chiapas, ran their own *consultas* (plebiscites) all over Mexico and hosted 'intergalactic *Encuentros*' (encounters) in 1996 and 1997 where activists from struggles around the world met in Chiapas to begin to create an international solidarity network against neoliberalism (see the quote at the beginning of this section). The Zapatistas also created networks of resistance within Mexico of labour unions and peasant federations, and hosted delegations of indigenous people from all over Latin America (Routledge, 1998). The Zapatistas marked the new confluence of indigenous and peasant groups, reaching new levels of organising through developments such as the

Latin American Congress of Rural Organisations (CLOG), which met for the first time later in 1994 in Lima, Peru.

By the mid-1990s, increasing global convergence between movements signalled a scale shift in what had hitherto been largely disconnected struggles. Though far from being the only example, the global campaign set up to support the Zapatista struggle symbolised this shift. In the same year, the International Forum on Globalisation (IFG) led a renaissance of praxis. It organised dramatic teach-ins at mobilisations of activists, published related texts, and put forward early topical analyses on frontier aspects of globalisation, such as the privatisation of water. The IFG was thoroughly internationalist and activist, centred on a Global South anti-imperialist perspective, and it united the Global North and South in solidarity on issues of globalisation (Starr, 2005).

From the mid-1990s onwards there was also an upsurge in trade union and labour militancy. In France, two million workers went on strike against 'austerity measures', that is structural adjustment policies implemented in Europe. French activists also formed the first European unemployed union, which quickly spread across the continent. Further afield, growing protests against neoliberal-driven reform were recorded in Canada, Peru, Korea, South Africa, Brazil, Argentina, Belgium, Italy (Cohen and Moody, 1998) and even China where Howells notes an 'almost relentless' increase in labour actions since 1989 (2006: 8). Within the trade union movement, the 1990s also witnessed the first effective global campaigns to support local labour disputes in cases such as the Liverpool dockers (Castree, 2000) and US-based campaigns against Ravenswood Aluminium, Continental Tyres and Bridgestone-Firestone.

The mid-1990s was also significant for an upsurge in worldwide protest against both neoliberal policies and global capitalism more generally. The year 1995 saw the creation of the WTO as a high (or low!) point of neoliberal global governance, but the following year, largely in response to problems of IMF and WB imposed policies, general strikes took place throughout Latin America. In Ecuador, Brazil and Bolivia, the strikes consisted of alliances of peasants, indigenous peoples and trade unions for the first time. In South Korea, trade unions held a series of general strikes in protest of a national labour law designed to increase employers' power in the interest of 'competitiveness'.

Meanwhile, commencing in July 1997 and continuing through 1998, a wave of economic collapses occurred throughout the Asian 'tiger' economies. As a result, diverse movements appeared resisting privatisation, austerities imposed by the Asian Development Bank and US militarism. In the same year the Fair Labour Organisation was established to oversee certification of Fair Trade products (Starr, 2005).

The beginning of 1998 saw the occupation by 24,000 people of one of the major dams in the Narmada Valley, and a scaling up of the struggle as it spread to Japan, Germany and the USA. The same year saw the formation of Peoples' Global Action (PGA, having been conceptualised at a Zapatista Encuentro), which put out a 'call to action' for the upcoming WTO meetings in Geneva. In May, the first 'human chain to break the chains of debt' of 70,000 people ringed the G8 meeting in Birmingham, England. This was the first global day of action during which simultaneous, diverse protests against the WTO were held in 30 countries on five continents. Later that month, 10,000 people protested the second WTO Ministerial in Geneva, held in the United Nations building. Following that protest, the first major direct action blockade of a globalisation meeting in North America took place at the Montreal Conference on Globalised Economies, at which the Secretary-General of the Organisation for Economic Cooperation and Development (OECD) was present. This action contributed to the international campaign, particularly strong in Canada, against the free-trade Multilateral Agreement on Investments which was ultimately scrapped at the OECD. This was also the year in which anti-biotech (GM) movements emerged across Europe, Latin America and South Asia, and anti-sweatshop movements – which had been developing in North America for nearly a decade – took powerful new shape with the formation of United Students Against Sweatshops (USAS) (Notes from Nowhere, 2003; Yuen *et al.*, 2004).

On 12 August 1998, José Bové and other farmers organised the dismantling of a McDonald's in Millau, France, as a response to the US trade attack on Roquefort cheese. Bove had been involved in the development of the French and European farmers' movement, helping to organise *Confedera-*

tion Paysanne in 1987. In preparation for the trial, the farmers' union built connections with other social sectors and international activists, ensuring that globalisation itself would be on trial. Many expert critics of globalisation testified as witnesses and over 100,000 people from Western Europe surrounded the courthouse on 30 June 2000, attended fora and festivities celebrating their growing international solidarity. October saw the formation of ATTAC (the Association for the Taxation of Financial Transactions for the Aid of Citizens), an organisation that adopted James Tobin's proposal for a small tax on international currency transactions. ATTAC subsequently organised chapters in 33 countries (Starr, 2005).

During 1999, PGA initiated an 'Intercontinental Caravan of Solidarity and Resistance' across Europe, consisting of 450 members, mostly peasant farmers from South Asia, undertaking 63 direct actions, including the destruction of biotech seed and crops. In June, the second 'global carnival of resistance' was held simultaneously in 43 countries at the time of the G8 summit in Koln. In November, at the Jubilee South-South Summit in Gauteng, South Africa, 35 countries gathered to devise a common analysis, vision and strategy regarding debt. Later that month, the protests in Seattle, USA against the WTO took place that heralded the entry of US citizens into the emerging networks of resistance against neoliberalism, and the establishment of activist-organised independent media centres (IMCs) that reported on the protests and posted reports and articles on the Internet. The protests saw 70,000 protesters successfully organise a direct action blockade against the WTO meeting, using entirely non-violent tactics. At the same time, solidarity protests took place in 100 cities in 40 different countries (Notes from Nowhere, 2003). The success of the IMCs led to the establishment of Indymedia, an activist-organised web-based news, eye-witness and analysis service that has over 150 sites around the world (Juris, 2004a; 2005a).

During 2000, an insurrection and general strike by farmers, unions, students and small business people in Cochabamba, Bolivia, successfully demanded the cancellation of a water privatisation plan in which the Bolivian government had sold the city's water to a US corporation, Bechtel.[2] The Cochabamba Declaration articulated the rights of free access to clean water for all. In April, the second major US mobilisation was organised at the joint meetings of the IMF and WB in Washington DC, while in June, the Soweto Electricity Crisis Committee (SECC) was formed in South Africa, in response to massive cut-offs of people unable to pay for privatised electricity. The SECC performed (illegal) reconnections and disconnected politicians' home lines. The broader Anti-Privatisation Forum was founded in South Africa in July, embracing issues concerning water, electricity and evictions. In September, the World Economic Forum meetings in Melbourne were successfully blockaded by protesters and the joint IMF and WB meetings in Prague were disrupted in another global day of action that saw solidarity demonstrations across the world. In December, a Global South summit on the debt met in Dakar to articulate strategies for resistance to neoliberalism, and resulted in the Dakar Declaration for the Total and Unconditional Cancellation of African and Third World Debt (Notes from Nowhere, 2003; Starr, 2005).

The year 2001 saw social movements from around the world gather in Porto Alegre, Brazil, to protest against the World Economic Forum. The World Social Forum (WSF) was established to discuss the alternatives to corporate globalisa-tion and plan collective international strategies against it. In April, the Summit of the Americas met in Quebec City to discuss further the Free Trade Area of the Americas (FTAA) and was met with massive protests. In June, protests at the EU summit in Gothenburg were greeted by the first use in Sweden since 1931 of live ammunition against protesters. During the same month well-organised general strikes along with massive and effective occupations and blockades forced the government of Peru to cancel the privatisation of the electricity companies. A month later, at the G8 meetings in Genoa, Italian police attacked peaceful marches, raided a sleeping place brutally (including lining people up along the walls and beating them) and fatally shot a protester, Carlo Giuliani (Juris, 2005c; Yuen et al., 2004). The month of September saw first World Forum on Food Sovereignty in Havana, Cuba, and in December, Argentinians reacted against IMF policies by ousting a series of presi-dents willing to collaborate with structural adjustment recommendations, and establishing autonomous factory takeovers and neighbourhood *asambleas populares* (popular assemblies) (Gordon and Chatterton, 2004).

In 2002, over 51,000 people from 123 countries went to the WSF, asserting that 'another world is possible'. In August, the first Asian Social Movements meeting was held in Bangkok, Thailand, wherein farmers, fisherfolk and workers again affirmed the continuity between issues of global economics and US militarism. Meanwhile, the WSF was organising 14 regional and national preparatory fora. The European Social Forum was held in Florence in November 2002. In 2003, 100,000 people went to Porto Alegre for the annual WSF. The coordinated international protests against the Iraq War on 15 February 2003 drew on the tactic of global days of action first realised in 1998. This day forcefully communicated a clear anti-imperialist message with solidarity among an estimated 30 million people internationally. In 2005, over 150,000 people participated in the WSF (Bramble, 2006). Clearly, a global resistance to neoliberalism is afoot, but just how connected are its constituent parts and to what extent can these pose a real challenge to neoliberalism and global capitalism?

Global justice networks

Many of the aforementioned struggles and initiatives – particularly those heavily mediated events such as the global days of action – have been considered to be examples of an 'anti-globalisation' sentiment. However, we are unconvinced by the 'anti-globalisation' terminology since many of the movements and organisations challenging neoliberalism articulate alternative 'globalisations' rather than a more spatially defensive politics (Routledge, 2003a).

'Grassroots globalisation' (Appadurai, 2000) refers to the process by which marginalised groups and social movements at the local and national level attempt to forge wider alliances in protest at their growing exclusion from global neoliberal economic decision-making. They struggle for inclusive, democratic forms of globalisation, using the communicative tools of the global system. While establishing global networks of action and support they attempt to retain local autonomy over strategies and tactics. Rather than being examples of 'anti-globalisation', such alliances represent struggles for inclusive, democratic forms of globalisation, using the communicative tools of the global system. What they are against is the neoliberal form of globalisation (see Graeber, 2002; Juris, 2004a).

In particular, such alliances involve the creation of networks: of communication, solidarity, information-sharing and mutual support. The core function of networks is the production, exchange and strategic use of information – for example, concerning oppositional narratives and analysis of particular events (Juris, 2004a; 2004b). Many information exchanges are informal such as by telephone, e-mail and the circulation of newsletters and bulletins through a variety of means including by hand, post and the Internet. Such information can enhance the resources available to geographically and or socially distant actors in their particular struggles and also lead to action (Keck and Sikkink, 1998). The speed, density and complexity of international linkages have grown dramatically in the past 20 years. Cheaper air travel and new electronic communication technologies have speeded up information flows and simplified personal contact among activists (Keck and Sikkink, 1998; Ribeiro, 1998; Cohen and Rai, 2000). Indeed, information-age activism is creating what Cleaver (1999: 3) terms a 'global electronic fabric of struggle' whereby local and national movements are consciously seeking ways to make their efforts complement those of other organised struggles around similar issues. Such networks, greatly facilitated by the Internet, can at times enable relationships to develop that are more flexible than traditional hierarchies (Juris, 2004a; 2004b; 2005a). Participation in networks has become an essential component of collective identities of the activists involved, networking forming part of their common repertoire of action and recruitment (Melucci, 1996; Castells, 1997).

From a geographical perspective, these developments are important because they represent attempts to connect up territorially-specific struggles to broader global networks of support, action and debate. However, despite claims that such initiatives herald the creation of a global civil society, and pose significant challenges to global capitalism (e.g. Brecher *et al.*, 2000; Klein, 2002; Callinicos, 2003; Kaldor, 2003; Drainville, 2004), there has been a relative lack of detailed scrutiny about these 'movements' component parts, their operational networks and their spatial dynamics, strategies and practices.[3] Indeed, many accounts consist of activist testimonies which, whilst valuable in providing grounded insights into particular struggles and mobilisations, tend towards hyperbole and inflated rhetoric about the capacity to achieve more sustainable and significant social change (e.g. Notes from Nowhere, 2003).[4] Juris's ethnographic work among global justice networks constitutes a notable exception, examining conflicts among different movement sectors, as well as the ongoing struggles of activists to build sustainable network-based organisations (Juris, 2004a).

Donatella della Porta et al. (2006) argue that 'global' events such as global days of action, counter-summits and campaigns have been sustained over time, and 'condensed' the diversity of networks resisting neoliberalism through the creation of 'tolerant identities',[5] thus contributing to an evolving global movement. Drawing upon two Italian-based events – the Genoa protests against the G8 in 2001 and the European Social Forum in Florence in 2002 – they cite several processes as their evidence. First, many activists identify themselves with a counter-globalisation movement and such a movement is acknowledged by the press, opponents and sympathisers alike. Second, global days of action have increased dramatically in number since 1999, and while participation in such actions is still dominated by local activists, there has been significant participation from activists from abroad. Third, there is increasing evidence of transnational coalitions of social movements and a growing number of locally active networks structured around global issues. Finally, local, national and transnational organisations agree in defining their scope as global: they address international government organisations and transnational corporations as their opponents, and they have transnational aims. Such claims have led some authors to claim that a 'global movement' (Yuen et al., 2004) or a 'movement of movements' (Mertes, 2004) exists. Others define a vague 'global justice movement' consisting of a loose network of organisations and other actors that are, on the basis of shared concerns, engaged in collective action designed to promote social, economic, political and environmental justice among and between peoples across the globe (Rootes and Saunders, 2007). In addition, it has been argued that a global movement is in the making, since counter-summits and campaigns have condensed the loose network of organisations and movements and been sustained over time, while local and national protests are also targeting international institutions and national governments' adoption of neoliberal policies (della Porta *et al.*, 2006).

However, given such diversity of aims, strategies and political identities of the political actors involved, Tarrow (2005) argues that networks' organisational structures are too weak, supranational protest events too scattered and collective identities too heterogeneous for there to be one coherent movement. Hence, domestic movements act in transnational arenas (at times with others) in order to strengthen their positions within their particular national contexts.

We also remain sceptical that a coherent global 'movement' actually exists. Every form of collective action has a plurality of analytical meanings, and *contra* della Porta *et al.* (2006), we do not accept that political actors' own beliefs provide sufficient ground for an adequate account of their actions. As Melucci (1996) argues, the broader system of relationships in which goals, values, frames and discourses are produced also need to be considered. We are concerned that there has been a tendency in some literatures to reify both the term 'global' and 'movement' when considering the upwelling of collective action against neoliberalism.

Therefore, in this book, our concern is to contribute to the emerging literature through an empirically grounded re-conceptualisation of this 'movement'. This involves acknowledging that the 'global movement' is composed of a diversity of struggles that are still territorially based, but are increasingly upscaling their actions to become involved in broader spatial networks. More specifically, we develop a critical analysis of three of its key constituents through detailed case studies. We analyse three contrasting networks – an international trade union network (the International Federation of Chemical, Energy, Mining and General Workers or ICEM); a network of Asian peasant movements (PGA Asia); and the Social Forum process, through research conducted at the European Social Forums in Paris in 2003 and London in 2004, and the World Social Forum of 2005.

Rather than a coherent global justice movement, our findings lead us to support a conception of a series of overlapping, interacting, competing, and differentially-placed and resourced networks (Juris, 2004a), or what we term Global Justice Networks (GJNs). While grassroots globalisation refers to the overarching process of movements working together across geographical space, GJNs are the specific operational networks that comprise this process. We term such formations Global Justice Networks because such networks, and the movements that comprise them, articulate demands for social, economic and environmental justice. Although precise conceptions of justice will differ between movements and unions in different cultural and political-economic circumstances, the participants in GJNs share common claims to broadly defined notions of justice pertaining to issues of redistribution (e.g. class) and recognition (e.g. identity), seeking to address and correct inequitable outcomes (e.g. concerning economic development) and the underlying processes that give rise to them (see Fraser 1997). Such notions of justice within GJNs act as a master frame enabling different themes to be interconnected and convincing different political actors from different struggles and cultural contexts to join together in common struggle (della Porta et al., 2006). These notions of justice require knowledge of processes of inequality and injustice in the world and activists' personal involvement in attempting to transform them, and incorporate all scales of transformative action – from the personal, the community, the state, to international arenas and institutions. Therefore, GJNs represent the ability of different movements to be able to work together without attempting to develop universalistic and centralising solutions that deny the diversity of interests and identities that are confronted with neoliberal globalisation processes. We will discuss GJNs in greater detail in Chapter 2, but our purpose at this stage is to set out our key arguments in this book.

We intend to challenge some of the key assumptions and claims made about the existence of a coherent 'global' movement against neoliberal globalisation and also, therefore, challenge some of the claims made about the existence of global civil society. Through an intimate consideration of the operational logics, strategies and spatial dynamics of GJNs, we will question the extent to which such networks fully engage and involve the grassroots activists who comprise the membership of participant social movements within GJNs.

We are particularly interested in how issues of heterogeneity and geography are negotiated through the structures and practices that have evolved in GJNs, and the implications of this for the development of coherent and effective social justice agendas. The diversity of GJNs participant movements may prove increasingly problematic due to the conflicting goals, ideologies and strategies of power that exist between the different participants (Juris, 2004a). Consequently, this leads to conflictual geographies which, we argue, are compounded by the uneven spatial operation of GJNs. When locally-based struggles become part of broader geographical networks, they become embedded in different places at a variety of spatial scales. Some networks remain relatively localised, while others become more global in scope with important implications for material and discursive resource availability in particular struggles.

We will develop the notion of convergence space (Routledge, 2003a, Cumbers et al., 2008) to recognise that GJNs are open, dynamic spaces in which power relations are worked through between different actors at a multiplicity of different spatial scales. We will explore the extent to which the forms of convergence space emerging through the practices of GJNs are successful in negotiating the entangled power relations that are an inevitable part of the network. GJNs vary greatly in their operational logics, and internally they comprise uneven distributions of discursive and material power and resources (Juris, 2004a). Although convergence spaces are rooted in particular place-based struggles, they are, of course, not necessarily local. We will argue that what gets diffused and organised across space is the 'common ground' shared by different groups – often the result of groups' entangled interests (Routledge, 2003a).

In contrast to claims that the contemporary resistance to neoliberalism has no leaders (Klein, 2002; della Porta et al., 2006), we will argue that much of the routine (international) organisational work of GJNs is conducted by key activists who have helped organise conferences, mobilise resources and facilitate communication and information flows between movements and between movement offices and grassroots communities. These people constitute the 'imagineers' of GJNs, who attempt to 'ground' the concept or imaginary of the network (what it is, how it works, what it is attempting to achieve) within grassroots communities who comprise the membership of the participant movements. They possess the cultural capital of (usually) higher education, and the social capital inherent in their transnational connections and access to resources and knowledge (Missingham, 2003; Juris, 2004a; Routledge et al., 2006). However, because of their structural positions, communication skills and experience in activism and meeting facilitation, they tend to wield disproportionate power and influence within GJNs (Juris, 2004a; King, 2004).

GJNs display considerable variety in both the extent and nature of their international solidarity activities, and the local and national scales remain vitally important for the mobilisation of resources and development of international agendas. Moreover, various collective gatherings – be they conferences or assemblies – provide performative spaces that play a vital role in face-to-face communication, the development of deeper interpersonal ties between activists, and the exchange of experience, strategies and ideas, and generate collective energy and sense of identity (Juris, 2004a).

Methodology

In this book, we use a variety of materials obtained from both direct political engagement within the networks studied (Routledge with PGA Asia, Cumbers with the Social Forums), and from in-depth interviews with activists in the three networks. For each network, the research focused upon a particular world region that was strategically important in the development of the network. For PGA, the Asian region was chosen because it is a region where PGA activities have expanded considerably and where some of the impacts of WB and IMF neoliberal policies have been most acute. For the ICEM, Western Europe was chosen as the world region where the union network is strongest, through membership levels and resources to campaigns. Within both networks, various movements were chosen to investigate diversity and different social, economic and political contexts of action. For the WSF, Latin America was the world region where the process emerged so Andy Cumbers visited the Porto Alegre Forum in 2005 as both researcher and participant (as a trade union representative). The European Social Forum was selected for participation in 2003 and 2004, both for ease of access and as the most successful and empowered (in terms of numbers attending) of the regional fora to date.

Research on the PGA Asia network was based upon participant observational research within PGA Asia conducted in South and Southeast Asia during 2002–2004 by Paul Routledge. He has been working in the PGA Asia network since 2001 helping to facilitate the network's organisational dynamics, through meetings with participant movement activists in South and Southeast Asia, participation in movement activities (such as workshops) and helping to coordinate network activities (such as the PGA Asia conference held in Dhaka, Bangladesh, in 2004, which is discussed in detail in Chapter 5).

The research was primarily focused around a set of semi-structured interviews with actors occupying different positions within the three networks. To enable an element of direct comparison between the ICEM and PGA networks, standardised questions were asked, analysing the operation of the networks regarding issues such as organisation, access to resources, levels of interaction with other actors, forms of conflict emerging between different actors, multi-scalar political action and the extent of local empowerment occurring through networks. For PGA Asia, 48 interviews were undertaken with both officials and ordinary members of the following movements: the Bangladesh Krishok Federation (25); the All Nepal Peasant's Association (10); the Karnatakan State Farmer's Association (India) (3); the Assembly of the Poor (Thailand) (4); the Bharatiya Kisan Union (India) (1); Vietnam Farmer's Union (1); Borneo Indigenous Peoples' and Peasants Union (2); and the Movement for National Land and Agricultural Reform (Sri Lanka) (2). Also some group discussions were conducted with activists in the participant movements of PGA Asia, both during and following the Dhaka conference.[6] Within ICEM,

47 interviews were conducted: 6 interviews with staff and officials involved with the global headquarters (Belgium), including interviews with the then General Secretary (as of 2005) and his predecessor; and interviews with trade unionists from national affiliates in Germany (2); the UK (17); France (14); and Norway (8). Group discussions were also conducted with 'grassroots' members of ICEM affiliate unions in the UK and France.

For the Social Forums, participant observation was complemented by 103 brief structured interviews (lasting between 15–30 minutes) at the London ESF (Chapter 7). As a more 'conglomerated' network, our concerns with the research undertaken here were more to do with evaluating the convergence and cross-fertilisation of actors and group-ings than purely with the operational logics and dynamics. In this sense, the material provided important opportunities to both triangulate our findings from the other two networks and build up a more general overview of the resistance to neoliberalism.

Whilst in all networks, the intention of achieving geographical diversity in respondents was achieved, the balance of interviewing tended to reflect the levels of activity within the network. Thus, for example, in the ICEM, more interviews were undertaken with British, Norwegian and French unions which have a higher number of affiliates within the ICEM and also a greater degree of ICEM-related activity than Germany where only one union is affiliated and international activities tend to be more restricted towards European issues. Within PGA Asia, interviews were conducted primarily with activists who had participated in a key event in the network, the regional conference held in Dhaka, Bangladesh, in 2004. The interview numbers reflected the differential participation of the respective movements' members in the conference. Our perspective on the Social Forum process was biased by our reliance upon largely English speakers for feedback although we were able, through one of our researchers, Corinne Nativel – to converse in German and French at the London meeting.

To enable an element of direct comparison between the networks, standardised questions were asked, analysing the operation of the networks regarding issues such as organisa-tion, access to resources, levels of interaction with other actors, forms of conflict emerging between different actors, multi-scalar political action and the extent of local empowerment occurring through networks.

Organisation of the book

As noted earlier, this book seeks to deepen and enrich our understanding of the resistance to neoliberalism through empirical engagement. To this end, Chapters 2, 3 and 4 develop our conceptual framework, which is then 'operationalised' in the case study Chapters 5, 6 and 7, prior to the concluding chapter. In Chapter 2, we consider theoretical approaches to the study of networks, including conceptions of networking as a political practice (Juris, 2004a). We will then briefly consider claims that have been made about networks and the emergence of global civil society. We will then turn our attention to a discussion of GJNs, and their key characteristics of diversity, creativity, convergence, scale politics and the creation of spaces of participatory democracy and solidarity. We will argue that they do not 'act' as a coherent actor in the manner of social movements, although some (or indeed many) GJNs may come together, in particular times and places, in order to prosecute specific campaigns or global days of action.

In Chapter 3, we begin to place GJNs in grounded contexts by examining their operational logics and strategies. By examining network relationality and power dynamics we will see that, contrary to claims that networks operate through horizontality, elements of both horizontal and vertical operational logics are present within the practices of networks (Juris, 2004a, b). We also examine how GJNs attempt to forge transnational (or as we term it, following Olesen, 2005) 'mutual' solidarities between their participant movements. We will also argue that the operation of GJNs require what we term 'networking vectors' to further the process of communication, information-sharing and interaction within grassroots communities, the most important being what we term 'imagineers': activists who conduct much of the organisational work necessary for these processes to be realised.[7]

In Chapter 4, we argue that the geographical concepts of place and space are paramount to the understanding of social movement behaviours and, therefore, social movement networks. We will consider the spatiality of GJNs exploring how they prosecute political action across multiple geographical scales. Pulling together all of the key conceptual analysis from Chapters 3 and 4 we conclude by introducing the concept of convergence space with which to understand the dynamics of GJNs. We will argue that convergence spaces (i) are comprised of place-based, but not necessarily, place-restricted movements; (ii) articulate certain *collective visions* (i.e. unifying values, organisational principles and positions), which generate sufficient common ground to generate a politics of mutual solidarity; (iii) involve a practical relational politics of solidarity, bound up in five forms of interaction and facilitation: communication, information-sharing, solidarity actions, network coordination and resource mobilisation; (iv) facilitate spatially extensive political action by participant movements; (v) are characterised by range of both horizontal and vertical operational logics; (vi) are sites of contested social and power relations; and (vii) require 'networking vectors', in particular 'imagineers' to further the process of communication, information-sharing, interaction and organisation within the network.

The next three chapters explore three case studies of GJNs, interpreting them through the conceptual frameworks established in Chapters 3 and 4. Our selection of case studies is driven by our desire to 'get to grips' with the different operational logics and geographical variety at the heart of the resistance to neoliberalism. Chapter 5 considers PGA (Asia), a recently established, non-hierarchical global network of diverse Asian grassroots social movements and activists, committed to decentralisation and political initiatives outside the realm of formal state politics. Its main function is to oppose the destructive consequences of neoliberal policies and to develop concrete alternatives. Chapter 6 focuses upon the ICEM, a longer established global union federation with more a formal hierarchical organisational structure, with power largely centred on national affiliates. Its primary objective is concerned with improving the working conditions of its membership worldwide and contesting employment change through formal state structures. These two cases represent important contrasts as GJNs with different types of convergence underway, one that could be considered as more 'grassroots' and another as a top-down form of convergence. However, as our chapters show, in practice some of their organisational logics, political dilemmas and geographical relations are similar, particularly with regards to how genuine transnational solidarity links are constructed that go beyond the elite 'imagineers' of constituent movements. Chapter 7 contains our analysis and interpretation of the Social Forum process and whilst, by its nature, its subject matter is broader and more discursive than the more specific case studies, it also is concerned with the fundamental issues of solidarity, democracy and grassroots engagement.

In the final chapter we summarise the key themes and findings of the book and evaluate current theoretical and empirical debates about global civil society, participative democracy and transnational solidarity within GJNs. We will argue that issues of space and scale are critical to the sustainability and future strategy of GJNs. Tensions arise between developing more horizontalist networks that facilitate democracy and grassroots participation, and the need to develop structures that can relay a global consciousness down to local activists. We will argue that understanding the potential for GJNs to develop a sustainable politics of international solidarity involves not just understanding the way that the 'local' is enmeshed in wider spatial relations, but also, and perhaps more critically, assessing how the 'global' is invoked in struggles that take place nationally and locally. Overall, our research leads us to be suspicious of analyses that conjure up an emergent global civil society, but instead to draw attention to the entangled operational logics, differential power relations and dilemmas surrounding the grassrooting of network imaginaries that characterise GJNs. The emergence of GJNs has not resulted in the finished construction of a global civil society but instead represents an ongoing, uneven process in which continuous effort is required by imagineers to link locally based struggles with a broader global consciousness.

Notes

1   Britain, Canada, France, Germany, Italy, Japan, Russia and the United States of America.

2   Peoples' Global Action held its next *Encuentro* in Cochabamba in September 2001.

3   However, see della Porta *et al.*, (2006) who begin to address this issue.

4   However, see Featherstone (2003); Routledge (2003a).

5   That is, framing differences as an enriching characteristic of the coalitions, emphasising the role of inclusiveness and placing a positive emphasis on diversity and cross-fertilisation of struggles. See della Porta and Tarrow (2005).

6   For a more detailed analysis of Routledge's positionality within the network, see Routledge (2008).

7   Juris (2004a) refers to those who conduct much of the routine work of maintaining networks (e.g. through information-sharing) as 'activist-hackers'. The concept of imagineers includes such networking tasks, but also emphasises the importance of ideational work and of grounding the network 'imaginary' in grassroots communities.

2

Networks, global civil society and global justice networks

In this chapter our purpose is to fuse together recent theorisations about the resistance to neoliberalism with broader debates that seek to conceptualise changes in society more generally, stemming from processes of globalisation. The latter, typified by the work of Manuel Castells, perceive of a fundamental qualitative shift in both the organisation and relations of human society brought about by globalisation processes. The network concept has been at the forefront of such debates, where its use depicts what are seen as flatter, dynamic and more fluid forms of economic and social organisation, emerging under globalisation. Network ontologies have also been highly influential within debates about global civil society and the resistance to neoliberalism. We use it in this book advisedly, recognising its methodological utility in encapsulating the global connections emerging through resistance to neoliberalism, hence the term GJN, but stressing also its limitations as a broader theoretical concept.[1]

After tracing the development of the term in recent sociological literature, we consider the ways in which it has been used by scholars and activists within the resistance to neoliberalism. We also explore the appeal to the network metaphor as part of global civil society discourses before developing a more restricted sense of network ontology; locating networks within the grounded realities and geographies of GJNs. The remainder of the chapter then outlines some basic features of GJNs as a prelude to further conceptualisation in Chapters 3 and 4.

Networks as theory and political practice

As Juris (2004a) has noted, the study of networks has increased in importance in recent years, analysis including the influence of digital technologies upon networks (Castells 1997, Cleaver 1999, Arquilla and Ronfeldt 2001, Bennett 2003, see also Juris, 2005a); the linguistic and textual practices of networks (Riles, 2001); how cultural codes, information and other resources are distributed and organised through network infrastructures (Diani, 1995, Keck and Sikkink, 1998); and how interactions between locally situated actors can create networks (Escobar, 2001). Meanwhile, actor-network theory (ANT) conceives of the world as a collection of heterogeneous activities, constantly in motion and of 'socio-technical' networks as links composed of the circulation of 'immutable mobiles' such as animals, tools, machines, money, people, etc. The world is made up of numerous networks of association which are constituted by that association, by the movement of 'traffic' through their links (Latour, 2005; 2006).[2]

As noted above, the conceptualisation of networks frequently implies flatter, dynamic and more fluid forms of economic and social organisation that are emerging to reflect the 'stretching out' of social relations under globalisation (Giddens, 1990; Castells, 1996; Melucci, 1996; Urry, 2004). The key work in this respect is Castells and his 'Network Society' trilogy (1996; 1997; 1998) where globalisation and the information technology revolution are seen as responsible for the emergence of a new set of social relations, whereby the 'space of places', in the territorially defined societies of nation states, is gradually giving way to a 'space of flows', in which locationally-defined communities are being replaced by delocalised networks of association. Subsequently, other theorists have made similar claims. John Urry, for example (2004: 110), talks of a 'shift from a heavy solid modernity to one that is light and liquid and where speed of movement of people, money, images and information is paramount'. With John Law, Urry suggests that '[w]ith it's many convergent, overlapping and irreversible interdependencies, "globalization" is remaking "societies" but not in a linear closed and finalised form' (Law and Urry, 2004: 403). The implication is that fixed and enduring

relationships centred on traditional communities and hierarchical forms of organisation territorialised at the level of the
nation state are giving way to more fluid, unstable and
deterritorialised social relations bound up in network forms
(see also Urry, 2003; Walby, 2003).

Because capitalism has itself changed through information
technology and the realities of globalisation – as we noted
in Chapter 1, Hardt and Negri talk of an 'Empire' based
upon a decentred and deterritorialising apparatus of rule
that progressively incorporates the entire global realm –
the social movements that emerge to resist it will also
be decentred, bound up in a variety of networked notions.
These include: the 'multitude' where place- and issue-based
singularities coalesce within and between movements
against a common enemy (Hardt and Negri, 2000; 2004); the
'swarm' which involves the decentralised yet coordinated
deployment of myriad dispersed networked groups (from a
variety of campaigns, movements, etc.) which converge on
a particular target or place from multiple directions, conduct
an action and then disperse (e.g. the critical mass bicycle
demonstrations) (Arquilla and Ronfeldt, 2001; Klein, 2002;
Notes from Nowhere, 2003); and 'rhizomes' which are
various types of communicative and political connections
that cross borders and reappear in distant places without
necessarily showing themselves in between (Deleuze and
Guattari, 1987).

Networks are used in this sense to emphasise the shifting
and temporary nature of many connections. For some, this
decentred network form is encapsulated in a shift from
a politics of solidarity associated with traditional social
movements, based around a more permanent sense of collective and shared identity, bound up in a particular struggle
(e.g. the democracy movements in Brazil or South Africa),
to one of 'fluidarity' whereby personal skills and experiences
rather than collective identities are mobilised in temporary
events and convergences (McDonald, 2002; 2006).[3] In
temporal terms, GJNs are non-permanent and unstable
assemblages where there are no clear beginnings and end
points but rather a system of multiple temporalities with
chaotic and multiple branching-points, so that people, actions
and ideas spill from one network to another. In this sense,
the type of social and political differences and competing

positions described above are celebrated rather than seen as problematic and used to argue for a politics of the moment, of temporary assemblages and resistances. This is what Maffesoli (2003: 37) terms the 'Einsteinsation' of time-space compression in which the present is experienced in the relational mode of an hedonistic *carpe diem*; the implication being that these 'transfigured politics' are more effective in combating global capitalism than longer term alliances that become increasingly fraught and contradictory (Chin and Mittelman, 1997).

Network imagery has also been taken up by anti-neoliberal activists themselves. Indeed, Juris (2004a; 2004b) argues that for many activists the network has become an important political and cultural ideal. For example, the editorial collective Notes from Nowhere, speak of:

> horizontal, as opposed to pyramidal structures of power, dispersed networks rather than united fronts. [. . .] Capital's dream of superfast networks that will spread consumerism across the planet was turned on its head. For while the networked money markets were tearing the planet apart, our grassroots networks were bringing us together. People were using the global communications infrastructure for something completely different – to become autonomous, to get the state and corporations off their backs. (2003: 63)

Reference is continually made to a 'global movement' without leaders (as noted in Chapter 1), that emerges spontaneously, that is constantly evolving, and takes place simultaneously in a multitude of different places. Metaphors of ants and birds – that swarm in a self-managed but decentred manner 'weaving' in and out of formation to connect with others in an unregimented and ungoverned fashion – are used to encapsulate the ability of one individual to make contact with any other in the network, independent of organisational or collective influence.

An important element of the network imaginary in this sense is a strong culture of self-identity (where generality gives way to individuality), again viewed as being in opposition to traditional social movements where belonging to a movement involves submerging your identity within a larger mass and developing a collective consciousness. Subjectivity increasingly constitutes the core of contemporary social conflicts: where political action is less concerned with defending collective identities and increasingly takes the form of a struggle for coherence of selfhood (Touraine, 1978). Hence it is important to retain the embodied subject at the centre of political action (McDonald, 2006). Networks involve the ability for individuals to become connected, but at the same time retain their autonomy and therefore potential to become disconnected and join other movements and alliances, as needs change or different issues assume greater importance (Juris, 2004a, 2004b; McDonald, 2002). Activism in this sense involves a more personalised and hybrid sense of identity; tied in with broader shifts towards a post-industrial society, with a class politics increasingly displaced by a fluid identity politics, in which activism takes more contingent forms.

In contrast to this emphasis on identity, Hardt and Negri (2004) argue in their notion of the multitude, that within contemporary networks, each struggle remains 'singular' and tied to its local conditions while also immersed in broader networks. Traditional forms of organisation have, they argue, been based upon what they term the 'identity-difference' couplet. This has taken two forms: first, where the identity of the struggle and its unity are organised under a central leadership such as a political party; and second, where struggle is based upon the right of each group to express its difference and conduct its own struggle autonomously (e.g. the 'identity politics' associated with struggles around race, gender and sexuality). However, networked models of political association transcend these: the multitude replaces the 'identity-difference' couplet with the 'commonality-singularity' couplet (2004: 217). We will draw upon this notion in more detail in Chapter 3.

This emphasis upon singularity reinforces the notion of activism around looser networks rather than submission to one totalising ideology and struggle. This discourse has also been extended to trade unions where there has been a lively debate about the need for unions themselves to become more hybrid and diverse in their make up if they are to survive under networked capitalism. The shift towards a more fluid, flexible and decentred workplace requires a move away from a territorially-based unionism centred upon the factory and the industrial worker towards a social movement unionism that appeals to more diverse social groups and develops a broader 'world of work' agenda (see e.g. Wills, 2000). In addition, it is argued that a new trade union internationalism is needed that transcends the nationally centred unions of the past towards organisational forms that are both more transnational and at the same time devolve more power down to grassroots activists (Moody, 1997; Waterman, 1998; Lee, 2004); in effect more networked forms of organisation.

However, recent accounts of networks have tended to downplay the embodied practices of the human actors (Diani, 1995; Diani and McAdam, 2002). Notable exceptions are Juris's (2004a) work on embodied practices in resistance networks against neoliberalism, and some Feminist accounts where the role played by empathy in solidarity-building (Eschle and Maiguashca, 2007), and jealousy in the operation of networks (Sperling et al., 2001) have been discussed. As discussed in Chapter 1, we have critically engaged with the movements, unions and fora that comprise the case study materials of this book. This is because such engagement throws into sharp relief the processes of social inequality (e.g. in terms of more and less powerful actors) that shape network interaction. Two points apply here. First, networks are always constructed through *a priori* social relations that include pre-existing forms of power (Juris, 2004a). Second, and frequently as a result of this, network practices, whilst partly generative in themselves, frequently embody uneven power relations. For example, some actors 'circulate' more than others within networks, creating differential social relations, whereby power is centred on certain people and things. This can be explained by taking fuller account of the embodied spatial practices of political action, in particular the way that power emerges from the actions and reactions of people as they act within networks (see Cresswell, 1999).

Of course, networks are always in process, expanding and contracting, evolving and adapting to changing circumstances and opportunities, such that power relations are unstable (Juris, 2004a; 2005a). They are, at the same time, embedded within broader societal relations and as such will be shaped (but not determined) by such processes as uneven access to material and discursive resources. To understand how these processes 'play out' in the operation of networks we will analyse some key events within the networks studied (such as conferences and meetings), and will argue that these represent crucial articulated moments in the practice and process of networking that embody the network in a variety of (more or less powerful) ways for participant actors (Juris, 2004a). These events act as moments of stabilisation and re-configuration within which networks are made manifest and transformed simultaneously (Chesters, 2003). A key question that emerges from such considerations is the extent to which such events signal an emerging global civil society.

Networks and global civil society

Despite claims that international NGO, trade union and social movement networks are representative of an emergent global civil society (Lipschutz, 1996; Anheier et al., 2001; McDonald, 2002; Keane, 2003; Anheier and Katz, 2005), the concept remains an ambivalent and contested concept (Amoore and Langley, 2004). Certainly, there are a range of networked initiatives that *might* attest to represent global civil society. These include: (i) the various global fora where actors from civil society meet to share ideas, discuss experiences and attempt to construct community, for example, the World and regional Social Forums and the various activist and NGO meetings that accompany the major summits of the international financial institutions and G8 governments; (ii) the networks of news and information that attempt to enhance connectivity and information sources for different organisations, for example, Indymedia, Social Watch, the Sustainable Development Communications Network; (iii) the various research networks where analysts from policy institutes and academia build knowledge bases, for example, the Third World Network, Focus on the Global South, the International Forum on Globalisation; (iv) the humanitarian and development aid organisations who respond to natural disasters, famines and poverty, etc., for example, Oxfam, the World Wildlife Fund, the Red Cross and the Red Crescent; and (v) the variety of 'global' campaigns and protests, including the alliances who mobilise around global days of action and international campaigns that link place-based struggles to transnational networks, for example, ATTAC, Amnesty International; the Climate Action Network, the

International Rivers Network (Kaldor, 2003; Notes from Nowhere, 2003; Starr, 2005).

As Juris (2004a) has argued, civil society has frequently been considered to be autonomous of both state and market and, as a result, a potential means for establishing political control over the global economy. Hence, Anheier *et al.* (2005: v) conceptualise global civil society as 'the realm of non-coercive collective action around shared interests and values that operates beyond the boundaries of nation states'; and which 'influences the framework of global governance' (2005: 2).

As Juris (2004a) notes, other scholars conceive of global civil society in more decentred and locally-rooted ways, resulting from varied ongoing grassroots attempts to jointly construct a 'globalisation from below' (Falk, 1987; Waterman, 1998; Appadurai, 2000). He also notes that the notion of global civil society has received criticism from different standpoints. First, the state remains the principal target of political action (Ayres, 2003), and the absence of a global state undermines claims for an emergent global civil society (Olesen, 2005). Second, transnational action on behalf of social movements, NGOs, trade unions, etc. is heterogeneous and occurs at multiple scales, and hence conceiving of a global civil society threatens to elide such differentiation (Keane, 2003; Eschle, 2001). Third, the notion frequently reflects the aspirations of its proponents who wish to see a coherent and coordinated challenge to neoliberal globalisation (Olesen, 2005). Fourth, the concept of civil society itself is interpreted in a variety of ways and, as such, lacks explanatory power (Comaroff and Comaroff, 1999). Moreover, certain civil society actors such as NGOs frequently collaborate with advanced capitalist states despite resistance by national governments (Gupta and Ferguson, 2002). In addition, government policies and practices of control frequently extend into civil society, dissolving the distinction between the state and civil society (Ong, 2003).

However, as Juris (2004a) argues, and what is clear from our research, is that for many grassroots activists the civil society discourse continues to be politically empowering. Thus we, like Juris, prefer to use the Gramscian notion of civil society as an open and permeable terrain of struggle where hegemonic actors (e.g. states and TNCs) are opposed by counter-hegemonic actors such as social movements and trade unions. In this respect, it is worth remembering that Gramsci's (1971) original formulation of civil society viewed it as an arena of struggle which dominant groups could also use to operationalise key institutions of power (e.g. the church). It is a space of conflict 'where different forces intersect, collide and cooperate, where resistance is accentuated rather than assimilated – a constituent space' (Chesters, 2003: 42).

Clearly, civil society, in its heterogeneity, contains differential power relations and forms of exclusion (Alvarez *et al.*, 1998). However, as Juris argues 'the spread of highly diffuse, decentralised network formations may represent not the withering of civil society, but rather its renewal as [a] . . . terrain of democratic intervention and struggle at local, regional, and global scales' (2004a: 409). On this terrain, civil society actors attempt to both influence political discourse and decision-making, and construct more democratic associational forms (Cohen and Arato, 1992; cf. Juris 2004a).

Contrary, to the celebration of flatter, decentred, topological networks in much of the literature about an emergent global civil society, we distinguish between networks and the movements that affiliate to them. In so doing, we ground in material reality both the grassroots movements and the networks to which they belong. In such an analysis, it is important to take into account 'the multiple differences in power, form, strategy, and ideology that exist between and within social movements' (Eschle, 2001: 72; see also Sperling *et al.*, 2001; Rai, 2003; Eschle and Maiguashca, 2007). It is our contention that this can best be achieved by a consideration of the intimate workings and characteristics of specific global justice networks.

Global justice networks

As we discussed briefly in Chapter 1, and will discuss in detail in the case study chapters, GJNs are networks and flows of communication, action and experience. Their forms of practice and communication are embodied and sensual as well as deliberative and representative (McDonald, 2006).[4] Rather than conceptualise GJNs as defensive practices against a globalising outside, we conceive of them as products of hybridities, overlappings and juxtapostions. Through their participation in GJNs, different place-based political actors such as social movements, trade unions, NGOs, leftist political parties, religious groups, etc., become connected to more spatially extensive coalitions with a shared interest in articulating demands for greater, social, economic and environmental justice.

GJNs work together on a range of events, including issue-specific campaigns, conferences, global days of action, social fora, etc. These events enable the embodiment of alternative social movement networks and the fashioning of 'trans-national counterpublics' (Olesen, 2005): 'open spaces for the self-organised production and circulation of oppositional identities, discourses, and practices' (Juris, 2004a: 401). These refer to the larger social contexts in which networks are embedded and 'are constituted by a range of geographically dispersed actors, and are often centered around local or national issues considered to be of relevance to people outside of the geographical location, or around issues with a cross border nature' (Olesen, 2005: 94). As mentioned in Chapter 1, GJNs are characterised by a range of general attributes that we will proceed to discuss below.

First, GJNs are characterised by diversity, as new alliances between social movements representing different terrains of struggle, experience the negative consequences of neo-liberalism (Wallgren, 1998). GJNs involve a variety of political actors as well as strategic foci, and have been celebrated for bringing together formerly disparate and often conflicting groups, such as trade unionists, environmenta-lists, indigenous peoples' movements and NGOs. In such networks, different groups articulate a variety of potentially conflicting goals (concerning the forms of social change), ideologies (e.g. concerning gender, class and ethnicity) and strategies (e.g. violent and non-violent forms of protest), and are embedded in specific national contexts (Juris, 2004a; Tormey, 2004a). The amalgamation and assemblage of these movements may be understood as resulting in a lack of congruence and 'weak ties'. For example, the claims of US trade unions may be seen as incompatible with some of the demands of environmental NGOs of the developing South. However, we prefer to see potential strength in the fact that such diversity of constituents results in the articulation of a diversity of place-specific solutions to economic and ecological problems. In this sense, we tend to agree with Subcommandante Marcos of the Zapatistas, when he calls for a 'world made of many worlds', rather than the potentially universalistic interpretation that accrues to the WSF claim that 'another *world* is possible' (our emphasis).

Underpinning such developments is a conceptualisation of protest and struggle that respects difference, rather than attempting to develop universalistic and centralising solutions that deny the diversity of interests and identities that are confronted with neoliberal globalisation processes. Hence:

> an international process of *recomposition* of radical claims and social subjects has been under way, a process which is forcing every movement not only to seek alliances with others, but also to make the struggles of other movements their own, without first the need to submit the demands of other movements to an ideological test ... [the] premise of recomposition is the multidimensional reality of exploitative and oppressive relations as it is manifested in the lives and experiences of the many social subjects within the global economy. (De Angelis, 2000: 14)

Within these coalitions, a variety of cultural and identity issues remain important (e.g. gender) but these are now being reframed within the context of broader critiques of the operation of economic and political systems, and they rejoin more traditional 'labour' and (re)distributive concerns about working conditions in the Global South, the effects of mobility of capital and job security in the Global North, etc. While struggles in the Global South have always tended to have a materialist focus, identity politics in the Global North have begun to rediscover a materialist critique (Crossley, 2001). However, because the globalisation of protest involves the inter-penetration and multiplicity of forces at local, regional, national and global scales, such a multiplicity raises the possibility of alliances that contain various contradictions (Chin and Mittelman, 1997). For example, place-based gender relations within particular autonomist social movements in the Global North may be at odds with those of more traditionally organised peasant movements in the Global South, with whom they participate in struggle. This raises questions about how social movements act effectively in coalitions across diverse geographical scales.

Concerning coalition diversity, Kaldor (2003) identifies at least six different types of political actor involved in contemporary political action – more traditional social movements (e.g. trade unions, and anti-colonial and revolutionary movements); more contemporary social movements (e.g. women's and environmental movements); NGO's (e.g. Amnesty International); transnational civic networks (e.g. those resisting the construction of large dams, e.g. International Rivers Network); 'new' nationalist and fundamentalist movements (e.g. Al Qaeda); and the anti-capitalist 'movement'. Meanwhile Starr (2000) identifies at least three different strategic foci present within contemporary anti-corporate protests, namely: (i) *contestation and reform* which involves social movements and organisations that seek to impose regulatory limitations on corporations and/or governments, or force them to self-regulate, mobilising existing formal democratic channels of protest (e.g. Human Rights Watch and the Fair Trade network); (ii) *globalisation from below* whereby various social movements and organisations form global alliances regarding environmental degradation, the abuse of human rights, labour standards. etc., to make corporations and governments accountable to people instead of elites (e.g. the Zapatistas, Labour unions, the WSF and PGA; and (iii) *delinking, relocalisation and sovereignty* whereby varied initiatives articulate the pleasures, productivities and rights of localities and attempt to delink local economies from corporate-controlled national and international economies (e.g. permaculture initiatives, community currency (LETS), community credit organisations, sovereignty movements, especially those of indigenous peoples, and various religious nationalisms (see also Hines, 2000). Furthermore, Juris (2004a) identifies four types of social movement response to neoliberalism: (i) *institutional movements* – these work within national structures of representative democracy, while seeking to establish social democracy or state socialism, and primarily involve political parties, unions and NGOs; (ii) *people's globalisation* – this refers to movements that are internationalist in scope, populist in orientation and aim to build a global civil society, and includes both reformist and post-capitalist varieties; (iii) *radical network-based movements* – these movements also stress autonomy and direct democracy, but further emphasise decentralised global networking; and (iv) *localisation and militant autonomy* – this includes movements that promote autonomous models of community production and democratic control, and which emphasise local forms of struggle and organisation rather than horizontal networking, although they may also take part in the latter (Juris 2004a: 141–142).

Second, GJNs are characterised by creativity. As discussed in Chapter 1, one of the most visible manifestations of GJNs has been the global days of action that have accompanied the international summits of the architects and implementers of neoliberalism. Della Porta *et al.* (2006: 238–239) argue that these contemporary protests specifically have tended to follow three types of logic. First, protests articulate the logic of damage, whereby protest seeks to generate material losses or damage, create disturbances, threaten disorder and challenge elites by enhancing uncertainty. Second, protests articulate the logic of numbers whereby large protests increase public disturbance and media coverage and threaten the potential for loss of consensus by a government refusing to negotiate. Third, protests articulate the logic of witnessing, whereby protestors demonstrate their commitment to act collectively for common goals, expressed through actions involving high costs or personal risks such as nonviolent direct action. Such techniques enhance the symbolic impact of actions and attract media attention (see Routledge, 1997c).

However, global days of action also involve a range of creative and productive activities that prefigure alternative worlds and in so doing summon them into being (Juris, 2004a). As Holmes (2004: 356) argues, the global days of action involve: collaborative research on the political, social, economic, cultural and ecological issues involved; coordination between numerous groups concerning the preliminary forms of mobilisation; global dissemination through a variety of channels of the research and preliminary positions; travel of tens of thousands of people and groups to specific sites of resistance; self-organisation of meeting and accommodation places (e.g. convergence camps and zones); the establishment of counter-summits through intellectual and political cooperation; the creation of artistic and cultural events;

minimal agreements of the basic parameters and forms of the actions to be taken; legal and medical coordination to ensure protestor safety; the installation of independent media centres to report on the events; social, political and legal follow-up on the aftermath of the protest; and subsequent analysis of the new situation that results from each confrontation.

Third, many of the aforementioned activities of GJNs embody a political vision and practice of autonomy, such as self-organised, cooperative, and interactive spaces and activities that seek to remain autonomous the state, capital and organised political parties (see Notes from Nowhere, 2003; Holloway, 2005). This is particularly pertinent in the creation of spaces for the practice of participatory democracy, such as the social fora, counter-summits, conferences and convergence camps, mentioned above and some of which discussed in more detail below (cf. Juris, 2004a). Other examples include the Zapatista autonomous communities in Chiapas (Holloway, 2005), Indymedia, the social centres that have emerged in many countries in Europe, especially Italy, the UK, Germany and Holland (Starr, 2005), food and housing cooperatives, and the *asambleas populares* (popular assemblies) in Argentina (Gordon and Chatterton, 2004). There are, of course, varying degrees of autonomy practised by different groups: varying degrees of interaction with the state, capital and political parties. Hence, whilst some social movements remain relatively autonomous of these institutions and processes, others frequently have working relationships with political parties or with the state (e.g. trade unions), or may participate in elections.

Even when attempting to embody autonomous practices, a range of problems can arise. For example, while purportedly an open, autonomous space of discussion between diverse social movements and NGOs, the WSF process has been criticised (Chapter 7). The Organising Committee of the WSF has been critiqued because of its hierarchical organisation and lack of transparency in decision-making (regarding who the decision-makers actually are, who gets to speak at the Forum, the allocation of spaces and resources at the Forum for different groups, etc). In addition, the Forum as a process has been criticised because of the special treatment and privilege allotted to celebrity speakers, and the privileging and co-optation of the Forum by institutionalised political structures, political parties, trade unions and mainstream NGOs (Juris, 2004a, 2005c; Osterweil, 2004). United States foundations have supported the WSF itself or various selected NGOs influential within it. The organisational space of the WSF is dominated by the official programme that has been conceived without notable discussion beyond the governing bodies. Many small or radical groups and events are marginalised geographically and politically (Juris, 2005c; Waterman, 2004). The WSF can provide alternative channels of communication, whereby particular voices that are suppressed in their own society may find articulation and their concerns projected and amplified. However, within the WSF these remain selective – some voices are still heard at the expense of others.

Fourth, GJNs are characterised by convergence. As noted above, among the obvious elements of convergence are the targets of GJNs: activists are especially opposed to the international institutions that are perceived to promote neoliberalism without regard to ethical standards. By identifying structures of power within the global political field, social movements have established common targets of protest – articulated through global days of action – that have included the meetings of the WB, the IMF, the OECD and the WTO, the G8 and 'free trade' treaties such as the NAFTA, the FTAA, the Multilateral Agreement on Investment (MAI) and the General Agreement on Trade in Services (GATS). Global days of action continue to represent a collective defiance to the business as usual of Empire and enable alternatives to be articulated and presented to wider publics. Other elements of convergence are collective events such as conferences and social fora such as the WSF, and collective campaigns such as the resistance against the MAI (see Notes from Nowhere, 2003; Starr, 2005). Convergence also implies a range of key characteristics that are of prime interest to us in considering GJNs. These are scale politics, the creation of spaces of participatory democracy and the forging of transnational solidarities.

Fifth, GJNs are characterised by spatially-extensive politics. What often mobilises place-based movements to construct broader spatial networks with distant others, is a growing awareness of common experiences arising from the implementation of neoliberal policies by compliant national or regional governments, or shared grievances emanating from the dispersed operational geographies of particular transnational corporations. When place-based struggles develop, or become part of, geographically flexible networks, they become embedded in different places at a variety of spatial scales. These different geographic scales (global, regional, national, local) are mutually constitutive parts, becoming links of various lengths in networks. Moreover, while networks can create cultural and spatial configurations that connect places with each other (Escobar, 2001), so can particular places be important within the workings of networks – the identification with particular places can be of strategic importance for the mobilisation strategies of particular resistance movements within GJNs.

Participation in GJNs allows activists to expand the spatial horizons of their own territorially-based struggles (Reid and Taylor, 2000). Most of the actors and movements that constitute GJNs derive their principal strength from acting at the local and national scales rather than at the global level (Sklair, 1995). Moreover, the process of trans-national politics also is dependent, in part, on place-specific processes. For example, the diffusion and domestication of different activist ideas, tactics and strategies from one location to another depend, in part, on a range of place-specific processes such as local activist narratives, the cultural contexts of protest, previous experience of actions, inter-connections with other campaigns and the place-specific physical terrain provided by a protest. Hence, forms of protest are spread and modified by the process of their application, which enable or constrain activist behaviours being internalised and legitimised between different cultural and political contexts (della Porta and Tarrow, 2005; Hayes, 2006).

At the same time there is considerable unevenness in the spatial reach of movements within GJNs, with some remaining relatively localised whilst others develop a dense web of broader connections and associations. In this sense, GJNs have to negotiate between action that is deeply embedded in place, such as local experiences, social relations and power conditions (e.g. see Routledge, 1993) and action that facilitates more transnational coalitions. We will argue in Chapter 4 that the spatialities of GJNs must be considered not as totalities but rather as 'convergence spaces' (Routledge, 2003a) for particular actors, movements and struggles at particular moments in time. Convergence spaces act as geographically dispersed social coalitions of actors and resources that are put into circulation in a continual effort to make political actions durable through time and mobile across space.

Sixth, GJNs attempt to create spaces for participatory democracy. Associated with the emergence of widespread resistance against neoliberalism, they have been the conferences and fora that have accompanied such protests. For example, at the global days of action against the WB and IMF in Prague, in 2000, there was a four-day conference among both the activists who had arrived to protest and other actors within civil society such as academics, etc. In addition, the protestors have organised convergence zones or camps where activists who have travelled to participate in global days of action can meet one another, sleep, cook, etc., and hold meetings to decide protests strategies and tactics (Juris, 2004a).

Such face-to-face meetings provide opportunities for activists to reflect and debate upon issues, and generate and exchange ideas (e.g. concerning alternatives to neoliberalism), resources and practices (Rai, 2003; Juris, 2004a). As Juris notes 'activist gatherings provide alternative mechanisms for generating affective attachments . . . that allow . . . movements to continue reaching out to a broader audience' (2004a: 467). Beyond the gatherings at particular protests, such processes have been 'institutionalised' since 2001 in the WSF and regional Social Forums that have taken place around the world. The notion of such fora has been to engender a process of dialogue and reflection and the transnational exchange of experiences, ideas, strategies and information between the participants regarding their spatially-extensive struggles and campaigns (Juris, 2004a; 2005c). We will return to an in-depth discussion of this process in Chapter 7.

One of the most powerful ways to take stock of the significance of such meetings is through the testimonies of the many actors who have taken part in global days of action and fora. Discursive resistance, like its material counterpart, acts as a political disruption in the unanimity implied by state and international institution discourses regarding neoliberalism. Testimonials of peasants, indigenous people, women, trade unionists, etc., through eye-witness accounts and speeches at public demonstrations and international meetings, are deployed to address state/corporate injustices such as encroachment on land, harassment, corruption and violence, as well as the effects of accumulation by dispossession (such as displacement and resettlement) upon communities. They personalise the denunciation of state or corporate violence and demonstrate resistance, and gain their narrative power from the metaphor of witnessing. They represent eye-witness experiences of injustice and violence and involve the act of witnesses presenting evidence for consideration by public opinion (Warren, 1997).

Testimonials also provide justification for action and resistance. The crucial power of these testimonials is to construct a reality where other people might consider becoming involved in resistance against neoliberalism. Testimonials act to reinsert the dispossessed and their experiences into a social system that marginalises them and makes them invisible. As such, it symbolises a revolt against invisibility. Although many such testimonials are never permanently recorded, some have found their way into print (e.g. see Notes from Nowhere, 2003; Mertes, 2004; Sen et al., 2004; Solnit, 2004). In addition, there are more journalistic accounts such as those of Klein (2002), and the plethora of accounts that have been published on-line on Indymedia (www.indy media.org), including those of Californian activist Starhawk (see her website at: www.starhawk.org/activism/activism-writings/activism-writings.html).

It has been argued that conferences and fora enable the practice of participatory democracy, in that the decision-making that takes place is more egalitarian, collaborative and consensual in character than the traditional hierarchical decision-making that characterises representative democracies (Juris, 2004a). In theory, at least, there are no leaders as such and all voices are equal: anyone/everyone can influence the course of debate, strategy and participation (see Klein, 2002; Notes from Nowhere, 2003; Starr, 2005). Indeed, it has also been argued that the very process of networking is conducive to more inclusive interaction and debates between actors, and allows for participatory democracy to unfold. It is argued that the virtue of deliberation is that it allows actors' preferences and identities to be modified so as to serve the greater good (della Porta, 2007). Hardt and Negri (2004) have even gone further, presenting the network organisation of social movements as the ultimate form of democracy (beyond representative and participative models) and as the ultimate emancipation of labour over capital. Our purpose in this book is less to engage within the voluminous critique that the theorists of the 'multitude' have sparked (e.g. see Chari, 2003; Corbridge, 2003; Welker, 2003), and to answer the normative question of whether or not this ideal has been attained, but rather to reflect on the spatial conditions of their existence and operation; in other words on how geography makes it possible (or not) for such networks to exist.

Finally, GJNs attempt to forge solidarities through the making of connections grounded in place- and face-to-face-based moments of articulation that occur at conferences, social fora, and joint campaigns and protests. The ongoing organising processes surrounding these events 'facilitate sustained exchange and interaction among diverse move-ments, networks, and organisations, generating common discourses, practices, and identities' (Juris, 2004a: 466). Moreover, temporary spaces of interaction and exchange are created whereby, it has been argued, practices of participatory democracy are realised. This will be discussed in more detail below.

Engaging with broader debates in the social science and activist literatures around the network concept, our purpose in Chapters 3 and 4 is to provide a more sophisticated conceptualisation of GJNs by analysing their operational logics, political strategies and some of their complex geographies. We will do this, in part, by drawing upon some of the key characteristics of GJNs that we have discussed above – particularly convergence, scale politics, the creation of spaces of interaction and the forging of mutual solidarity.

We will also (in Chapter 4) draw upon the concepts of convergence space (Routledge, 2003a) and relational spaces of responsibility (Massey, 2004; 2005) to consider the entangled geographies within which GJNs are embedded. We argue that issues of space and place are critical in understanding the operation of these networks and their potential to contribute to an alternative global politics. Spatially, the global linkages of GJNs can be seen as creating cultural and spatial configurations that connect places with each other in opposition to neoliberalism. However, the individual movements that comprise networks, while not necessarily place-restricted, remain heavily territorialised in their struggles, to the extent that local or national political priorities and objectives will in some cases shape trans-national network practices. It is important therefore to consider the spatial enactment of processes of interaction and facilitation, including communication flows, information-sharing, solidarity actions, coordination and resource mobilisation. In addition, as we shall show in this book, networks evolve unevenly over space with some groups and actors within them able to develop relatively more global connections and associations whereas others remain relatively more localised. Potential conflicts arise from such complex geographies which only become evident through analysing the specific operation and evolution of different networks.

Notes

1   See Cumbers *et al.* (2008) for greater development of these arguments.

2   ANT aims to reconfigure the notion of social agency through determining how power and organisation must be produced, stabilised and made to cohere through relations between collectives of people and things. ANT has also shown how productive and communicative social capacities (i.e. the exchange of information) are thoroughly relational and densely mediated achievements, and can only occur in the collective work of networks (Kirsch and Mitchell, 2004).

3   See also Diane Nelson (1999) on the concept of fluidarity.

4   Kevin McDonald (2006) makes a powerful case for inclusion of the embodied sensual experiences of networks. However, whereas he argues that these aspects of networks are more important than the deliberative and representative, our experiences within networks leads us to regard both as important.

Global justice networks: operational logics and strategies

Given the aforementioned variety of political actors and strategic foci of GJNs, detailed in Chapter 2, it is perhaps unsurprising that they comprise a series of political, operational and geographical 'fault-lines'. These include differences between ideological (e.g. Marxist, Feminist, Socialist, Social Democratic, Anarchist) and post-ideological (e.g. autonomist) positionalities; reformist and radical political agendas; the resource and power differences between movements from the Global North and the Global South; and different types of activism associated with NGOs, political parties, and direct action formations (Juris, 2004a; Tormey, 2004a). Here we draw significantly upon the recent work of Juris (2004a, b; 2005c), Tormey (2004a; 2005) and Robinson (Robinson and Tormey, forthcoming) in conceiving of the different operational logics at work within GJNs (see also Juris [2004a] on different operational logics in People's Global Action and the World Social Forum).

Operational logics of GJNs

Juris (2004a, b; 2005c), Tormey (2004a; 2005) and Robinson and Tormey, (forthcoming) argue that two principal political imaginaries – vertical and horizontal – are at work within the operational logics of political formations.[1] Juris (2004a, b; 2005c) specifically refers to a tension between 'horizontal networking' and 'vertical command' logics. In reality both tendencies may be at work within movements, but the distinction is a useful heuristic device for us here for characterising the broad differences in political and operational logics within GJNs. Tormey (2005: 2) argues that the vertical imaginary 'sustains the idea of a political party or a movement as a machine of transformation on the terrain of the social'. This 'modernist imaginary is one of an imagined *place* – a clearly delineated world that operates in accordance with clear maxims and principles of justice. It offers an image of how we should live and seeks to transform (or maintain) social life in accordance with its governing logic' (*ibid*).

By contrast social movements that are autonomous of political parties and eschew representative political structures (e.g. direct action formations such as Reclaim the Streets and Italy's *Ya Basta*) articulate a horizontal imaginary and are not concerned with generating a distinct *place* that can be seized or captured from a ruling elite, but instead are interested in generating *spaces* that resist overcoding or incorporation into a governing ideology (Tormey, 2005). Autonomous spaces are in this sense relational, open, contingent, and immanent (Juris, 2004a; 2005c).[2] Subcomandante Marcos[3] argues that the point is to create a *space* 'a world made of many worlds' (2003: 36). Space is an important concept in attempts to theorise a radical 'outside' of the present, from Harvey's (2000) 'spaces of hope', and Foucault's (1986) 'heterotopias' to Bey's (1991) 'Temporary Autonomous Zones' and Deleuze and Guattari's (1987) description of 'nomadic' or 'smooth' space (Tormey, 2005). The WSF was constituted as providing such spaces – spaces of discussion, comparison, affinity and affiliation. The Social Forums – at least theoretically – facilitate ways in which networks can coalesce, develop, multiply and re-multiply (Juris, 2004a, 2005c; McLeish, 2004; Sen, 2004b; Tormey, 2004b). We will return to the Social Forums as network encounters in Chapter 7.

Vertical operational logics

In more traditional movements (e.g. political parties, trade unions etc.) a 'vertical' logic of modernity predominates, where organisations display conventional hierarchical structures, with a recognised leadership, vertical social relations based on delegation, and formal organisational processes (Juris 2004a, b). As Tormey (2005: 2) notes: 'it is a politics premised on the necessity for the *development of a programme*, for the *building of a party* to win supporters to the programme and to *capture power* so as to use power' (italics retained from original; see also Robinson and Tormey, 2005) to establish a particular conception of how people should live. Here solidarity is achieved through renouncing particularities/singularities in favour of vertical relationships of representation and delegation expressed through the collectivity (e.g. established trade unions, political parties). Relationships between members are mediated through their relationship to the totality (McDonald, 2006).

As Tormey (2005) notes, the image of modernist politics is war (e.g. class struggle). Political programmes outline the ideological 'vision' of the parties or groups who espouse them, which frequently translate into a manifesto. Tormey notes:

> The objective is to capture (state) power in order to implement a vision, or to reshape the political environment, in accordance with the shared values of the group. This idea is based on an image of power as a macrosocial resource which one can possess, rather than as a microsocial relation which, as Foucault puts it, 'circulates' in social networks (Foucault, 2001). There is a 'centre' of power which can be occupied and which, once occupied, provides the power-holder with the basis for moulding society in a particular image. Once in power the object is the maintenance of power to ensure that the programme is realised and that rival visions are held at bay. (2005: 3; see also Robinson and Tormey, 2005)

Hence, vertical political organisations possess a teleological character, as do the processes by which parties can become exclusionary and alienating to members and non-members alike. The party controls the political line to be pursued by members and activists in their political interactions among themselves and with others they attempt to mobilise. It arbitrates in conflicts between members, being responsible for their discipline, and it provides the focus for the formulation of strategy and tactics. It generates political leadership and as such represents a government-in-waiting, mirroring the state apparatus itself. It is hierarchical and is based on a division of labour between an elite vanguard of activists that develops the ideological programme and apparatus, and a mass of party activists, who follow the vanguard's directives (Tormey, 2005).

The fact that there is a clear end point or vision to be reached pushes parties and movements in an 'oligarchical' direction (Michels, 1998). As Tormey notes:

> It is easier to effect a 'coalescence' around a programme where there are fewer people involved, just as it is 'easier' to come to a decision the fewer people are involved in making it. It is easier to pursue power if the lines of power and accountability are clear with a single leader able to project the message of the party without contradiction or mixed messages occluding the minds of potential supporters or voters. It is easier once in power to maintain power where decision-making is confined to a small number of officials. In this sense the quest for 'effectiveness' makes desirable and necessary the elaboration of vertical political structures. (2005: 4; see also Robinson and Tormey, 2005)

Vertical operational logics are able to mobilise large numbers through the articulation of clear goals and objectives (such as capturing state power), and frequently their democratic structures are accountable to needs and interests of movement members (Juris, 2004a). However, capturing state power invariably involves compromises, the moderation of political goals, and often corruption and the resulting singular political programmes frequently exclude others. For example, Holloway (2005) has argued that the state is embedded within social relations of 'power-over' others (contrasting with the power to do and create, in relations of solidarity with others). Hence, the capture of state power by revolutionary (or even reformist) movements inevitably leads to the exercise of power over others and the reproduction of the kinds of social structures and practices which were struggled against in the first place (e.g. witness the course of events in the USSR and China during the twentieth century). Verticalism is, from this point of view, an exclusionary and alienating mode of politics. The more ideas, people, variables are excluded, the more 'effective' vertical politics becomes in terms of seizing power, although the more contradictory it becomes in realising a genuine revolutionary politics.

Horizontal operational logics

As Tormey (2005) notes, following the events of 1968, notions of 'thinking for oneself' permeated political thinking

and the practices of movements. For example, the Situation-
ists and Immediatists both insisted on the necessity for
rejecting 'ideology' as a basis for acting, and the need to
accept both individual and collective responsibility for acting
(Debord, 1967; Castoriadis, 1991; Tormey, 2005; Robinson
and Tormey, 2005). This represented a continual process of
collusion and alliances, a practice of micro-power, as opposed
to the development of macro-strategies via traditional
political party forms. However, the practice of collective
action should also attempt to reflect the different desires,
emotions and perceptions that motivated people to resist
injustices and/or construct alternatives (Tormey, 2005).

Political practices that emerge from this approach attempt
to:

> create and sustain a network dedicated to resisting and
> confronting injustices as opposed to a party that promises to
> displace an unjust world with a just world, a model that of
> necessity presupposes the possibility of a final definition
> of 'justice' notwithstanding any difference of affect, need, want
> and desire that representatives suppose to be pertinent to such
> a question. A network model points to the need to generate
> spaces in which people can interact to mutual benefit – as
> opposed to the annual congress mechanism of traditional parties
> designed to create a line to which members will adhere. A
> network, unlike a political party, does not have a programme,
> nor does it need one. What it needs are zones of encounter, shared
> learning, solidarity and affiliation. (Tormey, 2005: 6; see also
> Robinson and Tormey, 2005)

Hardt and Negri (2004) refer to the multitude which is
created through collaborative social interactions and the free
expression of difference and commonality. The limiting and
exclusive logic of 'identity-difference' between struggles (e.g.
either through individual's subordination to the identity of
a particular struggle under a central leadership or through
the autonomously enacted struggles of identity politics)
is transposed into the expansive logic of 'singularity-
commonality'. This is where an open network of singularities
is established – in effect a global commons – that links
together movements and individuals on the basis of commonly held languages, ideas, relationships, enemies, dreams
of a better world, ways of living and methods of combat.
There is a danger that this presents a singular account of the

network, collapsing diversity into commonality, a point we shall return to later in this book.

Horizontal, inclusive, forms of political engagement are concerned with the continuous transformation of 'everyday life' – a succession of resistances and rebellions tied together through bonds of empathy and affinity (Vaneigem, 1983). Horizontal strategies are anti-statist, in that they abstain from the capture of power 'in favour of alternative strategies that maintain the integrity and autonomy of constituent singularities' (Tormey, 2005: 8). Such an operational logic implies that groups engage in a decentred, non-hierarchical network of rhizomatic relations (Juris, 2004a, b; 2005c). These are characterised by flow, multi-dimensionality, varying intensities of affect and affiliation, unpredictability, contingency – as opposed to stasis, hierarchy, loyalty, obligation, predictability of the kind found in representative structures (Deleuze and Guattari, 1987). Such groups tend to work outside of formal political structures, eschewing leadership roles and party structures. Their actions represent active challenges and alternatives to formal ways of making decisions (e.g. through governments), and they emphasise the need to accept responsibility for acting (Juris 2004a, 2008). This is exemplified through the practice of direct action, which implies taking responsibility for change yourself (e.g. through the blockading of military bases, or the occupation of land) rather than relying upon elected representatives (Carter and Morland, 2004) and is argued by some to be more effective than conventional party politics.[4]

Concerning the differences between vertical and horizontal operational logics, McDonald (2002) notes four recent political trends that have taken place in the Global North. These are:

> First, the decline of forms of organisation where individuals fulfil defined roles (e.g. president, secretary, treasurer) and the development of ways of organising where action expresses the person as opposed to the function they occupy. Second, the decline of organisational form structured in terms of hierarchy and delegation, where elections ascend and decisions descend. Third, the decline of the membership card and associated rituals of initiation. Fourth, the shift away from long-term involvement in organisations, and the development of forms of network and action built up around projects. (McDonald, 2002: 116)

McDonald (2002) argues that many 'northern' movements are composed of affinity groups which reflect the convergence of the people who act through them, as opposed to being an 'organised expression' of a group, class or community. Involvement draws on 'skill-sharing' brought by each person. This expresses different forms of connection and struggle than those expressed in the solidarity that characterises the labour movement, where members implement group decisions as an expression of solidarity. For affinity groups, the action of each participant will be different, and it is the recognition of that difference that comprises one of the group's core characteristics (McDonald, 2002). The action and ethic of such operational logics expresses 'fluidarity' (McDonald, 2002) characterised by individuality, mobility and more unstable forms of identity, with temporary and ever-changing coalitions of actors, rather than solidarity in terms of more stable modes of organisation and the relationship between person and group.

Key to the horizontal perspective on the operation of networks is the Internet (Cardon and Granjon, 2003; Juris, 2005a) which is seen as radical and democratic because it enables equal access to information compared with traditional forms of communications which would have been channelled through key gatekeepers within movements. Moreover, it is becoming increasingly difficult for ruling elites, usually located at the national scale, to play the gatekeeper role, through traditional territorialised hierarchies, with regard to information and communication flows across space. This is most evident in the emergence of some of the Internet-driven networks that connect local trade union activists and shop stewards with their counterparts in other parts of the globe to discuss common enemies in the form of particular MNCs (Lee, 1999). The implication is that everybody is involved as equals in decision-making and that the priority given to communication results in a more participatory politics. The Internet therefore helps to maintain non-hierarchical, horizontal relations within networks, whilst at the same time permitting more open and unrestricted dialogue about strategies and tactics (Juris, 2004a; 2005a). The enhanced ability for movements to communicate with distant others has undoubtedly been empowering for locally-based struggles facing more powerful and less territorially bound actors such as states and corporations. The ability to use the Internet, in particular by local activists as 'an early warning system' to relay information about corporate or state malfeasance to a multitude of others in distant places, the development of open publishing and alternative media sites such as Indymedia which critically challenge establishment media outlets and sources, as well as well as grassroots websites and discussion fora have undoubtedly created new and less 'regulatable' networks of association.

The Internet provides alternative information on specific issues, provides struggles with visibility via websites, links movements around the globe, and has been very helpful in the organisation of global days of action and long-term campaigns (Juris, 2004a; 2005a). It facilitates the construction of new flexible identities, enabling some people to accumulate a stock of latent ties that can be transformed into qualitatively superior relationships producing a growth of the weak ties and social networks in which an individual is embedded. Therefore, a horizonal politics, associated with the use of the Internet, attempts to generate an inclusive form of politics where, theoretically at least, all participants have a voice. The lack of hierarchies, leaders and permanent structures are deemed more difficult to contain, infiltrate, control and eliminate (Juris, 2004a).

However, while the Internet works well at developing flexible loose organisational structures, it performs badly for building trust, developing network coherence and resolving disputes (della Porta et al., 2006), which require a continuing level of face-to-face interaction (Rai, 2003; Juris, 2004a; Routledge et al., 2007). Moreover, the 'digital divide' remains, as we will discuss in the case studies. Those with access to, and competencies in, information technologies retain more 'powerful' positions within networks, resulting in vertical social relations (see also Routledge, 2003a; Juris, 2004a; Routledge et al., 2006). In addition, within most political projects, some leadership and strategy is needed (e.g. witness the World Social Forum debates in Chapter 7), since spontaneity alone is insufficient to maintain such projects over time. Localised actions by networked activists alone cannot drain power from local elites; instead coordinated action within and between political formations is required. Furthermore, many people are unable to 'exercise power' due to conditions of chronic poverty, illiteracy, etc. Finally, network activism tends to privilege communication over action. Networks generate their own reality by reflecting upon themselves: 'an ambition for political change through communication and information exchange' (Riles, 2001: 3). Network activity – particularly the day-to-day work of coordination and communication – can become a means to an end, and an end in itself (cf. Juris, 2004a, b).

As we have noted above, the binary between hierarchical or vertically organised established movements and newer decentred and networked forms is a useful heuristic device in thinking through the potential for GJNs to deliver new forms of political activity. However, it has its limitations as a concept for understanding the operation of GJNs in practice. In two of the case study chapters, we have chosen two contrasting GJNs, one with a seeming 'vertical logic' (ICEM) and one with a 'horizonal logic' (PGA Asia), in an attempt to show that such binaries are blurred in the practices of each GJN. Both operational logics are at work in an entangled way within each network. Similarly, whilst we recognise the limits to network thinking (Chapter 2), ontologically 'network analysis' can be used to shed light on the emergence of transnational social relations in an era of globalisation (Anheier and Katz, 2005).[5] A network methodology allows us to 'operationalise' the vertical/ horizontal binary in contrasting more participatory and decentred forms of politics with comparatively undemocratic practices at work in many older forms of social movement, notably trade unions, NGOs and certain peasant movements, where a culture of passivity among the membership (often fostered by elites) has developed through bureaucratic and hierarchical forms of organisation (Cumbers, 2005). Thus, we would emphasise its utility in mapping and categorising different forms of social relations and connections that are emerging, rather than as a theory explaining the workings of global society itself, in contrast to Castells (1996; 1997; 1998) and others. As della Porta *et al.* (2006) argue, networking alone is not enough to fully express political projects.

Networks, relationality and power with GJNs

Within network practices, there is an extensive focus on process as people within the network discuss how best to coordinate (via email, conferences, reports, etc.) (Juris 2004a). Indeed, Riles (2001) argues that the quotidian work of networks – the work of creating documents, organising conferences, securing funding, writing meeting minutes, conference evaluations, etc. – generates a set of personal relations drawing people together and also creating tensions and divisions, etc. She argues that personal relations are often the means of achieving network effectiveness, hence people and their actions and relations can be understood as an effect of the network: 'networks must be created, sustained, and made to expand, and this need enlists collective interest and commitment to Action' (Riles, 2001: 172–174).

There is a tension therefore in GJNs between the development of a flexible organisational culture that accommodates participants' autonomy and diversity, and unites them around common goals (Juris, 2004a). This is because the movements against economic liberalisation are too (culturally, ideologically) differentiated and locally rooted to be subsumed easily under a common global agenda.[6] For example, extensive inequalities exist among movements, and flexible coalitions have the advantage of ensuring more adaptable responses to changing circumstances (Bandy and Smith, 2005). Levi and Murphy (2004) argue that five factors influence the endurance of transnational coalitions: the framing of issues to create common interests and compatible tactics; trust; credible commitments by the members of the coalition; the ability to resolve tensions and conflicts regarding goals, tactics, ideology, culture and organisational structure; and how members benefit from cooperation. Meanwhile, Bandy and Smith (2005: 232–237) argue that five principal social conditions are important for the enabling of transnational network activity. First, the existence and activity of large, international nongovernmental organisations (INGOs) and, especially, international governmental organisations (IGOs) such as the United Nations facilitate the development of transnational social movement networks.[7] Second, the existence of well-organised national movements (e.g. witnessed by the role of peasant movements in the *Via Campesina* network) also facilitate the development of transnational social movement networks. Third, transnational coalitions are more likely to be sustained when they include NGO participation from the North. This is attributable to the fact that these NGOs often have more specialised knowledge, resources or, at the very least, access to centres of economic and political decision making. They have larger organisational capacity, financial power and abilities to enjoin IGOs, national governments or transnational corporations. Fourth, the existence of cultural similarities between different movements within a network (della Porta *et al.*, 1999). These may be grounded in a common language, ideology or the identity of activist leaders, if not members. These ultimately provide a basis for solidarity and a transnational vision of community and resistance. Fifth, the regular communication between national movements allows for more rapid and continuing diffusion of movement values, strategies and goals (McAdam *et al.*, 2001). In addition, the existence of government or corporate institutions that are open to change, the absence of international political conflict (such as the War on Terror) and the existence of mass public dissent also facilitate transnational networking.

della Porta and Mosca (2007) argue that three mechanisms enable individual and organisational networks to facilitate mobilisation, and by which mobilisations strengthen networks: cognitive ones related to the construction of collective and transnational identities (at the individual level, the formation of a collective 'we' and developing motivations for action; and at the organisational level facilitating the bridging between different visions and values); affective ones which facilitate tolerance and trust (collaborative interactions between movement leaders and rank-and-filers); and structural ones which refer to the creation of personal and organisational ties that favour collective action. Moreover, they also argue that individual and organisational participation in common campaigns, which involve mechanisms of tolerance, mutual trust, logistical coordination, cross-issue bridging and transnational identities generates cross-fertilisation and 'multiple belongings' between movements and networks. Hence GJNs have overlapping memberships in a multitude of different organisations, and a plurality of associative and thematic commitments. Particular campaigns, Social Forums and other 'solidarity assemblies' facilitate networking and cross fertilisation between different movements and networks (Juris, 2004a; 2005c; Saunders and Rootes, 2006; della Porta and Mosca, 2007).

Beyond these general factors that enable enduring network activity to take place, a consideration of political practices within networks leads to important questions of power and information control (Juris, 2004a). Although the ideal network imagines the free flow of information between all participants in all directions, the reality is invariably compromised by various factors and existing sets of social relations evident in capitalist society centred upon class, gender, ethnicity, etc., which continue to shape the functioning of networks. Whilst the Internet acts as a communicative and coordinating thread for movements, weaving different people, groups and struggles together so that they may converge in virtual space, it cannot simply be described in horizonalist or topological terms (Amin, 2002; 2004), as it is still underpinned by various topographies of social power. Indeed, network discourse, as it is applied both to networks and global social relations more generally, tends towards a rather westernised and elitist vision of globalisation. The principles of fluidarity, for example, may apply to elite middle-class activists from the Global North, or those able to sustain themselves in alternative lifestyle politics linked to affinity groups, but they are unlikely to apply to the majority of grassroots activists who are materially embedded and entangled in particular local contexts in the Global South.[8] In this vein, Anheier and Katz's (2005) study of networks participating in the World Social Forum at Mumbai (2005) and different groups' connections with other movements emphasise the global reach of Northern NGOs compared with the more localised connections of many Southern NGOs.

Resource conflicts and dependencies can compromise GJNs as resource-rich movements or individuals can often dominate social movement coalitions. They have greater access to communication technologies and travel funds, and their staffs can dedicate more time to facilitating coalition development. Thus they can exercise a disproportionate amount of power in defining international coalitions (see

Sperling *et al.*, 2001; Rai, 2003; Eschle and Maiguashca, 2007). This can (often inadvertently) deny the participation and interests of other, poorer participants, who may not be familiar with organisational forms and practices that have developed in the North (Bandy and Smith, 2005). In addition, identity conflicts may emerge in GJNs whereby identities that are relatively 'embedded' – i.e. those that are deeply bound to the patterns of everyday life such as those of nationality, region, gender, ethnicity, race, class, religion, sex and language – can inform or be displaced by differences concerning power, organisation or strategy, making them difficult to comprehend and resolve. One of the most common identity conflicts is that between activists of developed and developing nations, often between Northern activists who assume paternal or imperial roles and Southern activists who articulate chauvinistic forms of nationalism (Bandy and Smith, 2005).

Hence, the idea that no dominant group or person controls decision making within GJNs due to their horizontal networking logic is far from the truth (cf. Juris, 2004a). In terms of effectiveness, there can be a 'tendency for networks to create hubs as these provide more stability and robustness. Hubs establish a kind of 'hierarchy' within networks and this in turn gives a certain advantage to key positions of players' (Thompson, 2004: 418). Ironically, many of the people that proclaim the leaderlessness of the resistance to neoliberalism, such as Naomi Klein or Walden Bello, are proclaimed as leaders or spokespeople by the media, and tend to command certain positions of discursive power within GJNs. At the level of individual networks, few people can assume the necessary social position from which to make effective 'interventions' in practice (King, 2004). In any set of collective social relations, a set of informal conventions and rules emerge that govern decision-making and influence the value system of the group (Commons, 1931). Such institutional rules are, in practice, made and known only to a few, and awareness of power is curtailed by those who know the rules – providing the structure of the group is informal (see also Juris, 2004a). We will return to this important issue towards the end of this chapter.

In terms of sustainability and political effectiveness, Harman (2000) doubts whether decentred and topological network forms can develop into an effective opposition to neoliberalism, especially when corporate power is increasingly concentrated. He argues that the networks that function most efficiently are those that take on more conventional organisational structures over time, and either democratically, or through conflict, lead to the emergence of a vanguard or elite within a more defined political project. Even in movements that continue to espouse a decentred ethos: 'it is not good enough for everyone to do their own thing. There has to be some willingness to engage in democratic formulation of decisions that are binding on everyone involved' (Harman, 2000: 35).

Klein (2002) has conceded this point in her analysis of the debacle associated with attempts to close down a WB meeting in Washington in 2000, when allowing everyone to do their own thing led to one of the routes into the convention building being left open after one group of activists withdrew from the blockade. The blockade collapsed as a result and the meeting went ahead. The broader point that we would make here is that there are limits to horizontalist networking (cf. Juris, 2004a). As Harman points out, decentred forms of political networking are nothing new, but have been characteristic of many resistance and oppositionist movements throughout history, from French Jacobins to British Chartists with correspondence through letter writing – the modern communication of the time. However, at some point, if movements are to become more substantial political forces, they need to confront the problem of organisation and structure.[9] The weakness of the Chartists in achieving their immediate demand for universal suffrage in the 1830s and 1840s was arguably due to their fragmented nature – with significant mass mobilisations at the local level but weak relational linkages within the broader network, preventing it from coalescing into a coherent national movement (Foot, 2005). Indeed the 'new social movements' of the 1960s, noted at the time by theorists such as Touraine (1978) for their greater democracy and grassroots participation (in contrast to established movements), evolved into formal structured organisations – with 'leaders' or 'organisers' who increasingly set agendas and 'members' whose role was more passive, such as Greenpeace and Amnesty International (Mayo, 2005).

Tormey (2004a) argues that network activism fetishises communication, privileging communication over action. In this respect, a contrast needs to be made between the different networks, such as those of Northern activist-based networks which often number less than a few dozen dispersed members across continents; NGOs which vary from small relatively isolated groupings to more powerful and almost corporate organisations such as Oxfam; various Global Union Federations (GUFs) which are run by a small international cadre with a relatively passive locally rooted membership; to mass social movements such as the *Movimento Sem Terra* in Brazil which has a third of a million members regarded 'not as a passive, card-carrying membership but one defined by taking action' (Mertes, 2002: 102). Once networks reach a certain size, some measure of organisational structure, delegation and leadership become critical to their functioning and without it there is the danger of disintegration into their constituent parts.

Interestingly, organisational issues within GJNs – for example, those over representation, decision making, divisions of labour, leadership styles, hierarchy and centralisation – are the most common forms of conflicts between larger professionalised or bureaucratic organisations and those that are smaller and more locally- or community-based (Juris, 2004a, b; 2005a, b). Larger, more powerful NGOs often favour more centralised, bureaucratic and professional organisations, while community-based groups champion more participatory, decentralised coalitions that can preserve diversity, flexibility and member autonomy. However, as we have argued above, these may also run the risk of being loosely coordinated and politically ineffective. Both demands, efficient coordination and decentralised participation, are, we would argue, vital to coalition sustainability. However, these also come into conflict with differences over strategies and goals of GJNs that vary between radical and reformist, legal and illegal, nonviolent and violent approaches (Bandy and Smith, 2005).

Academic and activist discourses' omission of the social power and organisational realities residing in networks also reveal a lack of research into the actual functioning of networks or discussion about the particular forms and characteristics they take. Thus, until recently, the revolutionary potential of the Internet was theoretically asserted rather than empirically demonstrated. However, recent research has begun to address this omission (e.g. see Pickerill, 2003; Lee, 2004; Juris, 2005a; Olesen, 2005; della Porta *et al.*, 2006). Lee's work on union activism (2004) notes that whilst the Internet has the potential to revolutionise activist communication and action, current practices represent no more that the extension of traditional forms – for example, e-mail for telegrams, guestbooks for rallies, and messages of support – rather than qualitatively new forms of communication and action:

> No website has yet proven itself a substitute for a picket line, no web forum has replaced the need for union meetings and no one has been recruited to a trade union by clever marketing through the web. Unions are gaining strength or declining due to numerous other factors and the Internet remains insignificant compared to those. (Lee, 2004: 74)

Lee also makes the point that use of the Internet has been more important incrementally, in improving and deepening day-to-day routine communications within networks during periods of relative calm, rather than being pivotal at moments of crisis and rapid change. This is also the case for the dissent network, which coordinated the convergence site, and was involved in protests, during the G8 meeting at Gleneagles, Scotland in 2005. Although the Internet provides an important forum for communications, ultimately the key decisions and actions revolve around placed events and meetings, such as monthly mass meetings held in different cities, plus convergence around days of action at particular sites of protest.[10]

The problem with much of the network discourse is that it insufficiently theorises the social context from which networks emerge (Thompson, 2004; although see Rai, 2003; Eschle and Maiguashca, 2007). Networks in practice vary enormously in their make-up (Anheier and Katz, 2005); each network will have its own 'organisational culture' and politics reflecting the uneven power relations between its constituent parts (Juris, 2004a). In this sense, there is a lack of theorisation of the spatial and historical contexts of GJNs. Too little time is spent exploring and assessing the importance of the contexts from which different actors and groups have emerged. Whilst networks may be unstable and subject to always shifting coalitions and alliances, the movements that inhabit them are often not, but in fact are firmly rooted spatially and temporally in particular settings.

For example, the Zapatista rebellion emerged out of the protection of historic rights of indigenous communities in Mexico to communal land, which subsequently became articulated within a broader critique of, and resistance to, NAFTA. Indeed their name refers to the revolutionary leader, Emilio Zapata, whose original movement as part of the Mexican Revolution in the first two decades of the twentieth century was rooted in historical claims on land (Baschet, 2005). Thus, whilst there may well be networks of fluidity in McDonald's sense (particularly direct action and autonomous groupings in the Global North), the majority of GJNs are composed of movements that have more collective, stable and historically embedded senses of identity (Harman, 2000; Wallerstein, 2004), many of which were also involved in earlier moments of transnational political resistance, such as the upheavals across the globe in 1968. A key question for GJNs, then becomes how can they work effectively across geographic space, and the political-economic contexts in which they operate (Rai, 2003; Eschle and Maiguashca, 2007). Whilst we deal with the spatial dynamics of GJNs in detail in the next chapter, in the remainder of this chapter we focus upon the organisational dilemmas of network building and how these are resolved in practice (cf. Juris, 2004a). Recognition of the power relations that exist within the political practices of networks, the tensions between verticalism and horizontalism, leadership and democratic participation lead us to introduce the concepts of 'imagineers' and 'networking vectors' for improving our understanding of the workings of GJNs.

Networking vectors and imagineers

GJNs are defined not by social location *per se* but by forms of practice and doing. Hence the processes of circulation, information flows and domains of communication that people enter or leave (e.g. conferences) become crucially important for understanding network operational dynamics (Tarrow, 2005; McDonald, 2006). Key for enabling these processes to take place are the existence of networking vectors, particularly imagineers, within GJNs.

What we term 'networking vectors' are critical in understanding the operational logics of GJNs. These are mechanisms that intervene in the work of translation by which networks are formed and developed, furthering the processes of communication, information-sharing and interaction within the network at a variety of spatial registers. They are also critical in understanding how power is distributed within networks. Such vectors include the work conducted by those we term 'imagineers' (discussed below), conferences, meetings in which conference delegates provide feedback to the grassroots communities in which they work, activist caravans, and particular political-economic campaigns. Indeed, international fora such as conferences, workshops, activist exchanges, or protest events, represent the public spheres within which transnational civil society connections may be constructed (Juris, 2004a). The transnational public sphere(s) can be imagined as the medium through which various forms of collective action and social movement repertoires become transferable to distant locations and causes (McDonald, 2002; 2006).

As we will show in the case study chapters, much of the organisational work of GJNs – preparing, organising and participating in discussions, meetings, conferences and campaigns – is conducted by key activists who organise conferences, mobilise resources (e.g. funds), and facilitate communication and information flows across the network, for example between movements, movement offices and grassroots communities. They represent what Tarrow (2005) terms 'rooted cosmopolitans', that is, transnational activists who move physically and cognitively outside their origins; draw on, and are constrained by, domestic and international resources networks, and opportunities of the societies/places in which they live, and advance claims on behalf of external actors, against external opponents, or in favour of goals they hold in common with transnational allies. However, we use the term 'imagineers' because these activists attempt to translate the concept or imaginary of the GJN (e.g. what it is, how it works and what it is attempting to achieve in terms of campaigns and network goals) within the broader constituency that comprises the network participants (e.g.

the grassroots communities who comprise the membership of the participant movements within a GJN, as in PGA Asia, or the national union affiliates that comprise the source of GJN 'delegates' as in ICEM). Imagineers work relationally across space, although this does not mean that they work in an undifferentiated 'flat' networked space. Rather, imagineers may be working in relatively more (or less) local, national or international spatial contexts, depending upon the operational logics of a particular GJN, its internal power relations, levels of resourcing and specific spatial dynamics, etc.

Moreover, crucially, imagineers serve to embody the networks in which they work (see Olesen, 2005). They work to effect what Callon (discussed in Murdoch, 1997a) terms the 'moments' of actor network translation: they problematise network functions (in order to effect solutions that enable the network to act more productively); they attempt to designate networked roles for actors (e.g. by allotting key tasks for participant movement members and materials); they work to enrol other movements and materials into the network (e.g. though visiting social movements and fundraising activities); and they work to mobilise all enrolled entities (e.g. through events such as conferences, caravans and global days of action). For GJNs to be realised, these 'moments' work together with the four 'strategies' of network translation. These are: the durability of interpersonal relations, continually performed over time; mobility through space (the materials and processes of communication which enable acting at a distance); anticipation (the relationship between 'technologies' and the capacity to foresee outcomes); and scope (how translation strategies reproduce themselves in a range of network instances and locations) (Callon, 1986; Law, 1992).

Through these relational processes of translation, individuals, movements, materials and places are incorporated into GJNs. The imagineers represent the connective tissue across geographic space working as activators, brokers and advocates for domestic and international claims (Tarrow, 2005). In the spaces of GJN 'performance', such as conferences, workshops, activist exchanges or protest events, imagineers are able to promote all aspects of coalition-building (Juris, 2004a). They articulate international norms and permit movements to share worldviews and objectives. They help put human faces on what otherwise may be abstracted differences among distant organisations, allowing for greater interpersonal trust and intercultural education (Bandy and Smith, 2005).[11] Brown and Fox argue that:

> direct, repeated, sustained contact among bridging individuals appears to have been an important factor in the development of solidarity, trust, and shared values among participants. Many coalition participants mentioned the importance of developing close relationships across great differences in culture, wealth, and experience. Extensive interaction, particularly face-to-face, seems important to the development of trust and solidarity. (1998: 455)

Imagineers are engaged in what della Porta *et al.* (2006) term 'meaning work'. Through framing issues for GJNs, and negotiating shared meanings, imagineers work to convince others to engage in collective action. This is important in forging collective common actions within GJNs because of the heterogeneity of the constituency mobilised and addressed by GJN participant movements, the potentially different mobilising structures which each participant movement is located within (e.g. different political traditions, ideologies, etc.) and the geographically dispersed character of the structural and individual mobilisation structures of participant movements.[12] Bandy and Smith (2005: 240–243) argue that such skilled 'movement brokers' have five special sets of traits and skills to facilitate solidarity. First, they must be able to exercise legitimate authority (often through possessing a charismatic personality) among a wide diversity of GJN participants. Second, imagineers must be good communicators or translators. They may translate languages, but they also translate between different discourses of grievance and forms of action used by members. They promote dialogue among members, and thus mutual learning, trust and the sharing of resources (Barvosa-Carter, 2001). Third, imagineers must be educators; they mediate between members, they act as conduits through which movement ideas may be diffused or transmitted, regarding grievances, goals of social change, organisational development, strategic assessment, etc. (Snow and Benford, 1999). Through training workshops, conferences and protest events, these imagineers help to socialise and politicise members into a culture of resistance. Fourth,

imagineers may use common documents such as mani-
festos, mission statements, strategic goals and organisational
bylaws to codify the commitments of members to a common
framework of action. Fifth, imagineers must manage the
conflicts that arise in GJNs, allowing for an open discussion
of differences. Imagineers enable transnational diffusion (of
ideas, tactics, strategies, etc.) between different sites and
social actors, bridging cultural and geographic divides.

As a result, within movements in both the Global North
and South, certain activists possess the cultural capital of
(usually) higher education, and the social capital inherent in
their transnational connections and access to resources and
knowledge (Missingham, 2003; Juris, 2004a; Routledge et al.,
2006). They may also possess differential access to resources
and mobility (e.g. time and finances to travel internationally)
compared to others in the network (see Routledge, 2003a).
The existence of such 'informal elites' can also be partly due
to the attitudes of grassroots activists themselves, who at
times tend to defer authority to key movement contacts and
let them get on with the work of international networking, leaving activists free to build and sustain local bases
of movements (see Routledge et al., 2006). This certainly
applies to the international operations of most GUFs where
the head offices of national union affiliates are the key nodal
points for both communication and decision-making but also
can apply to some supposedly more grassroots movements
in the Global South where similarly hierarchical topographies of power exist at national, regional and local scales
(ibid). An added problem for grassroots activists in the
Global South is varying and often limited access to electricity, let alone computer technologies – concrete realities
that lead them to be more dependent upon key nodal points
(e.g. regional or national offices of particular movements)
than in the Global North where computer access is more
widespread and therefore information less susceptible to
selective filtering by gatekeepers.

Hence, within GJNs, whatever their founding ethos,
decision-making often devolves to a small elite of individuals
and groups who make a lot of the running in deciding what
happens, where and when. In his analysis of political
struggles within the European PGA network, Juris (2004a)
turns to Freeman (1970) who noted from her experiences in

the feminist movement that 'structureless' groups do not exist. As Freeman explains:

[T]he structure may be flexible, it may vary over time, it may evenly or unevenly distribute tasks, power and resources over the members of the group. But it will be formed regardless of the abilities, personalities and intentions of the people involved. The very fact that we are individuals with different talents, predisposition's and backgrounds makes this inevitable . . . Thus 'structurelessness' becomes a way of masking power. (Freeman, 1970: 1–2)

Juris (2004a) further builds on the work of King (2004), who updates Freeman's critique of informal hierarchies for the information age. In this sense, influential activists, who King refers to as 'supernodes,' dominate both the flow and content of information within networks. Although the degree to which they will 'speak for others' will depend upon the type of movements they emanate from and, not least, their diverse geographies, 'much unofficial doctrine nonetheless emanates from them' (King, 2004: 6; cf. Juris, 2004a). Within GJNs, such individuals and groups (often from better resourced organisations in the Global North) because of their structural positions, communication skills and experience in activism and meeting facilitation – tend to wield disproportionate power and influence (Sperling *et al.*, 2001; Rai, 2003; Routledge 2003a; Juris, 2004a). King argues that whilst they 'do not (necessarily) constituting themselves out of a malicious will-to-power . . . power defaults to them through personal qualities like energy, commitment and charisma, and the ability to synthesise politically important social moments into identifiable ideas and forms' (2004: 6). Moreover, what King (2004) terms 'crypto-hierarchies' can occur, whereby a core group, through its longevity in working together within a network, forms an unintentional elite. As we shall see in the case study chapters, this process gives these intermediaries great importance in shaping the information circulated, since within GJNs most activists remain rooted in, and constrained by, domestic realities.

Networking vectors constitute the embodied, articulated moments in the social relations of GJNs (Massey, 1994). They generate the communicative infrastructure necessary for the operation and sustainability of GJNs (Juris, 2004a). They need to be physically manifest within mass actions, global activist conferences, activist caravans, regional network gatherings and particular political-economic campaigns (see Routledge, 2003a). They fashion 'dynamic global fields of interaction involving diverse, overlapping, and unevenly distributed networks, where collective identities, discourses, strategies and tactics are continually (re)produced and contested and through which they circulate' (Juris, 2004: 407). This process of networking is always dynamic and constantly changing: it can involve conflict, expansion, convergence and dissolution (Juris, 2004a). However, at their root they are concerned with the primary strategy of GJNs: to generate mutual solidarity between social movements.

GJNs and mutual solidarity

GJNs are constantly in process, being produced and reproduced through various networking practices which involve conflict over issues related to power, language, authority and entangled operational logics within the network (Juris, 2004a, b; 2005a). Hence an important aspect of network dynamics entails deepening the process of network imagination within grassroots communities for whom digital technologies remain relatively inaccessible. Network imaginaries at the grassroots remain uneven and potentially 'biodegradeable' (Plows, 2004: 104), that is, they may dissipate without sufficient and constant nurturance. Protest itself may mean little for the social and participatory rights of groups at the bottom of social hierarchies, whose specific interests remain unrepresented. Social change is not about events by themselves (e.g. strikes) but particularly the processes that are entailed in, and result from, such events (Ettlinger, 2002). An over-emphasis on resistance events can ignore the lives of a variety of people with diverse relationships to globalisation, including unorganised workers, undocumented immigrants and those not involved in political movements. Thus it is important to attend to a range of social locations and power relations (e.g. gender, class, ethnicity, race, sexuality), 'that refract globalisation processes and the multiple ways that such processes are lived, created, accommodated and acted upon in different historical and geographic settings' (Nagar et al., 2002: 269–270).

GJNs can provide the organisational infrastructure that enable transnational terrains of meaning and action against neoliberalism to emerge (Juris, 2004a). As Juris notes:

> Periodic conferences and activist caravans, and the ongoing organising processes surrounding them, facilitate sustained exchange and interaction among diverse movements, networks, and organisations, generating common discourses, practices, and identities. By providing concrete tools for communication and coordination, these networks allow geographically dispersed and, more or less, locally rooted actors to reach out across space, [and] forge broader ties and connections. (2004a: 466)

They also enable the grounding of the notion of solidarity between different movements. Networking is based upon the making of connections, across difference and distance – shared experiences as well as shared interests, which articulate a politics of relations (Juris, 2004a, b). Thus networks consisting of different place-based movements are held together by commonalites. However, the construction of particular grievances by particular movements has a distinct spatiality (as a result of the particular political, economic and cultural contexts of movement action) which will also have effects on the conduct of solidarities between different groups. Hence, despite common antipathies to neoliberalism, some movements may articulate their resistance through exclusionary versions of nationalism, while others may articulate a multifaceted opposition rejecting alternatives based on a narrow articulation of the nation state (Bové and Dufour, 2001).

Networks facilitate multiple localised oppositions which articulate diverse critiques, approaches and styles in various places of action (Schlosberg, 1999). In particular, what can get transnationalised in the network imaginary are notions of mutual solidarity – constructing the grievances and aspirations of geographically, culturally, economically and, at times, politically different and distant peoples as interlinked (Olesen, 2005) (i.e. the singularity-commonality notion of the multitude [Hardt and Negri, 2004]).[13] The creation of mutual solidarity is also a means by which people attempt to challenge power inequalities (Eschle and Maiguashca, 2007).

The connections necessary for the forging of a politics of alliance are grounded in place- and face-to-face-based moments of articulation such as conferences and village meetings, which stress relationality, connectivity and commonality (Rai, 2003; Juris, 2004a). Tracing the routes and connections through which solidarities are constituted enables a more generative role for place-based political activity to emerge in the constitution of solidarities (Featherstone, 2008). This also alerts us to the politics of extension and translation of place-based interests and experiences (Katz, 2001). This approach – which we will return to in Chapter 4 – highlights the geographies of how associations are generated, and how through moments of togetherness – like eating meals together, sharing testimonies, planning collective strategies against common opponents – practical solidarities are effected. In this sense, 'places make the link' through everyday mundane activities (Maffesoli, 1992; 2003). Moreover, mutual solidarities are forged out of the collective articulations of different struggles, which themselves comprise different practices (of gender, class, caste, political strategy, etc.). Such practices are engaged in actively shaping the world (see Mol, 1999), and thus mutual solidarities are constituted as negotiated interconnections that mediate in the associations between humans and non-humans (e.g. resources and technologies such as the Internet, money, visas, telephones, fax machines, etc.) within networks (Whatmore, 2002; Featherstone, 2005). They become an active part in the constitution of the political identities of place-based struggles, and actively shape how GJNs 'act' in the world, both in terms of the collective political identity of the network (Massey, 2005), and the strategies and campaigns such a network adopts.

Of course, resistance is imagined and articulated in different ways by different individuals, movements and collaborators. The different ways that unequal geographies of power are contested is constitutive of different political identities. Such resistant identities may articulate very different 'maps of grievance' (Featherstone, 2003), which might involve exclusionary nationalisms, localisms or gender practices. This can have significant impacts on the conduct of mutual solidarities, since these are productive practices that form equivalences between different struggles (Laclau and Mouffe quoted in Featherstone, 2003). Hence, while such equivalences imply new, open, relational political identities, they also involve contested social relations (Featherstone, 2003; Routledge, 2003a; Juris, 2004a).

Mutual solidarity across place-based movements enables connections to be drawn that extend beyond the local and particular. Ideally, such mutual solidarity recognises differences between actors within networks while at the same time recognising similarities (e.g. in battles against neoliberal policies such as privatisation). However, the construction of mutual solidarities is not a smooth process: they involve antagonisms (often born out of the differences between collaborators) as well as agreements: they are always multiple and contested, fraught with political determinations (Sperling *et al.*, 2001; Rai, 2003; Juris, 2004a; Featherstone, 2005). Nevertheless, network imaginaries (cf. Juris 2004a; 2005a) may help to reconfigure distance in different ways – which emphasises commonalities rather than differences. As Olesen (2005) argues, 'mutual solidarity builds on a greater level of openness to different forms of social struggle' [and] 'entails a constant mediation between particularity and universality – that is, an invocation of global consciousness resting on recognition of the other' (2005: 111). A network imaginary that can invoke interconnectedness opens up the potential for mutual solidarity to enable a diversity of struggles to articulate their particularities while simultaneously asserting collective identities (Holloway and Pelaez, 1998). Such solidarity takes place in the form of changing and overlapping circuits of relations that are enacted both virtually through the Internet, and materially in particular forums such as conferences. Such face-to-face meetings enable the embodying of mutual solidarity. As Juris (2004a) notes:

> Beyond creating open spaces for reflection and debate, forums and conferences also provide 'temporary terrains of construction' where activists generate and exchange innovative ideas, resources, and practices, and within which alternative social movement networks are physically mapped and embodied . . . activist gatherings provide alternative mechanisms for generating affective attachments . . . [that allow] . . . movements to continue reaching out to a broader audience. (466–467)

The sustainability of such processes will depend, in part, on the extent to which network imaginaries are grounded successfully, and meaningfully, in grassroots communities.

Network imaginaries must thus be grounded in both material projects (i.e. inter-movement initiatives and campaigns) and the 'geopoetics of resistance' (Routledge, 2000), such as the cultural and ideological expressions of social movement agency drawn from place-specific knowledges, cultural practices and vernacular languages which inspire, empower and motivate people to resist (see Chapter 4). Due importance must be given to political and cultural meanings (e.g. femininity and masculinity, work, justice, activism), which will entail an engagement with power and the complex ways in which it works at multiple sites (body, household, workplace, movement, network) (Nagar *et al.*, 2002). GJNs thus entail hybrid mixings of 'horizonal' and 'vertical' imaginaries that require grounding in sustainable forms of material resistance. A concern with relationality and the creation of spaces of encounter brings us to the spatialised dynamics of GJNs that we will discuss in the following chapter.

Notes

1   The tension between verticalism and horizontalism in revolutionary politics goes back to the antagonisms between anarchists, syndicalists and orthodox Marxists in the nineteenth century and resurfaced in the 1968 uprisings between new social movements and a 'new left' and the more established communist and socialist parties and trade unions (Cleaver, 2000).

2   We shall return to the concept of relational space in Chapter 4.

3   The spokesperson of the Zapatistas.

4   James Scott recounts how peasants act in effective and concerted fashion against powerful forces without formal organisation of the party kind (Scott, 1987; 1992). Rick Fantasia demonstrates how unionised and non-unionised worker resistances operate on the basis of informal alliances and associations (Fantasia, 1988). Piven and Cloward show how informal networks are often capable of generating more effective forms of collective action than political parties seeking to represent the poor and needy (Piven and Cloward, 1988).

5   For example, Anheier and Katz (2005) identify five principles of networks: cohesion, where ties are relatively dense across a network of activists; equivalence, where social relations are relatively similar and equal between members of the network; prominence, where certain actors are empowered through multiple connections whereas others are marginalised through fewer linkages; and range and brokerage which relate to situations whereby certain actors bridge different networks or communities. We will explore the latter in some detail towards the end of this chapter, arguing that it represents a crucial process in the workings of our case study GJNs.

6 However, despite their diversity, GJNs have reached certain key areas of common agreement, such as: (i) the cancellation of the foreign debt in the developing world (which amounted to US $3,000 billion in 1999); (ii) the introduction of a tax on international currency transactions and controls on capital flows; (iii) the reduction in people's working hours and an end to child labour; (iv) the defence of public services; (v) the progressive taxation to finance public services and redistribute wealth and income; (vi) the international adoption of enforceable targets for greenhouse emissions and large-scale investment in renewable energy; (vii) policies which ensure land, water and food sovereignty for peasant and indigenous people; and (viii) the defence of civil liberties (Callinicos, 2003; Fisher and Ponniah, 2003).

7 Intergovernmental targets such as the WTO and the NAFTA helped activists articulate their common grievances and develop organisations and strategies for confronting the challenges of neoliberalism.

8 However, certain movement leaders, and NGO workers from the Global South do enjoy a certain degree of transnational mobility (e.g. attending international conferences and Social Forums).

9 Harman uses his critique of decentred networks to argue for more centralised forms of organisation and power, though we would reject this view, agreeing with Holloway (2005) about the limitations of vanguardist revolutionary projects. Nevertheless, the problems of developing effective organisation whilst retaining participatory political forms remain for horizontalist advocates.

10 However, it should be noted that the calls for the global days of action have been initiated over the Internet, and as a result of this, numerous protests have taken place around the world during the global days of action. Hence, during the demonstrations against the WB and the IMF in Prague in 2000, there were concurrent solidarity demonstrations in 40 countries around the world. Moreover, Arquilla and Ronfeldt (2001) show how the direct action tactic of 'swarming' at demonstrations is partly organised through the Internet.

11 Issues that may be intractable or difficult to resolve in relatively brief conferences or protests may be better addressed in long-term cross-border exchanges, in which coalition participants can shape more refined frames of coalition.

12 Multifacetedness is an instinsic element of GJNs' collective identity. Imagineers draw upon the frames of collective memory (e.g. global days of action), common opponents (e.g. the WB, WTO and IMF) and shared solutions pertaining to environmental, social, economic justice.

13 Much transnational solidarity in the Americas (between the North and South) has tended to be about activism in one (geographical, socio-economic, political) location working to defend the interests, rights and identities of folk in other locations (Passy, 2001; Olesen, 2005). In such circumstances, 'Southern' activists can be cast as victims. This paternalistic model of solidarity reinscribes power asymmetries (e.g. Northern activists as 'saviours'); erases the agency of Southern activists who construct their own solidarity networks; and risks erasing how Northern activists are also subject to neoliberalism. Northern activists embedded in their own situated struggles are 'in a better position to listen to and collaborate with others involved in equivalent struggles in different locations' (Sundberg, 2007: 162).

4

Global justice networks: geographical dynamics and convergence spaces

This chapter is concerned with analysing how the operational dynamics of GJNs are acted out across geographic space. The spatiality of GJNs concerns both the geographical context in which they operate (e.g. the conditions, opportunities and constraints that they face) and the strategies that they employ. It concerns the myriad ongoing connections that combine different parts of the world together (by connecting different place-based social movements) that are constituted through, and constitute, particular sites and places (Featherstone *et al.*, 2007). Of course, as we discussed in Chapters 1 and 2, GJNs comprise particular social movements involved in a variety of struggles. Geographical processes and relations across a variety of scales (e.g. local, national, transnational), as well as the particularities of specific places, influence the character and emergence of various forms of resistance, and social movement practices are constitutive of different relationships to space, through a range of different uses of space that may enable or constrain the articulation of resistance (Routledge, 1997b). Hence, we will firstly discuss how the geographical concepts of space, scale and place can be used to interpret the key processes involved in the emergence, development and death of social movements (Routledge, 1993; 1997a; Miller, 2000). Following on from these insights we will then develop the concept of convergence space which will act as the interpretive framework for understanding GJNs.

The spatiality of social movements[1]

Social movements are defined as collective actors that hold conflictual orientations to clearly identified opponents, are linked horizontally by dense informal networks, share a distinct collective identity and pursue collective goals, and privilege protest as a main form of action (della Porta and Diani, 1999). They generate organisational and relational dynamics that are different from those found in hierarchical and centralised parties and organisations, and employ distinct means (repertoires) for pressing their claims (Nicholls, 2007). As Nicholls (2007) notes, research on transnational social movements (e.g. Bandy and Smith, 2005; della Porta and Tarrow, 2005; Tarrow, 2005) indicates that the grievance structures underpinning social movements have been affected by neoliberal globalisation. Neoliberalism has not only exacerbated class and regional inequalities, it has also increased the control of large capitalist institutions (transnational corporations and governing institutions) over people's everyday lives. This has given rise to the re-emergence of working-class and peasant struggles alongside mobilisations concerned with culture, identity and autonomy (della Porta and Tarrow, 2005; della Porta, 2005; Nicholls, 2007). The consolidation of a global system of financial regulation has prompted the 'upscaling' of previously local struggles between citizens, governments and transnational institutions and corporations to the international level. Indeed, it is important to stress that the neoliberal project and the increased globalisation of capital were first and foremost a response to growing class struggle and resistance across North America and Western Europe in the 1960s and 1970s, but largely located at the national level (Harvey, 2006a) An understanding of spatial inequalities, the politics of scale and processes of place provides crucial insights into understanding both the behaviour of social movements and the dynamics of GJNs.

Spatial inequalities

As Nicholls (2007) argues, capitalist and state systems are articulated unevenly across space. Economic and political processes are articulated in geographically uneven ways which produce variations in the grievances and development trajectories of social movements (Routledge, 1992; Miller, 2000). The uneven nature of capitalism both differentiates grievance structures across space, and concentrates and disperses the resources needed to make social movements possible (Nicholls, 2007). For example, the urbanisation process within the southern states of the USA resulted in the concentration of organisational resources of Black Americans (e.g. churches, people, money, social networks) in a handful of urban centres (McAdam, 1982). As Nicholls notes: 'the spatial concentration of people and resources was an important step in the emergence of the Civil Rights movement because it allowed insurgents to strengthen their networks and to facilitate the pooling and deployment of their collective resources' (2007: 612). Conversely, there are a range of factors that hinder the development of social movements. Nicholls (2007) goes on to argue that the increased mobility of people and resources can diffuse the resource base available to movements, weaken important social networks between potential collaborators (hence limiting the usefulness of networks for procuring key resources) and place movements into territorial competition with one another (see also Auyero, 2005; Coleman, 1988; Diani, 1997).

As Miller (2000) notes, the uneven character of economic cycles creates differential conditions of social movement mobilisation. Rapid economic growth, or state investment in particular areas, may create conditions of environmental degradation, gentrification or urban redevelopment. Conversely, economic decline, or state disinvestment in particular areas, may create conditions of unemployment, factory closures or inner-city decline. Hence, the uneven articulation of economic and state power – at the macro-level – geographically differentiates the grievance structures of social movements (Nicholls, 2007).

State power is articulated unevenly across space which presents different sets of political opportunities for actors in different locations (Nicholls, 2007). Both between states and within them, geographical variations in the relationship between states and civil society actors are important in understanding the context from which social movements emerge. For example, trade unions are still accepted as legitimate 'social partners' in much of western Europe though they have been under attack in North America, UK and Australia and are heavily censored or often state-dominated in parts of Asia, Eastern Europe and the former Soviet Union. Social movements are confronted by a range of more or less democratic political systems, and hence must operate within political spaces that are more or less coercive, which may increase the barriers to cooperation. In addition, the degree of political opportunities available to movements differs profoundly across political regimes (Nicholls, 2007). The coercive powers of the state are deployed differentially across space, which creates an uneven pattern of regulatory and repressive controls to contain those places where social and political contention is articulated (Mitchell and Staeheli, 2005; Dikeç, 2006; Nelson, 2006). At the sub-national level, variations are also evident in the relations between local state actors and civil society. For example, in the USA, the American Federation of Labour (AFL-CIO) has faced a more favourable organising environment in northern states than unions in the southern states (Moody, 1987; Herod, 1998), because unions are accepted as more legitimate social actors in the former and there is a more long-standing tradition of local union membership and organisation. In a similar vein, recent research in the UK has found that the imposition of local workfare regimes in traditional Labour-run local authorities tend to be more favourable to the participation of trade unions and voluntary sector organisations in policy design and delivery than elsewhere, where business interests are more dominant (Sunley et al., 2005).

The politics of scale

Political power is unevenly articulated across national space and geographic scale, and social movements mostly operate at the intersection of a series of overlapping scales – from more local municipalities, through regions, to the nation state and, increasingly international forums (Nicholls, 2007). These different politics of scale provide movements with a range of opportunities and constraints (Miller, 2004; Sikkink, 2005). As Nicholls (2007) notes, the uneven scaling of political opportunities has an important effect on the geographical strategies developed by both social movements in the pursuit of their claims and political elites in their challenges to movements. Indeed, 'states often shift policy making processes to those scales where popular pressure can be muted or diffused' (Nicholls, 2007: 614). For example, subsuming national labour regulations to international conventions reduces the opportunities for social movements to use electoral threats to pressure national political leaders. Also, devolving welfare policies to local government diffuses resistance because social movements must make claims in countless local bodies rather than a single national one (Nicholls, 2007).

Of course, movements that are local or national in character derive their principal strength from acting at these scales rather than at the global level (Sklair, 1995). For example, transnational corporations such as Nestlé, McDonalds and Nike have usually been disrupted primarily due to the efficacy of local campaigns (Klein, 2000). Where international campaigns are organised, local and national scales of action can be as important as international ones (Herod, 2001). For example, the Liverpool Dockers international campaign was grassroots-instigated and coordinated (by Liverpool Dockers) and operationalised by Dockers beyond the UK working within established union frame-works (Castree, 2000). However, Sikkink (2005) has argued that political opportunities for transnational social movements differ markedly between national and international scales, depending on the political character of countries, international institutions and the nature of the political issues at stake. National scales may be more effective for organising at some times, and international scales at others. She argues that movements often utilise political opportunities at one scale to create opportunities at other scales.

The persecution of multi-scalar strategies is also an interactive and relational process that requires the development and reorganisation of social networks across geographical and social boundaries (Nicholls, 2007). In their work on the American Civil Rights movement, Tarrow and McAdam (2005) term this process 'scale shift', which is achieved through two mechanisms. The first is 'relational diffusion', which refers to the extension of a movement through pre-existing relational ties containing trust and shared identities. This provides a durable base for sustainable mobilisations and facilitates the spread of social movements. However, because the spread is dependent on existing relational ties, the social and geographical reach of this scale shift tends to be limited and localised, which reduces the spatial and political impact of these types of mobilisations (Nicholls, 2007). The second mechanism is 'brokerage' which refers to the spread of social movement mobilisation (through various brokers) resulting from linking two or more social movement actors who were previously unconnected (Tarrow and McAdam, 2005). As Nicholls (2007) notes, 'this results in new relations across traditional geographical and social boundaries, enhancing the potential reach and effect of collective actors' (615). Though brokerage can expand the scope of social movements, they are also more fragile because they are made up of many different groups and possess weak mechanisms of social integration (Nicholls, 2007).

Putting social movements in their place

Because different social groups endow space with an amalgam of different meanings and values, particular places frequently become sites of conflict where the social structures and relations of power, domination and resistance intersect. This is most evident in instances where different ethnic or nationalist groups contest the same political space (e.g. Israel/Palestine, Northern Ireland/Ulster). Collective action is often focused upon cultural codes which are themselves spatially specific, since culture and ethnicity can create 'imagined spaces' (Harvey, 1989) reflecting a community's sense of place, such as the subjective orientation that can be engendered by living in a place. This plays a distinct role in shaping both the political claims of actors and the perception of political opportunities (Martin, 2003). The ideology which emanates from this, articulates a process of positive assertion (of local values and lifestyles) and resistance to intervening values of domination.

Place, then, is important to sites of resistance, the creation of alternative knowledges and the interplay between local and global practices. Places comprise an interwoven web of specific symbolic meanings, communicative processes, political discourses, religious idioms, cultural practices, social networks, economic relations, physical settings, envisioned desires and hopes. Sensitivity to such processes when considering particular practices of resistance acknowledges the subjective nature of people's perceptions, imaginations and experiences when they are involved in political action. It locates such action in dynamic spatial contexts, as it sheds light upon how spaces are transformed into places redolent with cultural meaning, memory and identity under conditions of conflict. For example, the Zapatista spokesperson, Subcommandante Marcos, has written widely about the place-specific political and cultural economy of indigenous people in the Mexican state of Chiapas, and how this has informed the Zapatista insurgency (Routledge 1998). 'Place' has a central role in shaping the claims, identities and capacities of mobilised political agents, helping to explain why social movements occur where they do, how the particularities of specific places influence the character and emergence of various forms of resistance, and the context within which, movement agency interpolates the social structure (Routledge, 1992; 1993; 1997b). Such a context-based analysis of social movements seeks to understand how the geographically uneven modes of exercising state and economic power intersect with people's everyday lives, combining to generate particular 'terrains' of resistance.

Sustained and proximate interaction over time in particular places can create strong trusting relations between actors, which can then be drawn on to enable collective action (Granovetter, 1983; Coleman, 1988; Diani, 1997; Miller, 2000; Tarrow and McAdam, 2005; Tilly, 2005). Indeed, despite globalisation, proximity remains crucial to the processes through which strong social and cultural ties are established, bound up, for example, in kinship networks, ethnic and religions affiliations, common history, shared language and traditions, etc. Places are particularly critical in facilitating the repeated contacts and bonding experiences between people which in turn favour stronger ties (Coleman, 1988; Collins, 2004; Nicholls, 2007). Morevover, social movements frequently draw upon local knowledges, cultural practices and vernacular languages to articulate their resistances. The body, performative rituals, work, ceremonial life, individual and collective identities form a reservoir of meanings embedded in the practices of everyday life, from which people shape and articulate their struggles (see also Juris, 2004a). The songs, poems, stories, myths, metaphors and symbols which are used to inform and inspire collective action form a poetics of resistance (Comaroff, 1985; Thrift, 1997; Coleman, 2004). Such cultural practices can evoke a sense of place, history and community which give potent expression to social movements struggles. These may also remain despite defeat, often latent for long periods, but bound up in the local collective memory as discursive resources that may bring to life future forms of resistance.

The particular cultural, economic and political milieu from which a movement emerges – its place of performance – can influence the character and form that a movement's resistance takes, evoking a community's sense of place and history. Indeed, the material, symbolic and imaginary character of places can powerfully influence the articulation of resistance. Spatial imaginaries – i.e. individual and collective cognitive frameworks constituted through the lived experiences, perceptions and conceptions of space – mediate how actors evaluate the potential risks and opportunities of joining social movements. For example, in the context of agricultural restructuring, political openings and religious mobilisation in southern Brazil, landless farmers used and reformulated their spatial imaginaries to embrace land occupation through the MST; while in the northeast, unemployed rural workers overcame the spatial imaginaries put in place by the local sugarcane economy to join the movement (Wolford, 2004).

The myriad cultural expressions of movement resistance frequently form a place-specific discourse of dissent which motivates and informs social movement agency, and articulates a movement's resistance identity. The poetics that emerges from such place-based resistance – i.e. the *geopoetics*[2] – acts as a political disruption and intervention, expressing emotions, hopes, desires – that which gives social movements their 'feeling space' (Routledge, 2000). In addition to being redolent of particular places of struggle, the geopoetics of resistance are deployed in order to mobilise, to educate, to propagandise, to teach tactics and explain strategies. As such they can also form 'vectors of dissent' in that they may 'travel' within and between civil and political societies, and potentially relay messages to a variety of audiences (including movement supporters and opponents), across a variety of scales (from the local to the global).

Castells (1997) has conceived of place-based struggles as representing defensive responses to the network society. He views the cultural and economic specificity of particular places as being deployed as part of a broader articulation of resistance to the space of flows, that is capital investments and developments increasingly detached through the use of information technologies, from the social constraints of cultural identities and local societies. However, place-based struggles can be both offensive and defensive with regard to the emergent spaces of globalisation. For example, the Zapatista peasant insurgency in Chiapas, Mexico, has been exemplary in the scaling up of its resistance through the development of global support networks. A completely different, though less cited, example was the US union, the United Auto Workers' successful action against General Motors in the mid-1990s, that demonstrated how strategic intervention by workers at a local plant in Flint, Michigan could bring a global just-in-time production system to a standstill as part of 'upscaling' their struggle (Herod, 2001). Both examples illustrate the relationality between place-based action and broader spatial dynamics that is missing in Castells' formulation of a binary between local and global processes, trapping social movements within territorially defined spaces. Moreover, the increasing globalisation of financial, technological and human flows and spatial extension of particular social movement struggles poses important criticisms for territorialised conceptions of place and scale that we shall discuss below.

Relational spaces of resistance

Massey (2004) has argued that stressing the distinctiveness and internal cohesiveness of place-based worlds can reinforce essentialised differences between people and the exclusive characteristics of belonging, where actors in specific places can be seen as possessing homogenous interests and identities which set them apart from actors in other locales, placing 'insiders' and 'outsiders' into perpetual struggles over the realisation of conflicting interests (see also, Nicholls, 2007). Rather, places are internally multiple with pluralistic exchanges between actors within these areas, and the possibility for relational interactions across different sites (Massey, 2004). Moreover, places are not only internally plural, they are also connected to extensive economic, political and cultural networks with varying geographical reach (Nicholls, 2007). As Amin argues, notions of internal spatial coherency and boundedness reify rather than reveal the logic of socio-spatial relations in a globalising world:

> In this emerging new order, spatial configuration and spatial boundaries are no longer purposively territorial or scalar, since the social, economic and political inside and outside are constituted through the topologies of actor networks which are becoming increasingly dynamic and varied in spatial constitution. (2004: 33)

Therefore, in order to make sense of the complex nature of transnational movements we need to avoid counter-posing notions of local and global, space and place (Featherstone, 2003). As we will show in the case study chapters, social movement actors are not internally homogeneous and externally different from others. Movement interests and identities are formed through relational exchanges between multiple actors within and between different sites (Featherstone, 2003). Particular locations are crossed by a variety of power networks, with actors in different sites engaging with one another through multiple relational exchanges (Featherstone, 2005).

However, while social movements may be increasingly made up of extensive and pluralistic relational flows, a number of factors continue to require their territorialisation (Martin, 2003; D'Arcus, 2005; Bosco, 2006; Nicholls, 2007). Certainly, political power continues to be primarily institutionalised through discrete territorial boundaries despite increased interdependencies and relational exchanges across state spaces (Mann, 1997; Tarrow, 2005). As Nicholls, notes: 'this has meant that the targets, opportunities, and strategies of social movements continue to be shaped through territorialised political structures and institutions' (2007: 618). This is certainly the case with the empirical examples studied in this book, and supported by recent work on transnational social movements (Bandy and Smith, 2005; Sikkink, 2005; Tarrow, 2005).

As a result we agree with the view that both territorially intensive and geographically extensive relations contribute distinct yet complimentary resources to social movements (Beaumont and Nicholls, 2007). As Nicholls argues:

> Whereas territorially intensive relations permit the genera-tion of certain high-grade resources (lives, reputations, tacit knowledge), geographically extensive relations facilitate the circulation of more generic ones (money, codified information, political support) between distant actors ... [hence, social movements] ... tend to depend on both territorially intensive and geographically extensive relations for pooling and deploying resources. (2007: 618–619)

As we argue in this book, processes of territoriality continue to be important in a world of increased relational flows (see also Routledge, 2003b).

The spatiality of GJNs

When place-based struggles develop, or become part of, geographically flexible networks, they become embedded in different places at a variety of spatial scales. These different geographic scales (global, regional, national, local) are mutu-ally constitutive parts, becoming links of various lengths in the network. Networks of agents act across various distances and through diverse intermediaries. However, some net-works are relatively more localised, while others are more global in scope and the relationship of networks to territories is mutually constitutive: networks are embedded in territories, and at the same time, territories are embedded in networks (Dicken *et al.*, 2001).

To quote Massey, 'each place is the focus of a distinct *mixture* of wider and more local social relations' (Massey, 1994: 156), and hence places can be imagined as 'articulated moments in networks of social relations' (*ibid*: 154). Networks can create cultural and spatial configurations that connect places with each other (Escobar, 2001). Moreover, particular places can also be important within the workings of those networks. For example, in his research on the *Madres de Plaza de Mayo* in Argentina, Bosco (2001) shows how collective political rituals enacted in different places across space (e.g. the public meetings of *Madres* in Plazas across Argentina) enabled the sustainability of different movement communities and movement identities. By reinforcing moral commitments and group solidarity, activist identities were maintained both within particular groups and between movements and activists in wider solidarity networks.

Bosco (2001) argues that the identification with particular places can be of strategic importance for the mobilisation strategies of particular resistance movements. These can contribute to the construction of strategic network ties with other movements in the same locality or in other localities. Activists may deploy symbolic images of places to match the interests and collective identities of other groups and thereby mobilise others along common cause or grounds. Hence the ties to particular places can be mobile, appealing to and mobilising different groups in different localities (Bosco, 2001). For example, concerning the opposition to the construction of the Diablo Canyon nuclear plant in San Luis Obispo, California; Diablo Canyon occupied a central place in the history and mythology of different anti-nuclear groups' subcultures. Activists' sentimental attachment to the place motivated them to travel from distant localities to participate in protest against the nuclear plant. Local activist groups constructed an alternative identity for the place as a sacred site for all folk concerned with the environment and strategically framed this identity to mobilise others outside the area (Jasper, cited in Bosco, 2001).

However, because places are important loci of collective memory, then social identity and the capacity to mobilise that identity into configurations of political solidarity are highly dependent upon the processes of place construction and sustenance (Harvey, 1996). Such particularities of place may come into conflict with those of other places. This, for example, often occurs where different place-specific understandings of gender relations operate, with highly patriarchial local social systems clashing with more progressive forms. As a result, these may vitiate against multi-scalar mobilisations and pose important problems for the development of GJNs. To discuss this issue requires a consideration of the work of David Harvey.

Militant particularism/global ambition

Borrowing a term from Williams (1979), Harvey argues that place-based resistances frequently articulate a 'militant particularism' (1996; 2000). This is where the ideals forged out of the affirmative experience of solidarities in one place have the potential to get generalised and universalised as a working model for a new form of society that will benefit all humanity – what Harvey terms 'global ambition'. However, Harvey notes that militant particularisms are often profoundly conservative, resting upon the perpetuation of patterns of social relations and community solidarities. He wonders whether there is a scale at which militant particularisms become impossible to ground let alone sustain. Indeed, he argues that:

> Anti-capitalist movements . . . are generally better at organising in and dominating 'their' places than at commanding space. '[R]egional resistances' . . . can indeed flourish in a multitude of particular places. But while such movements form a potential basis for that 'militant particularism' that can acquire global ambition, left to themselves they are easily dominated by the power of capital to coordinate accumulation across universal but fragmented space. The potentiality for militant particularism, embedded in place runs the risk of sliding back into a parochialist politics. (1996: 324)

Successful international alliances have to negotiate between action that is deeply embedded in place, such as local experiences, social relations and power conditions (e.g. see Routledge, 1993), and action that facilitates more transnational coalitions. Social movements, according to Harvey, can either remain place-based and ignore the potential contradictions inherent in transnational coalitions (e.g. concerning different gender relations within participant movements) or treat the contradictions as a nexus to create a more transcendent and universal politics, combining social and environmental justice that transcends the narrow solidarities and particular affinities shaped in particular places. In short, movements need to develop a politics of solidarity capable of reaching across space, without abandoning their militant particularist base(s) (1996: 400). This is especially pertinent for those militant particularisms that arise to protest those disguised particularisms – such as masculinism and heterosexism – that masquerade as universal (Fraser, 1997).[3]

However, even if social movements are capable of reaching across space, differential power relations exist within the functioning of the networks that are created. Particular actors are often dominant within networks, due to their control of key political, economic and technological resources (Dicken et al., 2001). Moreover, different groups and individuals are placed in distinct (more or less powerful) ways in relation to the flows and interconnections involved in the functioning of resistance networks. Thus, while the working of networks involves the intermingling of geographic scales, contradictions and tensions remain – either tied to the militant particularisms of particular movements or in the placing of specific actors within the network.

Katz (2001) has suggested that within specific places a useful strategy is to construct what she terms 'counter-topographies'. By this she means a detailed examination of some part of the material world, whereby the layers of process that produce particular places are excavated in order to determine their intersections with material social practices at other scales of analysis. Importantly, such an approach enables the examination of relationships across spaces and between places, in order to determine shared commonalities between places, in terms of their experience of the effects and particular relations to the process of neo-liberal globalisation. Such commonalities imply connection between places, and hence the production of counter-topographies link places analytically, and also potentially enhance struggles in the name of common interests (Katz, 2001: 1223–1224). This is particularly pertinent in the construction of mutual solidarities between social movements within GJNs. We have developed the notion of 'convergence space' (Routledge, 2003a; Cumbers et al., 2008), to draw together these spatial insights into the behaviour of movements and networks, and to provide a conceptual framework with which to interpret the operational and spatial dynamics of GJNs.

Convergence spaces

Our starting point for thinking through the spatialities of GJNs is to consider them first and foremost not as totalities but rather as 'convergence spaces' (Routledge, 2003a) for particular actors, movements and struggles at particular moments in time. Participation in GJNs allows activists to expand the spatial horizons of their own territorially based struggles (Reid and Taylor, 2000). Convergence spaces act as associations of actors and resources (intermediaries such as texts, humans, non-human materials, money), which are put into circulation in a continual effort to make political actions durable through time and mobile across space. Constantly redefined in interaction through active resources, and utilising materials of association such as the Internet, which are able to act at a distance, time and space are constructed within spaces (Latour, 1993; Murdoch, 1998). Convergence spaces as geographically dispersed social coalitions are defined by a range of characteristics.

First, they are comprised of place-based, but not necessarily place-restricted, movements. Most of the actors and movements that constitute GJNs derive their principal strength from acting at the local and national scales rather than at the global level (Sklair, 1995). Hence, for many grassroots activists, whether it is in peasant or indigenous people's movements, trade unionists or even consumer activists, it is their own locality, sense of community or even a national or ethnic collective consciousness that remain the most important (but not necessarily only) source of collective and individual identities. In this respect, 'stubborn chunks' (Valins, 1999) of territorialised identity persist. Indeed, it is this local diversity and differentiation that is often under threat from capitalist modernisation. Hence, regarding the Zapatista uprising: '[t]erritory comprises ancestors, knowledge, the use of plants, their evolution, the perception of the cosmos, customs and community and living history' (Cecena, 2004: 361).

More prosaically, the realities of making a living, social reproduction and links to family and community structures continue to embed movements in particular places. Also, even those actors whose lifestyles engender high degrees of mobility (e.g. movement leaders and NGO workers from the Global South who regularly attend international conferences and social fora) are never completely disembedded from these sorts of place-based social relations. Whilst there may be varying relations of connection to distant others, the continuing reality that everyday life is meaningfully territorialised is difficult to escape. But, crucially, immediate issues of survival and livelihood can act as motivations for people to participate in GJNs (see Routledge *et al.*, 2006). In addition, social identities within movements and the capacity for solidarity-building are still heavily dependent upon place-based processes of social production and repro-duction (Routledge, 1993; Harvey, 1996). Indeed, activists are often constrained by the political and institutional contexts and opportunity structures available to them, which are place-specific. These can include local and/or national decision-making processes, the degree of political account-ability of elites, and the absence of legal frameworks governing availability of information (Fagan, 2006).

Moreover, the process of transnational politics is also dependent, in part, on place-specific processes. As della Porta and Tarrow (2005) have noted, transnational politics takes three forms: the diffusion of ideas and actions from one country to another (e.g. sit-ins from the US civil rights movement spread to European student movements in the 1960s); domestication within national politics of conflicts that had external origins (e.g. the protests against national governments for accepting SAPs imposed by international financial institutions); and externalisation, where inter-national institutions are challenged to intervene in domestic affairs (e.g. International NGOs and Brazilian rubber tappers putting pressure on the WB and the Brazilian government to account for development projects in the Amazonian rainforest (Keck and Sikkink, 1998). These processes of diffusion and domestication depend, in part, on a range of place-specific processes such as local activist narratives; the cultural antecedents to protest (e.g. established modes of contention), previous experience of actions; interconnec-tions with other campaigns, the place-specific 'topographical opportunities' (i.e. the physical terrain) provided by a protest, and the specific experience of iteration as forms of protest are spread and modified by the process of their application, which enable or constrain innovative behaviour being internalised and legitimised (Hayes, 2006).

Hence, GJNs must negotiate between action that is deeply embedded in particular places and territories, and the fostering of coalitions that are more spatially extensive, and the impacts that such coalitions have upon the political identities of those involved. It should be recognised that the particularities of place may also vitiate against broader spatial mobilisation and pose important problems for the development of GJNs.

This emphasis upon 'place' as the cornerstone of live material existence does not mean that we hold to a closed or territorially-bounded view of the 'local'. Rather we would concur with Massey's view of places as open and relational such that 'each local struggle is already a relational achievement, drawing from both within and beyond "the local"' (2005: 182). Harvey argues that 'it is only when relationality connects to the absolute spaces and times of material and social life that politics comes alive. To neglect that connectivity is to court political irrelevance' (2006b: 293). Indeed, Featherstone (2005) has pointed out that even 'militant particularisms' (Williams, 1989; Harvey, 1996) are relational, in the sense of being formed out of broader non-local connections. This seems to us to be particularly true of GJNs where what often mobilises place-based movements to construct broader spatial networks with distant others, is a growing awareness of common experiences arising from the implementation of neoliberal policies by compliant national or regional governments, or shared grievances emanating from the dispersed operational geographies of particular transnational corporations.

In ontological terms, we would emphasise here that when place-based struggles become part of transnational networks, they become entwined in a complex set of spatially extensive relationships and connections, rather than the flatter topology of social relations suggested in the networks discourse (Chapter 3). Returning to the celebrated Zapatista example, the development of global networks of support for the struggle reflected the imperative to extend solidarity building to a transnational level in the face of a hostile state (Johnston and Laxer, 2003). The national state therefore remains an important site for both constraining and facilitating networking and coalition-building. The significance of the global solidarity network was its novelty in providing discursive and material resources for the Zapatista movement at the transnational scale for a struggle that remained ultimately a territorial one. But the transnational support network remained 'one scale of struggle among many' (*ibid*: 73).

Second, convergence spaces articulate certain 'collective visions' (i.e. unifying values, organisational principles and positions), which generate sufficient common ground to generate a politics of mutual solidarity (see below). Ideally, these collective visions are representative of a 'prefigurative politics' (Graeber, 2002), prefiguring not a future ideal society, but a participatory way of practising effective politics, articulating the (albeit imperfect) ability of heterogeneous movements to be able to work together without any single organisation or ideology being in a position of domination. Collective visions approximate the universal values that Harvey (1996) discusses, recognising differences between participants within convergence spaces, but attempting to provide common platforms of collective actions. While united in broad common desires for economic and environmental justice, perhaps the strongest collective vision is that of opposition to neoliberalism. However, contrasting, but not necessarily disabling, tensions exist between the articulation of a universalist politics and the militant particularisms of movements within the functioning of convergence spaces. Differences between movements concerning practices of gender, class, caste and ethnicity may also generate conflicts, not least if the collective visions of the convergence create homogenous activist environments that elide important issues of diversity. In addition, the immediacy of place-based concerns – such as movements' everyday struggles for survival under conditions of limited resources – can mean that the global ambitions articulated by GJNs remain unrealised.

Third, convergence spaces are relational achievements (Massey, 2005; Latour, 2006), involving a practical relational politics of solidarity, bound up in five forms of interaction and facilitation: communication, information-sharing, solidarity actions, network coordination and resource mobilisation. Such solidarity takes place in the form of changing and overlapping circuits of relations that are enacted both virtually through the Internet, where interactions within virtual space act as a communicative and coordinating thread that weaves different place-based struggles together, and materially, in particular fora such as global conferences, meetings and days of action and protest, where connections are grounded in and face-to-face-based moments of articulation (Rai, 2003). As we argued in Chapter 3, such territorialised meetings enable the embodying of mutual solidarity (cf. Juris, 2004a) – constructing the aspirations and grievances of geographically, culturally, economically and, at times, politically different and distant peoples as interlinked (Olesen, 2005), whereby activists draw upon feelings of empathy for others to contest power inequalities (Eschle and Maiguashca, 2007).

Mutual solidarity across place-based movements enables connections to be drawn that extend beyond the local and the particular. The creation of solidarities as part of the constitution of networks helps to reconfigure distance in different ways, emphasising commonalities rather than differences (Olesen, 2005). Mutual solidarity is concerned with articulating a transnational public sphere, space(s) of dialogue and debate, where the open exchange of differing opinions does not presuppose a unified movement or transnational space simply in need of a single common strategy. Rather, they are multiple, embodied and affected by historic influences (Marion Young, 2001). Hence the participants, or publics, of civil society are multiple and open to one another:

> they take account of one another, challenge one another, engage one another (with more or less conflict and cooperation) to such an extent that boundaries and identities become ambivalent, rather than fixed, and that the entire pattern of publics in civil society gains a fluid, dynamic quality. (Torgerson, 2006: 716)

This presupposes shared collective visions that form a point of departure from which opinions are discursively shaped and shared in patterns of convergence and divergence. These common spaces are hybrid, with the discourse depending upon plurality rather than unity, any meaning constituted in a tension of dialogue/ intersecting discourses (Torgerson, 2006) and (ideally) resolved within a particular discussion but never closed off for future projects.

Convergence spaces are, therefore, those of variation and flux, where the links between various intermediaries tend to be in process and are contestable. Networked actors fashion their political identities through the way that they engage with, and struggle against, different spatial configurations of power relations. Rather than having pre-determined, fixed identities, political identities are crafted through the connections, associations and solidarities that are made in active struggles, and the multiplicities within which such identities are formed. Hence convergence spaces can be seen as generative, actively shaping political identities rather than merely bringing together different actors (activists, movements) around common concerns. Forms of solidarity are thus diverse, multiple, productive and contested (Braun and Disch, 2002; Featherstone, 2003; Juris, 2004a).

Recognising the potential for GJNs to develop a sustainable politics of mutual solidarity involves not just understanding the way that places are enmeshed in wider spatial relations but also, and perhaps more critically, assessing how the 'global' is invoked in struggles that take place 'locally'. Massey (2004; 2005) recasts the politics of place by considering how political intervention at the local scale might develop against neoliberalism. She uses the phrase 'geographies of responsibility' (2004) to make the point that because places are relational and social relations flow through them, connecting us up increasingly to 'distant others' in complex ways, we should think more about the political impacts – both positive and negative – of our own actions and interventions 'locally'.

This spatial thinking adds to the temporal dimension developed by German philosopher Jonas (1984) who argues that the ethics of responsibility need to be fundamentally recast in the light of technological change: the human capacity to conquer and alter nature means that the principle of responsibility should always be constructed in anticipation of the potential harm that human actions may cause instead of being expressed *ex post*, for example, repairing harm already incurred. Of course, this type of time–space consciousness has been the motif of the environmental movement for some time: to think globally and act locally. But there are other interesting implications. For example, different places have different capacities for resistance to neoliberalism; reflecting the uneven power geometries described earlier:

> a local politics of place that took seriously the relational construction of space and place [. . .] would understand that relational construction as highly differentiated from place to place through the vastly unequal disposition of resources. This

is particularly true of capitalist globalisation. The mobilisation of resources into power relations between places is also highly differentiated and a local politics of place must take account of that. (Massey 2004: 13)

Another implication is the question of how a wider spatial imaginary – in other words, a broader 'global' consciousness and understanding – is embedded in the activities of place-based or territorial struggles. In other words, to what extent do resistance movements against neoliberalism foster a spatially extensive mutual solidarity, rather than pursuing a more reactionary and defensive politics? As Massey (2004) argues '"challenging globalisation" might precisely, in consequence, mean challenging, rather than defending, certain local places' (ibid). At root here is the need to develop a more self-reflexive local politics that recognises global responsibility with 'distant others'.

Interestingly, it is this type of perspective that fuelled the development of the socialist internationals from the time of Marx onwards. The construction, and nurturance of mutual solidarities between workers, peasants, indigenous people, etc. are likely to be predicated upon the common experiences of alienation and exploitation through the workings of capital (Harvey, 2003), and how movements in their everyday practices attempt to take account of, or are reflexive about, responsibilities to distant others. Crucially, the development of an effective and sustainable politics of mutual solidarity will necessitate sustaining effective place-based politics. Much ultimately depends on the ways in which a more 'global' consciousness is fostered among the grassroots of movements to the extent that broader spatial imaginaries become embedded in everyday actions.

Fourth, convergence spaces facilitate spatially extensive political action by participant movements. As noted above, social movements are engaged in grounded material struggles and articulate place-specific concerns, but also increasingly participate in forging non-local networks with other movements. Indeed, particular local-based social movements may develop transnational networks of support as an operational strategy for the defence of their place(s) (Escobar, 2001). Certain places may be of symbolic importance in the collective rituals of the network, for example as sites for international conferences, or global days of action (Bosco,

2001). These transnational collective political rituals contribute to the creation of activist and movement identities, and practically and symbolically articulate the common ground shared by different placed-based social movements. Such participatory fora represent moments of temporary but intense network stabilisation where the groups, organisations, individuals, ideologies and cognitive frames that constitute particular GJNs are made manifest (Juris, 2004a). The places in which such fora are held become 'articulated moments' (Massey, 1994) in the enactment of GJNs. These meetings and days of action provide a reflexive impetus for GJNs, an opportunity to recognise 'itself' and the embeddedness or otherwise of its participants; to accommodate and negotiate differences in strategies, visions, goals, etc.; to reflect upon particular strategies and tactics; to share skills; construct means of communication and information exchange; to formulate political projects and new spatialities of action, whereby mutual solidarity can be expressed (Chesters, 2003). As a result of these types of action, there are differential impacts on particular place-based struggles, due in part to the extent to which a particular struggle is projected onto the global arena by virtue of its involvement in a globalising network.

However, the practices of solidarity-building in convergence spaces are uneven from the outset, because of the inequalities between the constituent movements (e.g. the different resources available to movements), and because of the different geographies within which these movements are located (Bob, 2001; Sperling et al., 2001; Anheier and Themudo, 2002; Rai, 2003; Eschle and Maiguashca, 2007). Movements will vary enormously in their spatial reach and ability to generate support and political legitimisation with implications for political outcomes. Some movements remain relatively 'localised', others become linked into national coalitions, whilst others develop more transnational and even global networks of support. There are considerable (place-specific) differences between movements located in the Global North and the Global South (and between movements located within different countries within these 'blocs'). These include different political opportunity structures such as the character of democracy and political traditions in a particular country and the availability of financial resources; and the different ideologies and strategies espoused by different movements (e.g. concerning approaches to the environmental issues, such as climate change and air pollution). Such differences, despite the existence of collective visions, can pose major obstacles to efforts to develop transnational collective identities and common action (Smith, 2002; Doherty, 2006; Doyle and Doherty, 2006).

Moreover, particular places and movements become empowered whilst others remain marginal within the operations of GJNs. Indeed, a range of place-specific conditions enable or constrain movements in their capacity to organise their struggles and participate within GJNs. Place-specific economic conditions – particularly the availability and deployment of financial, human, organisational, political, informational or cultural resources – are crucial in movement mobilisations. Moreover, transnational alliances are facilitated when movements possess significant mobilisation capacities already underway; when they have the capacity for regular communication with other movements; and when each organisation's members take some responsibility for brokering bonds of solidarity (Bandy and Smith, 2005). In addition, the ability of movements to participate in transnational alliances is also shaped by the actions, policies, limitations and challenges posed by the governments of the states in which they are located (Burawoy et al., 2000; Glassman, 2001). In these ways, networks are both influenced by, and replicate, the existing 'power geometries' (Massey, 1999) that characterise connections between places under economic globalisation. Within a particular network, one would expect an activist grouping operating from London to have greater global connectivity and reach than one operating out of Dhaka.

Moreover, rather than fostering broader networks of mutual solidarity, some convergence spaces may (over time) become dominated by the politics of particular movements which might cause a retreat into a more narrowly defined and more conservative territorial politics. In addition, while convergence spaces are spatially extensive in their operation, many of their participant movements (particularly in the Global South) may see defence of particular places, and opposition to national governments (pursuing neoliberal policies), as their most appropriate sites of political action.

Even within the context of internationalised struggle, principal arenas of conflict for political actors frequently remain within national states (Glassman, 2001; Mertes, 2002). As a result, geographical dilemmas arise in the attempt to prosecute spatially extensive politics compounded by the uneven character of processes of interaction and facilitation.

Fifth, as we argued in Chapter 3, in order to 'ground' the idea of a convergence space within the communities that comprise the active membership of participant movements, it is essential to have 'networking vectors'. These vectors work to intervene in the work of translation by which networks are formed and developed, acting to further the process of communication, information-sharing and inter-action within a network's participant movements and the communities in which they operate. Such vectors include the work conducted between activists at conferences, meetings in which conference delegates provide feedback to the grassroots communities in which they work and activist caravans. Networking vectors constitute the embodied, articulated moments in the social relations of convergence spaces (Massey, 1994). They generate the 'communicative infrastructure' necessary for the operation and sustainability of convergence spaces (Juris, 2004a).

The most important networking vectors are what we termed in Chapter 3, 'imagineers', who conduct much of the organisational work of convergence spaces – preparing, organising and participating in discussions, meetings, conferences and campaigns. These key activists organise conferences, mobilise resources (e.g. funds) and facilitate communication and information flows between movements and between movement offices and grassroots communities. The imagineers attempt to 'ground' the concept or imagi-nary of the network – what it is, how it works, what it is attempting to achieve – within grassroots communities who comprise the membership of the participant movements. Moreover, crucially, imagineers serve to embody the net-works in which they work (see Olesen, 2005). The imagineers represent the connective tissue across geographic space working as activators, brokers and advocates for domestic and international claims (Tarrow, 2005).

Sixth, convergence spaces are characterised by a range of different operational logics, spanning from more horizontal (decentred, non-hierarchical) to more vertical (hierarchical, centralised) operational logics. The networking logic of GJNs is always entangled with more verticalist practices as a result of traditional movement structures, power relations inherent within and between participant movements, and the role played by key network actors within convergence spaces. (Juris, 2004a, b; 2005c). As a result, operational dilemmas arise in the attempt to prosecute spatially extensive politics.

Finally, convergence spaces are sites of contested social and power relations, because the diversity of groups that comprise them articulate a variety of potentially conflicting goals (concerning the forms of social change), ideologies (e.g. concerning gender, class, ethnicity) and strategies (e.g. institutional [legal] and extra-institutional [illegal] forms of protest) (Sperling et al., 2001; Rai, 2003; Eschle and Maiguashca, 2007). Moreover, unequal discursive and material power relations exist that result from the differential control of resources (Dicken et al., 2001) and placing of actors within network flows (Massey, 1994). These in turn may give rise to problems of representation, mobility and cultural difference, both between the social movements that participate and between activists within particular movements. The alliances forged necessarily involve entangled power relations, where relations of domination and resistance are entwined, that create spaces of resistance/ domination (Sharp et al., 2000). The construction of mutual solidarities is not, therefore, a smooth process: they involve antagonisms (often born out of the differences between collaborators) as well as agreements: they are always multiple and contested, fraught with political determinations (Sperling et al., 2001; Rai, 2003; Featherstone, 2005).

We conceive of GJNs in both vertical and horizontal terms, and argue that it is essential to consider how and why territorially based movements become involved in GJNs, and how the convergence of differently resourced and placed actors in such networks are played out in practice. Whilst global days of action are symbolic of GJNs as convergence spaces, a question remains about their ability to foster a broader geopolitical consciousness among the grassroots members of movements and produce genuine transformative political projects. While global days of action are always accompanied by solidarity protests throughout the globe (which enables a broader geography of dissent to be articulated), effective and sustainable mass mobilisation can only come about if global networks can themselves relate to the direct and lived experience of exploitation from those communities at the sharp end of neoliberalism (Burawoy, 2003).

Perhaps more fundamentally we might ask, following Ettlinger and Bosco (2004), whether a network is really a single network or, rather, a federation of cells that share common strategic goals and coalesce into temporary networks for individual missions only to dissolve and form again in another constellation for the next mission. In this sense, we might make a distinction between GJNs as the discursive and convergent spaces within which 'transnational counterpublics' (Olesen, 2005) meet to challenge dominant neoliberal discourses and practices (Juris, 2004a); and their participant movements as the territorially based organisations that are able to mobilise (or not) for particular struggles both within and without GJNs. Developing a sustainable counter-hegemonic politics to neoliberalism ultimately depends on the success in which GJNs are able to foster and sustain the involvement of territorially based movements in broader struggles outwith a movement's immediate ('local') interests. This is intimately connected to whether the sustainability of GJNs are based upon the existence of a stable core and a periphery of temporary activism that reinforces it at crucial times, and the spatial politics within which such cores are situated. In the next three chapters, we proceed to respond to these key issues through an empirical analysis of the operational dynamics of three GJNS: PGA Asia, the ICEM and the Social Forum process.

Notes

1   This section draws significantly upon Nicholls (2007).

2   Brandt (1997) has used this term to refer to the interrelatedness of poetry, poststructuralist theory and socio-political practice. While acknowledging this interelationship, the term has been expanded in Routledge (2000) to refer to the geographical embeddedness of political and cultural action.

3   Harvey's use of militant particularism conflates the local/global and particular/universal binaries, producing topographies of political engagement where the local is elided with the particular, thus making

it impossible for political activity to break out of this particularism in ways that shape political imaginaries, thereby marginalising the agency and dynamism of political activity (Featherstone, 2005, 2008). In this book, we are concerned with foregrounding the dynamism of political agency, through an ethnographic analysis of three different networks.

5

People's Global Action (Asia): peasant solidarity as horizontal networking?

People's Global Action (PGA) represents a network for communication and coordination between diverse place-based (but not place-restricted) social movements, whose membership cuts across differences in gender, ethnicity, language, nationality, age, class and caste. The PGA network owes its genesis to an international encounter between activists and intellectuals that was organised by the Zapatistas in Chiapas in 1996. At the encounter, the Zapatistas' Subcommandante Marcos declared that those present would construct an intercontinental network of resistance against neoliberalism. In Spain the following year, the idea of a network between different resistance formations was launched by ten social movements including MST (Landless peasants movement) of Brazil, and the Karnataka State Farmers Union of India. The official 'birth' of the PGA was February 1998, whose purpose was to facilitate the sharing of information between grassroots social movements. The PGA organised an alternative conference (at the 1998 Ministerial Conference of the WTO in Geneva) between social movements from Asia, Africa and Latin America that called for resistance to neoliberal globalisation.[1]

The broad objectives of the network are to offer an instrument for coordination and mutual support at the global level for those resisting corporate rule and the neoliberal capitalist development paradigm, to provide international projection to their struggles, and to inspire people to resist corporate domination through civil disobedience and people-oriented constructive actions. PGA has established regional networks – e.g. PGA Latin America, PGA Europe, PGA North America and PGA Asia – to decentralise the everyday workings of the convergence. It purports to be an example of horizontal networking (cf. Juris, 2004a), an issue that we will discuss in depth below.

PGA Asia as a convergence space

As we will discuss below, the PGA Asia convergence space involves a relational politics of mutual solidarity between movements, imagineers, spaces of interaction and facilitation, collective visions, networked political action across multiple places in Asia and beyond, entangled operational logics, and contested social relations (see Routledge, 2003a; Routledge *et al.*, 2006; Routledge *et al.*, 2007). The network involves place-based social movements, including: the Karnataka State Farmer's Association (*Karnataka Rajya Raitha Sangha*, KRRS) – a 5 million-strong peasant farmers' movement in Southern India; the *Bharatiya Kisan Union* (Indian Farmer's Union, BKU) comprised of predominantly wealthier segments of the 'Backward Castes'[2] (*Jats*): farmers; the Save the Narmada Movement (*Narmada Bachao Ando-lan*, NBA) – a 50,000-strong peasant farmers' and indigenous people's anti-dam struggle in central India; the *Andhra Pradesh Vyavasaya Vruthidarula Union* (APVVU) – a federation of agricultural workers and marginal farmers' unions in Andhra Pradesh, India; the Bangladesh *Krishok* (peasant) Federation (BKF) – a federation of peasants and landless agricultural workers from Bangladesh;[3] the All Nepal Peasants Association (ANPA) – a 500,000 person-strong movement of landless, bonded labourers, small and middle peasants, women; fisherfolk, etc; the Borneo Indigenous Peoples' and Peasants Union (*Panggau*), Sarawak, Malaysia; the Assembly of the Poor, (AoP) – a 200,000 person-strong network of anti-dam, peasant, student and labour movements in Thailand; and the Movement for National Land and Agricultural Reform (MONLAR) – a 20,000 person-strong network of (small and landless) farmer organisations, NGOs and people's organisations in Sri Lanka.

PGA Asia acts as an association of actors and resources (intermediaries such as texts, humans, non-human materials, money) that are put into circulation in a continual effort to make political actions durable through time and mobile across space. Constantly redefined in interaction through active resources, and utilising materials of association – such as the Internet – which are able to act at a distance, time and space are constructed within this network (Latour, 1993; Murdoch, 1998). The links between various intermediaries in PGA Asia tend to be in process and are contestable.

PGA Asia is concerned with five principal processes of facilitation and interaction between movements. It acts as a facilitating space for communication, (e.g. using letters, e-mail, websites, newsletters, telephone, fax and face-to-face meetings such as conferences); information-sharing (e.g. concerning the effectiveness of particular tactics and strategies, knowledge on place-specific legal issues and local geographies, etc.); solidarity (e.g. demonstrations of support for particular struggles such as protests, letter-writing campaigns, etc.); coordination (e.g. organising conferences, meetings and collective protests, etc.); and resource mobilisation (e.g. of people, finances, and skills) (Routledge, 2003a). The network articulates certain 'hallmarks' or unifying values – what we would term collective visions – to provide common ground for movements from which to coordinate collective struggles (see also Juris 2004a).[4]

As a convergence space, PGA Asia actively shapes political identities in addition to bringing together different actors around common concerns. Forms of solidarity are diverse and contested, hence in PGA Asia, the various components of the network continually re-negotiate with one another, forming variable and revisable coalitions. During PGA Asia's existence social movements have left the network while others have joined it, and many of the movements that compose this convergence are enrolled in alternative networks in addition to their participation in PGA Asia. Particular campaigns, social fora and other 'solidarity assemblies' facilitate networking and cross-fertilisation between different movements and networks (Saunders and Rootes, 2006; della Porta and Mosca, 2007).

For example, for the participant movements in PGA Asia, these 'multiple belongings' (della Porta and Mosca, 2007) include: the participation of the KRRS, BKU, ANPA, the BKF and MONLAR in the international farmers' network *La Via Campesina* and in the Asian Peasants' Network; the participation of KRRS, BKU, NBA and APVVU in the all-India social

movement network, the Indian Coordinating Committee;
ANPA, KRRS, MONLAR and BKF, in the Pesticide Action
Network; the NBA and parts of AoP (i.e. the movement to
stop Thailand's Pak Mun Dam) in the International Rivers
network and other anti-dam networks; the participation of
Thai Labour Camapign (a pro-union NGO) in both PGA
Asia and ICEM; and the participation of all of the afore-
mentioned movements at various WSF events since 2001.

Operational logics

The PGA network claims to be constituted by decentred and
horizontal forms of organisation. As Juris (2004a) has argued
(see Chapter 3), 'such networking processes generate the
communicative infrastructure necessary for the emergence
of transnational social movements', or what Olesen (2005)
refers to as 'transnational counterpublics' (Juris 2004a: 401).
Nevertheless, despite this attempt to foster a grassroots-
based, decentralised network, PGA Asia's participant movements – while comprising significant grassroots involvement
– tend to be organised through more verticalist structures
and logics: hierarchy, elections, delegation and, in some
cases, political party structures too. For example, the BKF
holds internal elections for a series of functional positions
within the movement; the ANPA operates similarly, and is
also affiliated with the Communist Party of Nepal (Unified
Marxist-Leninist, [CPN-UML]); the NBA has a powerful core
group of activist organisers (Routledge, 2003b); the Panggau
has an elected secretariat that operates along more 'horizontalist' lines, with a mobile 'core catalyst' group of between
20–30 people, who organise local communities throughout
Sarawak, Malaysia; and the AoP comprises a network of
grassroots-based anti-dam, peasant, student and labour
movements, with their own differing modes of operation.

As we have noted, contemporary networking logics stress
the process of exercising power, rather than attempting to
seize it. Hence within PGA Asia, there is an attempt to
decentre power, with a diversity of movements practising a
diversity of tactics, and no one governing ideology or strategy
dominating the process (see PGA hallmarks 2 and 5).
However, the operational logics of some of the constituent

movements within PGA Asia are predicated upon taking political power in the more traditional sense of revolutionary politics (Holloway, 2005), although the relationship with the state varies. For example, while the BKF operates autonomously from Bangladesh's principal political parties (the BNP and Awami league), the KRRS participates in electoral politics in order to draw attention to rural, grassroots issues, and the ANPA is affiliated to the CPN-UML, which has participated in Nepal's government at different times. Moreover, the existence of 'imagineers' in the network also compromises its supposed horizontality, generating unequal power relations within the network, as will be discussed below.

Sustaining collective action over time is related to the capacity of a group to develop strong interpersonal ties that provide the basis for the construction of collective identities (Bosco, 2001). PGA has periodic international and regional conferences and meetings that provide material spaces within which representatives of participant movements can converge and discuss issues that pertain to the functioning of the network (Juris, 2004a).[5] Such conferences and meetings also enable strategies to be developed in secure sequestered sites, beyond the surveillance that accompanies any communicative technology in the public realm (Routledge, 2003a). Moreover, such gatherings enable deeper interpersonal ties to be established between different activists from different cultural spaces and struggles, as will be discussed in detail below.

While an important aspect of networking is to build such interpersonal relationships, another is to coordinate joint actions across space, for example against particular neoliberal institutions such as the WTO. Such joint actions, when embodied in collective experiences such as conferences, enable connections and exchanges between activists to be made, and such interrelations can build trust between activists and shape collective political identities and imaginaries (Juris, 2004a). For example, through the re-drafting of the networks collective visions at the international conferences in Bangalore, India, 1999, and Cochabamba, Bolivia, 2001, the network was able to define who it was (in terms of its political beliefs and practices, see hallmark 2 and 5), what constituted its common problems (e.g. poverty), who constituted its opponents (see hallmark 1) and how the network operated through the creation of common political strategies (see hallmark 4) (Featherstone, 2005; Wood, 2005).

PGA also organises activist caravans. These are buses of activists from various struggles around the world, which visit social movement struggles in countries other than their own. These caravans have a certain historical precedent in the solidarity convoys that took North American activists to Nicaragua, El Salvador and Guatemala during the 1980s. These convoys brought humanitarian aid to communities in those countries, and articulated opposition to US government policies in the region – particularly the US government support for the military *juntas* in El Salvador and Guatemala, and for the contra war attempting to destabilise the *Sandinista* revolution in Nicaragua. Rather than being forms of political tourism, the PGA caravans are organised in order for activists from different struggles and countries to communicate with one another, exchange information, share experiences and tactics, participate in various solidarity demonstrations, rallies and direct actions, and attempt to draw new movements into the convergence. The emphasis on such processes is movement-to-movement communication regarding struggles, strategies, visions of society, and the construction of economic and political alternatives to neoliberalism.

The Internet acts as a crucial immutable mobile within the PGA Asia network, a communicative and coordinating thread that creates a multiplicity of partial connections between locally, regionally and globally placed human and non-human actors. The Internet acts as one of the key mediators within PGA Asia (in addition to conferences and activist caravans). It enables activists to maintain contact with one another, discuss issues and strategies, plan network events and keep informed about network-relevant news. It also provides one of the means for announcing and mobilising actions: through e-mail lists and the PGA website, the PGA network, among others, have put out the calls for global days of action against capitalism, such as the protests in Seattle 1999 (against the WTO), Prague 2000 (against the WB and IMF), Genoa 2001 (against the G8), Cancun 2003 (against the WTO) and Gleneagles 2005 (against the G8) (see also Juris, 2004a). Of course, in the Global South, grassroots movements have varying and often limited access to electricity, let alone computer technologies. Hence participant movements in PGA Asia effect communication and information relays via the imagineers (who have various international contacts owing to their participation in various networks, including PGA Asia). They are the points where information accumulates: the movement offices in Kathmandu, Dhaka, Bangkok, etc. and the imagineers' lap tops and office computers. Rather than what Cleaver (1999) would term an 'electronic fabric', the Internet acts as a communicative and coordinating thread in the PGA network, which weaves different place-based struggles together so that they may converge in virtual space.

The PGA website is translated into seven languages and provides information about the history of the network; PGA international and regional conferences; various actions and initiatives that the convergence has organised; upcoming events and reports on struggles from around the world (see also Routledge, 2003a; Juris, 2004a). There are several e-mail lists that provide spaces for discussion, communication, information-sharing and coordination. Many activists participate in these discussions in PGA Europe, although PGA Asia and PGA Latin America tend to witness less activist participation. Although mass movements participate in these regional networks, those with e-mail contact who tend to participate in PGA discussions are usually only individuals who can communicate in English and who have access to the Internet.

The PGA network is facilitated by a Convenors' Committee, which comprises social movements within the network. The current Committee comprises movements concerned with ethnic, women's, labour and indigenous issues. The Committee organise the PGA conferences (see below), decide about the use of resources, advise local organisers about technical and organisational questions, and decide about the content of the PGA information tools. In practice there have been problems with the workings of the Convenors' Committee. First, the convenors have not been able to take the time to fully assume their responsibilities, owing to the exigencies of movement work in their respective localities. Second, the convenors have had great difficulty in functioning at a distance, having problems of access to necessary information, as well as language and cultural problems. The process has tended to remain haphazard, abstract and dependent on e-mail access.

Hence, much of the organisational work – preparing, organising and participating in discussions, meetings, conferences and caravans – has been conducted by 'free radical' activists and key movement contacts (usually movement leaders or general secretaries) who have helped organise conferences, mobilise resources (e.g. funds) and facilitate communication and information flows between movements and between movement offices and grassroots communities (see also Routledge, 2003a; Juris, 2004a). These free radicals and key contacts – who must possess English language skills (the lingua franca of PGA Asia) and be computer literate – constitute the 'imagineers' of the network, who attempt to 'ground' the concept or imaginary of the network across a range of spatial registers and, in particular, within grassroots communities who comprise the membership of the participant movements. As discussed in Chapter 3, they work to effect the 'moments' of translation: they problematise network functions (in order to effect solutions that enable the network to act more productively); they attempt to designate networked roles for actors (e.g. by allotting key tasks for participant movement members and materials); they work to enroll other movements and materials into the network (e.g. through visiting social movements and fundraising activities); and they work to mobilise all enrolled entities (e.g. through conferences, caravans and global days of action). Through these relational processes, individuals, movements, materials and places are incorporated into the PGA Asia network. In PGA Asia, as of 2004 there was an all-Asian convenor (ANPA), a South Asia convenor (BKU), a Southeast Asia convenor (AoP) and a 'free radical' group of one Thai and four European activists.[6]

Relational dynamics: the Dhaka conference

PGA is constituted and made durable by the circulation of numerous 'immutable mobiles': people, the Internet, airplanes, buses, taxis, rickshaws, pen and paper, etc. Its operational dynamics in this sense have always been more fluid than those of ICEM, which operates through more fixed structures. However, the formation of the crucial common grounding that enables the network to act politically necessitates communication between people, eye to heart to mind, replete with intonations and gestures. This is because:

> Trust, friendship, reputation, predictability, hierarchical position within a social network, and even charisma are elements of political activity that certainly cannot be reduced to technologies of communication. There are features of face-to-face interaction. (Ribiero, 1998: 341)

Hence the durability of collective action over time in PGA Asia (as in many other networks) requires the development of strong interpersonal ties between the imagineers and between participant movement activists that provide the basis for the construction of collective identities (Bosco, 2001). This requires face-to-face processes of communication that facilitate the exchange of experiences and ideas between activists (Rai, 2003; Juris, 2004a; Routledge et al., 2007). One of the most effective means of achieving network durability and spatial coordination has been the PGA international and regional conferences and meetings that provide material spaces within which representatives of participant movements can converge and discuss issues that pertain to the functioning of the network (Juris, 2004a). As we discussed in Chapter 3, the quotidian work of networks (e.g. organising conferences) generates a set of personal relations that enables the various 'strategies' of network translation. A consideration of the PGA Asia conference, held in Dhaka, Bangladesh, 2004, will highlight how these strategies were worked through, and how moments of network translation are effected.

The holding of a second PGA Asia conference[7] was first discussed by PGA Asia imagineers at the PGA international conference in Cochabamba, Bolivia in 2001, who saw it as a means of enabling the network to act more productively. Key networking tasks such as fundraising and planning for the conference were designated to the imagineers. They also decided to work to enroll other movements into the network by visiting them, holding meetings and discussions about the PGA Asia network, and inviting them to the conference.

The six-day conference was formally called the PGA Asian and Gender conference, with a decision by the network to conduct two days of workshops on gender issues, and to consider gender as an integral aspect of all conference issues, workshops, discussions and decisions. The conference was held at the Institute of Social Science in the semi-rural outskirts of Dhaka, and the first day of the conference was slow to start, with delegates arriving throughout the day, and the on-site conference office taking time to install telephone line, Internet and printer services. All of the delegates lived on-site for the duration of the conference and the hosts, the BKF and the *Kisani Sabha*, had organised food, dormitory accommodation and temporary 'bucket' showers and toilets. Collective meals were eaten from plates on people's laps.

The PGA Asia conference in Dhaka saw the convergence of 150 delegates from Bangladesh, India, Nepal, Thailand, Malaysia, Philippines and Vietnam representing 46 grassroots peasant movements (of farmers, fisherfolk, indigenous people, women and labourers). Forty per cent of the delegates were women. All conference proceedings were conducted in Bengali and English, with other translations (e.g. Nepali, Thai, etc.) being conducted in 'language clusters' as the proceedings progressed. Much like the European PGA conference described by Juris (2004a), the PGA Asia conference consisted of activist testimonies concerning their movement's struggles; workshops (followed by plenaries) on a variety of issues to facilitate discussion,[8] the exchange of information, role-playing and the formulation of possible issue-based campaigns; language-based group discussions on operational processes and strategic coordination within PGA Asia; and the setting up of political campaigns.

Every evening, delegates enjoyed activist videos from different parts of Asia, and a group of musicians and dancers performing *Quawali* music. The purpose of the conference was to generate deeper interpersonal ties between different activists from different cultural spaces and struggles, and in so doing, develop solidarity between different social movements in Asia in the form of communication, exchange of information, coordination of Asia-wide actions, mutual support and the mobilisation of collective resources.

The Dhaka conference represents one effect of the moments and strategies of network translation. It provided a convergence space for 'performing, representing,' and embodying the network (Juris, 2004: 419), representing 'an important mechanism through which alternative transnational counterpublics are produced and reproduced' (Juris, 2004: 435). It played a vital role in face-to-face communication and exchange of experience, strategies and ideas, providing spaces where social movement participants could meet, represent themselves to others (through movement testimonies), generate effective connections with others, articulate oppositional discourses and lay bare certain political determinations (Juris, 2004a: 434).

The conference saw the expansion of the PGA Asia process, with groups from Thailand, Malaysia, Vietnam and the Philippines being formally enrolled into the network for the first time, and the mobilisation of network actors through three calls to action: (i) Global days of action across Asia, against the WTO during its meeting in Hong Kong in 2005; (ii) a global day of action focusing on violence against women on International Women's Day 2005; and (iii) an PGA Asian caravan for 2006.

At such conferences, the institutional, geopolitical and material aspects of people's identities are opened up for negotiation, and the possibility for social categories to be created, enacted and transformed in and through peoples' interactions emerges (Nagar and Geiger, quoted in Nagar, 2002). In so doing, mutual solidarity between activists and their movements becomes possible, a key process in the constitution of the network. For example, a Malaysian activist in Panggau noted:

> We wanted to share our experiences of struggle. We don't have many linkages to other movements or the space to speak. The Dhaka conference provided us with that opportunity and the space to speak. (interview, Kuching, Borneo, Malaysia, 2004)

Moreover, people's positionality in relation to others could be re-assessed, as a Thai activist noted:

> There was a real chance for exchange between activists. We usually stereotype people by nation but when we meet face to face it breaks down the borders between us, and generates collective strength to make change. (interview, Bangkok, 2004)

As Juris (2004a) has pointed out with respect to the WSF, a PGA conference can also be conceived as a 'performative ritual', where diverse acts of articulation produce an event and 'where diverse activist networks constitute themselves and symbolically map their relationship to one another through verbal and embodied communication' (*ibid*). As an activist in the Bangladeshi Floating Women's Labour Union noted, referring to the PGA Asia conference in Dhaka, 2004: 'I was able to meet many different people from different movements in Asia, and it made me realise that they face similar problems to us' (interview, Dhaka, Bangladesh, 2004).

As with the WSF and PGA events described by Juris (2004a), the PGA Asia conference provided the space for a great deal of informal networking conversations and opportunities between geographically distant and culturally different activists. Such communication enabled the creation of common ground between movements, which is a necessary precursor to the development of mutual solidarity, as explained by a Nepali activist:

> Dhaka provided a forum to share our work and experiences with others in different parts of Asia, others who have similar problems to us. We were able to share political views and to identify our common ground. The local and the national are not enough because globalisation has intensified the exploitation process across the world. We need to develop global solidarity. (interview, Kathmandu, Nepal, 2004)

However, movements are differentially empowered by their participation in GJNs. Particular places and movements may become empowered whilst others remain marginal within network operations. Certainly, the BKF benefited particularly from being the co-host of the conference, receiving political kudos from its involvement in the PGA network. A BKF activist explained it thus:

> BKF has got an image via its involvement with PGA. In Bangladesh other movements know BKF is active in a global network against imperialism, and thus what we are for, and fighting against, is clear. It is useful to have a mass image and recognition within society as a growing movement, with international links. We are seen to be against imperialism and *for internationalism* (our emphasis), unlike some anti-imperialist groups in Bangladesh. (interview, Dhaka, Bangladesh, 2004)

Through its embodiment in collective experiences such as the Dhaka conference, the PGA network enables connections and exchanges between activists to be made, and such interrelations can shape political identities and imaginaries: a recognition of common opponents (such as the WTO) and common problems (such as poverty), and the creation of common political strategies (see Featherstone, 2005). Such identities and strategies are not place-bound, but fashioned through interconnections facilitated by actor-networks, and circulated through these networks (Juris, 2004a). For example, the Dhaka conference produced a 'PGA Asia Declaration' (agreed upon by all those present at the conference), that stressed the solidarity between movements, the issues of common concern and the planning of collective action by participant movements in the network. Some of these (more general) outcomes could be, in part, anticipated, in that previous conferences had also generated connections between movements and collective strategies for action. For example, the Cochbamba conference had led to both the Dhaka conference, and a tour of Europe by Colombian activists in 2002. Other outcomes – such as how many activists would finally attend the conference, precisely what kinds of strategies would emerge and what the longer-term achievements of the conference would be – only emerge from the particular face-to-face interactions that take place between activists on the 'ground' during such embodied moments of the network as the Dhaka conference.

However, various problems attend the networking process. First, there is a constant problem of securing funding to provide key resources to reproduce network actions. For example, the PGA Asia conference in Dhaka was delayed almost two years due to the problems associated with fund-raising, and was further hampered by the late availability of some of those funds, as noted by a BKF activist:

Fund-raising takes time, and was uncertain right up to the conference. Funds were located in Europe and it was difficult to access them. There was a delay in getting the funds and thus we did not prepare for the conference very well. This had effects on both logistics and resources. Uncertain funds meant that the logistics were not fully organised until the last minute, and delegates did not have enough information on gender before the conference. (interview Dhaka, 2004)

Second, the commitment of certain movements might wane, or be attracted to other networks (see also Juris, 2004a). Hence the formation of the WSF (and the regional Asian Social Forum) has seen both the participation of several of the movements also involved with PGA Asia (such as BKF, ANPA) and the loss of movements within the global PGA network such as the Federation of Indonesian Peasant Unions (FSPI) as they have directed their energies towards the WSF. In addition, several movements involved in PGA Asia, such as ANPA, the BKF, and KRRS, alongside FSPI, are also participants in the *La Via Campesina* network. Third, a network can be compromised by the ineffectiveness of the communication and operational links (i.e. the networking vectors) between its participant movements, or inappropriate actions (or inactions) of the imagineers. According to an ANPA activist, there had been little ongoing communication between the participant movements in the PGA Asia e-mail list: 'the problem is that no one responds to the emails, there is no activity in the PGA list' (interview, Kathmandu, 2004). Based upon interviews with Dhaka participants in Bangladesh, Nepal and Thailand (during 2004), many people felt also that the conference language translation process was inadequate. For example, an activist in the Nepal National Fish Farmer's Association noted: 'the PGA objectives are very good but there are problems of translations. We are farmers and we don't know English. There were insufficient translators. Only two Nepali delegates spoke English' (interview Kathmandu, 2004). Not only were there many different languages present at the conference but also many different Bangladeshi regional dialects:

> The Dhaka conference was a good start to the Asia process. We need to strengthen the process but there are diverse languages and many local languages within countries, thus it is difficult to coordinate movements. But also there is a big possibility to spread the PGA process, since most Asian countries are agrarian-based and people are victims of globalisation and there are many movements because of this. People have different cultures and languages but common enemies, so there are differences but also potentials. (BKF activist, interview Dhaka, 2004)

Delegate participation during the Dhaka conference was uneven because there were few interpreters and thus they missed much of the discussions. As an activist in the AoP noted: 'language was a real obstacle, because the full experience of activists was unable to be communicated' (interview Chiang Mai, Thailand, 2004). Moreover, certain concepts, such as gender, do not translate into mother tongues. This was recognised by the support group in their evaluation of the Dhaka conference:

> There were ongoing problems with language. First, the lack of an adequate number of interpreters meant that during the workshops and plenaries, there were problem of translating from one language into another. Also, the main conference document was only in English (due to lack of time to produce one in Bengali) and there is a necessity in the future to have all documents in local languages. It became clear, that, for example, in Bangladesh there is a need to create a local project to support language and computer-literacy training for women. (PGA evaluation of Dhaka conference: see www.agp.org)

Thus, an associated problem is that interpreters themselves accrue power and influence by virtue of their language skills. For one Thai activist, the operational logic of the network is underpinned by 'literate' and conceptual communicational forms (e.g. the writing of e-mails and documents, the analysis of how networks function), whereas the operational logic of most grassroots movements is based upon oral communication:

> There is a real limitation to the capacity of grassroots movements to take ownership of the process. Movements do not know each other very well, and some Southeast Asia movements do not really know the PGA process at all. Thus participation is limited and language affects this too. Most movements are based on oral communication, whereas the PGA process is more literate and concept-based, thus it is difficult for grassroots movements to understand. (interview, Bangkok, Thailand, 2004)

It is ironic, but a clear example of the limitations of insufficient resources, that in a network whose *raison d'etre* is to facilitate communication, the problem of interpretation continually arises. In Dhaka, each language group would sit together in a cluster with one interpreter providing simultaneous verbal interpretation, against the background noise of the conference. Interpretation would be approximate (given that the interpreters were activists rather than professionals); interpreters would get burned out since there were so few of them (and hence the quality of the interpretation would decline over time); the content and nuance of debates would be lost because of the time taken to interpret; frequently interpretation would be partial rather than full (i.e. activists would 'sum up' a debate for others); and frequently the interpreters would be movement leaders who might reframe issues for their grassroots.[9]

Two responsibilities seem to arise here. First, there is a responsibility of movements to provide sufficient and competent interpreters, and second, for the network to help ensure resources to enable movements to do this. In Thailand, few activists have English language skills, and thus there is a danger that, when Thai activists (for example) participate in PGA conferences, rather than there being interpretation clusters, there ends up being interpretation ghettos, where folks barely communicate outside of their language group. This wastes resources and the potential of meaningful (cultural-political) exchange. Clearly, language access for activists is a crucial component of sustainable solidarity.

Moreover, what Featherstone (2005: 264) terms a 'dynamic topography of relations' exists between different political actors in networks such as PGA Asia. Different geographically-specific political opportunities and constraints, and movement characteristics vitiate against smooth unproblematic alliances and network participation. First, social movements' primary political terrain of struggle continues to be the state (Burawoy et al., 2000; Glassman, 2001; Mertes, 2002). This is exemplified by a consideration of three PGA Asia participants: ANPA, AoP and the BKF. Concerning ANPA, since 2004 the movement's political energies have been consumed by the political turmoil in Nepal. This has included: the ongoing Maoist insurgency within the country; the enforcement of martial law and suspension of the government in 2005 by Nepal's King Gyanendra; ANPA's participation in a Seven Party Alliance to oppose the royal coup; and its subsequent involvement in the country's peace process. Concerning AoP, although the issues that they confront are similar to those confronted by many movements in PGA Asia (e.g. an AoP participant, the Pak Mun anti-dam struggle, has liased with the NBA in India in anti-dam networking activities), their processes of mobilisation focus their struggle within and against the Thai state. This is reinforced by the languages problems described above, the fact that few have resources to travel abroad and ongoing discrimination by the Thai state over the obtaining of visas. Moreover, there is limited contact between Thai movements and other international activists due, in part, to the selective participation of AoP in international alliances (interviews, Bangkok, Thailand, 2004; see also Glassman, 2001). Indeed, as of 2007, AoP had failed to ratify their position as PGA Asia Southeast Asian convenor, despite being nominated as such at the Dhaka conference. This has been due in part to poor communication and competition between different factions within the AoP network (interview, Bangkok, Thailand 2006). Concerning the BKF, a series of government-enforced land evictions of 2000 landless families – all members of the BKF and *Kisani Sabha* – in northern Bangladesh in 2007 have consumed the energies of the movement. Their primary responsibilities have been to recover land for the landless and resettle displaced families (personal e-mail communication, 2007).

Second, as argued in Chapter 4, convergence spaces comprise contested social relations because different groups articulate a variety of potentially conflicting goals, ideologies and strategies (cf. Juris 2004a). For example, in PGA Asia there are caste differences and, at time prejudices, between participant movements within South Asia and within South Asian movements. Hence, the BKU is comprised of predominantly wealthier segments of the 'Backward Castes': farmers who have, at times, either ignored the grievances of landless labourers and lower castes (Gupta, 1998) or organised them through coercion (Bentall and Corbridge, 1996; Corbridge and Harriss, 2000). Moreover, some South Asian movement leaders are of higher caste (and/or class) status than their movement members.[10] In the KRRS, the (now deceased) leader of the movement, Professor Nanjundaswamy, excluded the State Committee of the KRRS from involvement in the PGA Intercontinental Caravan (see below), acting as an imagineer appropriating various global links that the KRRS enjoyed, and the only mediating point between Indian movements and the different European welcoming committees of the caravan (Featherstone, 2003).

Another issue is that gender inequalities and discriminations prevail within every movement within the network – although they take different geographical and cultural forms. For example, during a networking meeting prior to the Dhaka conference, a *Kisani Sabha* activist explained the process of the landless occupying Charhadi island in the Ganges delta:

> In 1992 [. . .] in the Ganges delta, the BKF instigated a series of land occupations. Landless peasants, armed with brooms and chilli powder, occupied four uninhabited islands. On Charhadi, peasants began by having to eat boiled grassroots, before planting trees, and subsequently taking loans from local landlords to buy livestock and tools to cultivate the land, which they repaid (at high rates of interest) in *padi*. Charhadi forms one of twenty two islands occupied by eleven thousand people. On some islands, people have been dispossessed of their land by landlords from the mainland, who employ armed *goondas* (thugs) to drive the people off the islands. On Charhadi, people have resisted the landlord and their armed *goondas*. Through a series of signals the communities are warned of impending attacks. Despite successfully remaining on the island for ten years, people still have no education or health care, and no flood shelters for their cattle when the river floods during the Monsoon. Since the occupation nearly one hundred, mostly children, have died. (interview, Charhadi, Bangladesh, 2002)

Clearly, the life of a peasant woman in a poor village on an occupied island in the Ganges delta is very different to that of a male movement leader living in Dhaka and connected to the Internet, which in turn is different to that of a Western imagineer temporarily visiting the island. There are pronounced differences in physical mobility across space, access to resources such as money and technology, etc. The causes of a *Kisani Sabha* activist's relative lack of network circulation (in comparison to network imagineers) are due to a complex web of political, economic and cultural determinations attendant to rural Bangladesh: that include, for example: the oppressive economic conditions (e.g. loans) that delimit everyday possibilities of peasant life; the local political power of landlords in the Ganges delta area, which necessitate the defence of occupied islands by the landless; and the gender relations that circumscribe women's mobility beyond their villages.

Such problems serve to introduce a hierarchy of relations between network participants, differentiating between network imagineers and grassroots movement members in what is meant to be coordinated horizontality. These are exacerbated by the importance of the imagineers in effecting the moments of network translation, as well as their key roles in facilitating the processes of network durability and mobility as we discuss below. Some actors have far more capacity to direct the course of relations than others, which partly stems from their ability to collect 'power' and condense it within networks (Castree, 2002). Within PGA Asia this is related to the process of network relays of communication and information.

Relays of communication and information:
imagineers

The abstract view of networks as horizontal relations is clearly not realised in practice, with the reality of network agency giving rise to more vertical relations. PGA Asia is organised primarily through the Internet, which acts as a communicative and coordinating thread weaving different place-based struggles together to create a convergence space. Of course, as we noted in Chapter 3, grassroots movements in the Global South have limited access to electricity and computer technologies. Hence the communication and information relays between participant movements in PGA Asia are conducted by the imagineers. As a result of their participation in a variety of activist networks, imagineers have a range of international contacts. Hence they, and their work spaces, become key nodes in the PGA network where informational traffic converges and disseminates. Hence, within the diversity of a network such as PGA Asia, there has developed 'controlled heterogeneity' (Riles 2001: 120), where decision making often devolves to a small number of individuals.

Power becomes the ability to enroll others on terms that allow key actors to 'represent' the others (Castree, 2002). As a result of the uneven access to (financial, temporal) resources and network flows, differential material and discursive power relations exist within PGA Asia (see Routledge, 2003a). As key networking vectors, the imagineers – because of resource access and skills such as communication and experience in activism and meeting facilitation – tend to wield disproportionate power and influence within the network, not least in effecting moments of network translation. Globally mobile (both physically – in that they have the time and resources to travel outside of their home countries – and through their access to distance-shrinking technologies), they perform much of the routine work that sustains the network (see also Juris, 2004a). They possess the cultural capital of (usually) higher education, and the social capital inherent in their transnational connections and access to resources and knowledge (Juris, 2004a; Missingham, 2003).

Moreover, as discussed in Chapter 3, 'soft control' by 'crypto-hierarchies' (King, 2004) can occur whereby the core group form unintentional elites (Juris, 2004a). These elite groups can act as covert structures in open consensus. For example, the details of meetings and discussions are published and circulated, but this information is primarily received by those connected to certain technological and social networks. PGA's 'hallmarks', language and phraseology are a point of 'soft control' (King, 2004). The documentation of meetings and decisions usually only tells half the story. Points of serious contention are frequently left out on grounds that the parties involved in the disagreement might not want them to be published (King, 2004). Juris (2004a) has examined in detail the ongoing struggles over organisation and decision-making within the European PGA network. For example, in an open letter to the PGA by the *Sans Titre* network in advance of the PGA Europe conference in Leiden, Holland (2002), this critique was articulated thus:

> Whenever we have been involved in PGA-inspired action, we have been unable to identify decision-making bodies. Moreover, there has been no collective assessment of the effectiveness of PGA-inspired actions ... [There are] flaws in our *de facto* decision-making process: Who decides what? When? And how? ... [T]he lack of clearly defined procedures and structures induces a new and more perverse form of hierarchical control. (Sans Titre, 2002: 1–2)

However, the existence of an 'informal elite' can also be partly due to the attitudes of grassroots activists themselves who at times tend to defer authority to key movement contacts and let them get on with the work of international networking. Hence an activist in the KRRS explained:

> We need to involve the grassroots in the PGA process, but the attitude of local activists can be a barrier. When I report back about PGA events such as Dhaka, no-one really takes it very seriously. This is also accentuated by the fact that few people in the movement speak English. But movements need to take responsibility for the PGA process. (interview, Kathmandu, Nepal, 2004)

Agency is a relational effect generated by interaction and connectivity within the network. Hence differential social and power relations comprise the convergence space of the PGA Asia network. For example, the gender inequalities and discriminations that exist within movements are not only being (differentially) addressed by movements, they are also being addressed as part of the process of transnational networking. At the Dhaka conference two days were devoted to the consideration of gender issues with a range of workshops, discussions and films. Here, while mutual solidarities are forged recognising differences between participant movements, certain differences – such as those of discriminatory gender relations – lead to antagonisms that can be addressed as part of the ongoing constitution of the network.

Hence, network processes are unequal, since certain social relations may be disproportionately directive (Castree, 2002). Certainly, in PGA Asia, actors vary greatly in their powers to influence others; and that power, while dispersed, can be directed by some (namely specific 'social actors') more than others (Castree, 2002). This is because, not least, powerful actors are able to deploy important materials such as money and technology. As noted in earlier chapters, the durability of interpersonal relations between key movement contacts and the free radicals, their 'mobility' and their ability to enroll others, is what enables the operation of the network.

When asked specifically whether he thought that an elite group was forming within the PGA Asia process, a key movement contact in the BKF stated:

> This will continue because we are working with illiterate people and it is difficult for them to formulate actions and theories. They can only give their opinions based on their experiences. Thus the educated have to meet in a small group. Also we need to meet in a clandestine way for decision-making because in

open meetings not all those present are our friends (i.e. some may be state agents). We are creating a hierarchy but what does this mean? The actual hierarchy is very different: it is those in Washington, etc. We discuss with the people and refer our thoughts to them and listen to their opinions. Later in small groups we try to formalise their opinions, then we take these back to the people and see if they agree. The support group has an important role, because they have valued opinions, but it would not be wise for them to impose their ideas on the process. The support group should not be decision-makers, they can facilitate the process. I don't see any support group people trying to dominate. The Dhaka declaration was presented to and accepted by the conference. It was able to synthesise/formalise the feelings and decisions of the conference. (interview, Dhaka, Bangladesh, 2004)

What is interesting about this reply is how an internal hierarchy/binary is encoded and accepted (by this activist) within the functioning of the network. An educated, literate 'us' will guide an illiterate 'them'; 'we' will meet in secret, while 'they' will hold open meetings; 'our' hierarchies are not as damaging as the hierarchies of 'our' enemies (e.g. in Washington). However, within PGA Asia, the support group's own analysis of the PGA process, following the Dhaka conference, suggests concern with the emergence of an 'informal elite' within the PGA process:

There was a failure to decentralise initiative-building. Much of the calls to action came from a coordinating committee that consisted of activists from ANPA, BKF, BKU, KRRS, and four support group members. More work needs to be done to decentralise the PGA Asia process, and to make social movements self-reliant in all aspects. The continuation of the support group is problematic, in that it was hoped that the support group could dissolve after the conference. While the delegates voted unanimously to keep the support group, there are real, ongoing questions about the power that the support group has in the PGA process – not least because of its ability to raise funds, etc. (PGA Dhaka conference evaluation, 2004: see www.agp.org)

Hence, there is an acknowledgment that the dynamics between support group and movements is one of relative dependency. Interestingly, for a Thai activist in the AoP, this mirrors a broader differential dynamic between activists of the Global North and Global South that she has witnessed in over 12 years of political organising in what she terms the 'process', referring to the processes of political mobilisation, networking and facilitation:

> The relationship between North and South is unequal. Activists in the North have more skills, knowledge, and higher levels of education and therefore they tend to dominate the process. They guide the process, often with goodwill, but they have the advantages of resources, power, and strategy. Northern activists are always involved in the process in the South but Southern activists are never involved in the process in the North. I have worked with Focus on the Global South, *Via Campesina*, the World Social Forum, the Asia Social Forum, Trade unions, womens' groups and NGOs. It is the same everywhere. The Northern activists provide the analysis and control the process; the Southern activists provide the testimony. (interview, Bangkok, Thailand, 2004)

Interwoven with the problem of differential activist powers (and the vertical social relations that this implies), is the issue of the network's imaginary, played out across material and virtual space.

Spatial dynamics of the PGA Asia convergence

Networks are a means of acting upon space, in that spaces are arranged so that certain types of action can be conducted. For example, gatherings in particular places remain critical to the sustainability of a sense of collective identity when in a spatially extensive network such as PGA. Places have been used strategically to sustain PGA. For example, specific symbolic sites have been chosen for the location of the PGA international conferences. The PGA conferences in Bangalore and Cochabamba were chosen partly because they had been the sites of successful resistance by popular mass movements against transnational corporations pursuing a neoliberal agenda. In the case of Bangalore, Monsanto and Cargill had both faced successful opposition to their attempts to introduce GM cotton-seeds and field trials in the Indian state of Karnataka, by the Karnataka State Farmers' Association – the host of the PGA conference. In Cochabamba, Bechtel Corporation faced successful opposition to their attempts to privatise the city's water supply by a popular coalition of students, business people, labour unions and peasant movements. This included the Six Federations of the Tropics (coca farmers) who jointly hosted the PGA conference with the National Federation of Domestic Workers.

These conferences have differential impacts upon the struggles that occur in those places where they are organised. When movements act as hosts for PGA international or regional conferences, their struggles are given a certain amount of national and international projection and legitimacy (e.g. through the media) as a result. Moreover, the grassroots members of a movement can receive a boost in morale when activists from around the world visit and articulate support for their struggles (as noted earlier regarding the BKF's hosting of the Dhaka conference).

Hence, particular places and movements become differentially empowered and connected within the operations of networks. Within PGA Asia, Dhaka – as the locale for the conference – became an articulated moment of the network as a result of the collective activities of imagineers (deciding upon the need for a conference and its time and place); movement activists in the BKF (setting up a conference coordination office); government officials (granting visas to foreign delegates); and numerous nonhuman others (computers, printers, airplanes, trains, etc.) A longer-lasting effect was that the conference led to the beginnings of the development of a national PGA process in Bangladesh and Nepal commencing in late 2004.

While the decision to hold a PGA Asia conference was taken by Asian delegates at the 2001 PGA international conference, the decision to hold the conference in Dhaka was the result of discussions between some of the free radical activists and members of the BKF, during a visit that the former made to Bangladesh in 2002.[11] The Dhaka conference enabled the BKF to secure its first office space in order to coordinate the conference logistics.[12] This office was equipped with computers, internet, printers, etc. for the purpose, became the 'hub' of connections during the lead-up to the conference, and subsequently became the BKF national office. Because the conference took place in Bangladesh, the majority of the participants were Bangladeshis (110 out of 150 total participants). Their presence at the conference increased the ability of the BKF to organise peasant communities within the country (not least because of its increased status as a result of co-hosting the conference [with the Bangladesh *Kisani Sabha*]), and also generated a deeper sense of participation in the PGA Asia network of many of the peasant delegates involved (interviews, Dhaka, Bangladesh, 2004).

In addition, the routes of the PGA caravans focus around those places where social movement struggles are occurring. Caravans attempt to create a spatially-extensive politics of solidarity through communication and support actions within particular countries between activists from those and other countries involved in different struggles. For example, in 1999, an Intercontinental Caravan was organised which brought 450 representatives of grassroots movements from the Global South to visit 12 European countries, meet with grassroots European movements and conduct joint solidarity actions (e.g. against transnational corporations involved in the production of genetically modified crops (see www.agp. org and Featherstone, 2003). Such an initiative required massive coordination by the various local-based groups who were organising the specific elements (e.g. meetings and rallies) of the caravans' activities. In the aftermath, regional strategy meetings of those groups who were involved had been organised to plan for future protests and initiatives, such as the PGA conference in Bangalore in 1999, and the creation of PGA Asia.

PGA Asia is a network where the links between actors and intermediaries are in process, at times divergent and unstable. The components (imagineers, movements) continually re-negotiate with each other forming variable and revisable coalitions (Callon, 1992; Murdoch, 1998). The PGA Asia network could be seen as what Ettlinger and Bosco (2004) term a 'constellation' or 'federation' of overlapping relations between imagineers, social movements and other regional 'constellations' of the PGA network that coalesce in conferences such as at Dhaka, caravans and actions. At other times, these same individuals and movements are engaged in other projects and actions (e.g. within their own national and regional movement contexts, within other networks such as *La Via Campesina*, etc.). While certain movements have left the network, such as FSPI, others have joined the process, including AoP, the Vietnam Farmers' Union and the Panggau.

A focus on process necessitates an understanding of network growth and contraction strategies, coalitional development and change, an identification of the groups to which a network may connect and the circumstances and strategies of connection and dissolution. This must take into account the fact that while networks of resistance operate transnationally, the struggles and the identities of resistance are often born locally through activists' sense and experience of place (Pile and Keith, 1997). What also gets diffused and organised in convergence spaces is the 'common ground' shared by different groups – in this case the PGA hallmarks (Routledge, 2003a).

However, the technology for reaching out cannot extend networks where the notion of extension or enrolment fails to capture the imagination (Riles, 2001). Conflicts between networking and more vertical operational logics result in confusion among some activists over the relation between their constituent movements and the broader network (cf. Juris, 2004a). Moreover, many grassroots members are unaware of the difference in operational logics between their own movements and the networking logic of PGA. For example, many activists interviewed expressed the need for more familiar operational logics and structures in the PGA Asia process. Hence an activist in the Bangladesh *Kisani Sabha* thought that the network was too loose and needed tangible structures to facilitate coordination, communication and contact:

> PGA is a process but it should have particular institutions where people can get training, for example via an education program, and we need a communication point from where people can get information and use as a contact point. The network is too loose. We need an operational secretariat. *Kisani Sabha* is interested in coordinating a national PGA process in Bangladesh, but we need a tangible structure in Bangladesh for coordination, communication and contact. The Dhaka conference was the start of this. (interview, Dhaka, Bangladesh, 2004).

Some grassroots activists interviewed in Nepal and Dhaka thought of PGA as an organisation which arranged events for them, rather than imagining themselves as being part of the PGA Asia network. The need for more traditional, tangible (verticalist) organisational structures rather than horizontal ones, may be attributed to the entangled character of PGA Asia's organisational logics, discussed earlier. The PGA imaginary remains abstract to many grassroots activists, for whom the networking logic of many direct action groups (and PGA) is unfamiliar. As one BKF activist remarked:

> We have to disseminate information to people in rural areas, but so far they have not been able to visualise what the network is. We need a national conference to begin the process of visualisation of the PGA process in Bangladesh. (interview Dhaka, Bangladesh, 2004)

In addition, as noted earlier, activists do not see a link between their movement and their daily lives, and the PGA network. This leads us to a discussion of how the PGA process is networked across space, and in particular, if and how it is 'grassrooted' in the countries of participant movements.

Networking vectors

In order to 'ground' the idea of a network such as PGA Asia, it is therefore essential to have 'networking vectors' which work to intervene in the work of translation by that networks are formed and developed, acting to further the process of communication, information-sharing and interaction within grassroots communities. Such vectors include the Dhaka conference, feedback by conference delegates to their grassroots communities, activist caravans and the imagineers. Most activists who attended the PGA Asia conference in Dhaka, had been invited by one of the key movement contacts of the network. Many had only recently heard of the PGA network, but the conference enabled them to learn more about the PGA process. According to the activists who attend them, PGA regional and international conferences have enabled grassroots activists to (a) learn about other struggles in other countries and decrease their sense of isolation; (b) communicate with other activists from other countries; (c) share tactics and strategies; and (d) generate a sense of solidarity between movements (interviews, Dhaka, Bangladesh, 2004; Kathmandu, Nepal, 2004). Hence a BKF activist noted:

> PGA can provide information about struggles around the world; about how economic globalisation works, and how this is

affecting grassroots communities, and agriculture in Bangladesh. This increases consciousness of international issues and struggles and thus we are able to identify common enemies. With PGA support, the BKF struggle will be more effective. Information on other struggles also provides information about how others struggle and also knowledge about the history of different struggles. This inspires other movements when they know they are part of an international process. (interview, Dhaka, Bangladesh, 2004)

Participation in PGA Asia activities can also benefit particular social movements in their own organsing practices, as noted by an ANPA activist:

Indirectly, PGA conferences and caravans support ANPA's work. When PGA supports delegates to go to these events they can gain knowledge, share experiences, learn from others, and experience actions when they participate. This supports the long term work of ANPA. (interview, Kathmandu, Nepal, 2004)

Moreover, communication has enabled the creation of common ground between movements, as a precursor to international solidarity, as explained earlier.

The Dhaka conference was an inspiration since we were able to meet so many committed activists from other groups. We learned about others, and shared the experiences of others. We are also exploited, and therefore we share similar problems and issues with other movements such as food sovereignty and biodiversity. Solidarity between farmers is important because we face the same problems. (interview, Kathmandu, Nepal, 2004)

In addition, many movements held post-conference debriefing meetings at national and district levels to explain to people about the conference and the PGA process. As a Bangladesh *Kisani Sabha* activist explained, concerning the process in Bangladesh:

The Dhaka delegates disseminated information into the rural areas. I held several meetings for *Kisani Sabha* members in villages to discuss the PGA conference and process. Rural women and members of *Kisani Sabha* now know about PGA, have got new impressions and the sense that *Kisani Sabha* has an international role. So, rural women have got a sense of empowerment. (interview, Dhaka, Bangladesh, 2004)

As noted, activist caravans enable activists from different struggles and countries to communicate with one another, exchange information, share experiences and tactics, and participate in various solidarity actions. Through these processes of articulation the ground for mutual solidarity between activists and social movements is nurtured, other movements are potentially drawn into the network, and political, economic and cultural alternatives are posed in opposition to neoliberalism. Caravans also enable collective strategies to be developed between movements, facilitate the development of movement-to-movement projects and initiatives, and enable deeper interpersonal ties to be established between different activists from different cultural spaces and struggles (Featherstone, 2003; Routledge, 2003a).

The caravans have included the Intercontinental Caravan in 1999; a United States caravan (on which certain Asian activists participated) that culminated in the WTO protests in Seattle in 1999; and caravans before and after the PGA conferences in Bangalore, India (1999) and Cochabamba, Bolivia (2001).[13] In addition, there have been speaking tours, workshops and seminars, concerning neoliberalism and its alternatives, on several continents.

The role of the imagineers has also been important in networking the PGA imaginary. For example, for poor BKF peasant communities in Bangladesh, or the AoP's peasant communities in Northern Thailand, their only source of connection to the network is primarily through the activist organisers who operate from the movements' offices, and who visit the communities as part of their organising practices. 'Free radical' activists (accompanying activist organisers) have also often travelled to visit social movements in Asia before PGA events such as conferences to discuss with them the PGA process, attend meetings, conduct workshops and invite them to participate in forthcoming events.[14] The imagineers (and to a lesser extent Dhaka delegates who conducted feedback sessions) are important networking vectors and, at times, 'grassrooting vectors' within PGA Asia. They frequently act as the agents of translation's moments and strategies, displacing the network's collective visions (including the shared experiences of oppression, problems, opponents) from one context to another in order to further the processes of connectivity and affinity among peasant communities who comprise the 'grassroots' of PGA Asia's participant movements.

For the poor of grassroots movements, such relational dynamics can constitute an expansion of their geographical imagination and practical political knowledge. The presence of imagineers in grassroots communities embodies the network and can constitute proof of sorts of the international character of the network – a tangible, visual example that peasants are part of something wider and larger. It also enables the concept of PGA to begin to take root in people's imaginations. The imagineers tend to act as the driving force of the network imaginary, coordinating and controlling the majority of informational traffic. As noted earlier, certain decision-making power accrues to them by virtue of access to resources (time, money, technology, language skills, etc.), as well as personal qualities such as commitment and charisma (Juris, 2004a; King, 2004). Social capital accrues to these imagineers by virtue of their networking capacities. Disproportionate power accrues to networking vectors as a result of their capacity to enroll others into the network, to travel and to act as channels of communication between activists located in different places who are not as 'mobile'. This belies the decentralised horizontal coordination that supposedly operates within PGA Asia, since networking vectors constitute a hierarchy of communicational, informational and decision-making 'powers' within the operational and relational dynamics of the network. However, networking vectors are essential (at least at present) for networks such as PGA Asia to 'act'. They help to forge connections between PGA Asia and its participant (and other) movements: they conduct the primary work that organises the network.

Horizontal (and within movements somewhat vertical) networks interconnect villagers at the grassroots (of social movements), the imagineers, and even some NGO workers, who act and speak in various contexts to construct PGA Asia. These networks are also, at times, interlinked with a variety of media (such as the Internet), journalists (especially during conferences), academics (who conduct research on the networks), other social movements and organisations (e.g. who participate as guests at conferences), and those networks which PGA Asia participant movements are also involved in (such as *La Via Campesina*). These interactions are also entwined with the ideas, information and resources which flow through the skein of networks. Through the collective rituals of the network – the practices of meetings, conferences, protests, caravans and other forms of networking – participants come to embody activism and cultures of solidarity (Juris, 2004a).

However, for most of the grassroots activists of PGA Asia's participant movements, their most immediate source of self-recognition and autonomous organisation is their locality: they mobilise to protect their community, their land and their environment (Castells, 1997). Moreover, particular experiences of neoliberalism, and the formulation of understandings and responses, differ from place to place. These immediate issues of survival and livelihood nevertheless can act as motivations for people to participate (as social movement members) within transnational networks such as PGA Asia, in order to meet activists in other movements, to learn from them, and increase their understanding of the issues that affect them. They can also form the basis for common grievances between movements, as a prelude to forging mutual solidarity.

However, many activists believed that an important step in bringing the PGA imaginary to the grassroots, lay not only in having local post-conference debriefing meetings, or meetings where imagineers spoke, but also to create a national PGA process within their respective countries (which would also involve caravan activities such as meetings between activists from different countries):

> We need to bring the PGA process to the national level and then down to the grassroots workers, we need a national PGA process to which the grassroots are linked, via conferences, workshops, discussions, trainings. I have begun to talk to the grassroots communities in my district (Saptari) and in my union about my Dhaka experiences. But this has to be a collective process of growth. We also need to bring other international activists to the grassroots communities. The problem with the grassroots process is that we do not talk in depth, we need a national action plan for PGA. (ANPA activist, interview, Kathmandu, Nepal, 2004)

In addition, activists articulated the need to establish more ongoing grassroots programmes, whereby some of the experiences that activists would normally only get at conferences (such as learning about the dynamics of globalisation and the struggles of other movements) could be provided: 'we need training programmes to exchange experiences about struggles and tactics, because our knowledge is not enough, it is only knowledge about Bangladesh' (BKF activist, interview, Dhaka, Bangladesh, 2004). This was seen as the responsibility of the participant movements in PGA Asia:

> Movements need to take responsibility for the PGA process. We need to make each local district organisation have representatives on a PGA committee, and responsibility for international matters. (KRRS activist, interview, Kathmandu, Nepal, 2004)

Hence, networking vectors, while important, are insufficient for the construction of durable networks. The vertical power relations that they embody require replacement with more horizontal relations between movements within countries and between movements from different countries. Grounding network imaginaries necessitates forging mutual solidarity.

Mutual solidarity

The nurturance of mutual solidarity within GJNs such as PGA Asia not only requires that networks be 'constantly produced and reproduced through concrete networking practices (Juris 2004a: 469)' but also the deepening of the network imaginary within grassroots communities. Key network moments, embodied in networking vectors such as conferences, caravans and global days of action, constitute the networking vitality of PGA Asia, while the ongoing organising that surrounds such events, facilitates sustained exchange and interaction among diverse movements, networks and organisations, generating common discourses (such as the network's collective visions), practices and identities (Juris, 2004a). However, whether such networking is sufficient to enable transformative political projects to be realised remains to be seen.

Protest events in themselves may mean little for the social and participatory rights of groups at the bottom of social hierarchies, whose specific interests remain unrepresented. As one Panggau activist noted with regard to global day of action events:

Demonstrations are not sustainable forms of resistance – for communities like the Iban,[15] they are artificial forms of resistance, inappropriate to their culture and their communities' local realities. Symbolic demonstrations may get into the press for a day, but afterwards little will change, and these communities are only left with memories. We need to develop consciousness (e.g. through educational trainings) about legal rights, and how to develop sustainable economies and sustainable forms of resistance. We need to discuss ways that movements can meaningfully support one another. (interview, Kuching, Borneo, Malaysia, 2004)

This view reflects broader concerns about the establishment of lasting alternatives to neoliberalism (interviews, Nepal, Thailand, Bangladesh, 2004). Such concerns have led to the emergence of certain projects from within the relationships generated through the PGA Asia convergence. For example, activists from the KRRS and Bangladesh *Kisani Sabha* have begun a long-term project in southern India to establish an agro-ecological community for women's empowerment (personal communication, Kathmandu, Nepal, 2004).

Sustainable connections between movements are grounded in place- and face-to-face-based moments of articulation such as conferences and village meetings (Rai, 2003; Routledge *et al.*, 2007). Through moments of togetherness – like eating meals together, sharing testimonies, planning collective strategies against common opponents – practical solidarities are affected. They become an active part in the constitution of the political identities of place-based struggles, and actively shape how transnational networks such as PGA Asia 'act' in the world, both in terms of the collective political identity of the network (Massey, 2005), and the strategies and campaigns such a network adopts.

For example, two of the women's movements participating in PGA Asia, the All Nepal Women's Association (ANWA) and the Bangladesh *Kisani Sabha*, have commenced the development of an exchange programme, exchanging various products (such as legumes and citrus), and are investigating the development of an alternative cross-border market system between communities in Nepal and Bangladesh. As an ANWA activist commented:

In Dhaka, we leant about other struggles, shared the experience of others, and saw that we shared similar problems and issues with other movements. We need to share the experiences of Dhaka with women at the grassroots, and need to develop a separate network of women – where our struggles are connected to other women's struggles in Asia, where we can include gender issues in our organising. (interview, Kathmandu, Nepal, 2004)

The sustainability of such processes will depend, in part, on the extent to which network imaginaries are grounded successfully, and meaningfully, in grassroots communities. Network imaginaries require grounding in both material projects (i.e. inter-movement initiatives and campaigns) and the geopoetics of resistance (i.e. the cultural and ideological expressions of social movement agency that inspire, empower and motivate people to resist (Routledge, 2000)). Within PGA Asia, this process remains in its nascent form, particularly since participant movements' time and resources are primarily devoted to movement-specific issues within their own countries. Moreover, there are concerns among movement activists that while certain activists (such as the imagineers) are empowered within GJNs such as PGA Asia, grassroots communities are left largely untouched. Hence, a PGA Asia caravan project, called for during the 2004 conference in Dhaka, has yet to be organised owing to activists' concerns that, while it would benefit those who participated, most grassroots communities would be left unaffected (interviews, Kathmandu, Nepal 2006). Thus, while PGA Asia exemplifies a decentred networking logic in theory (cf. Juris, 2004a, b; 2005a), in practice certain hierarchies persist and powers are unevenly distributed.

Notes

1 This was convened by such groups as MST (Brazil), Karnataka State Farmer's Association (India), Movement for the Survival of the Ogoni People (Nigeria), the Peasant Movement (Philippines), the Central Sandinista de Trabajadores (Nicaragua) and the Indigenous Women's Network (North America and the Pacific).

2 'Backward Caste' is an official category employed by the Government of India, being lower castes (but not 'untouchables') who are economically depressed but not landless (Gupta, 1998).

3 The BKF is part of the *Aaht Sangathan* (eight organisations). The eight organisations have a membership of 1.3 million people and comprise:

the Bangladesh Krishok Federation (landless peasants organisation, 700,000 members); the Bangladesh *Kisani Sabha* (women peasants organisation); the Bangladesh Floating Labour Union (migrant labourers); the Bangladesh Floating Women's Labour Union; the Bangladesh *Adivasi Samiti* (indigenous people's organisation); the Bangladesh Rural Intellectual Front; the *Ganochaya Sangskritik Kendro* (cultural centre); and the Revolutionary Youth *Sabha* (youth front).

4   The collective visions of PGA, are as follows: 1. A very clear rejection of capitalism, imperialism and feudalism; and all trade agreements, institutions and governments that promote destructive globalisation. 2. We reject all forms and systems of domination and discrimination including, but not limited to, patriarchy, racism and religious fundamentalism of all creeds. We embrace the full dignity of all human beings. 3. A confrontational attitude, since we do not think that lobbying can have a major impact in such biased and undemocratic organisations, in which transnational capital is the only real policymaker. 4. A call to direct action and civil disobedience, support for social movements' struggles, advocating forms of resistance which maximise respect for life and oppressed peoples' rights, as well as the construction of local alternatives to global capitalism. 5. An organisational philosophy based on decentralisation and autonomy. (Taken from the PGA website: www.agp.org).

5   There have been three international conferences, held in Geneva, Switzerland (1998), Bangalore, India (1999) and Cochabamba, Bolivia (2001), and regional PGA conferences have been held in Europe (Milan, Barcelona, Leiden), Nicaragua, Panama, Brazil, Bangladesh, New Zealand (Aotearoa) and the United States.

6   The European members of this group were established during the PGA international conference in Cochabamba, Bolivia in 2001. Several of the European delegates to the conference volunteered to carry out this work in response to requests by Asian (movement) delegates for a team of activists to support the work of PGA Asia. With their access to possible European funding sources and the time and resources to carry out 'support' work, these volunteers were readily accepted by the Asian delegates. Several of the European-based activists have spent prolonged periods of time in Asia working with movements during the past four years. This group had wanted to devolve their work to the social movements in Asia over time, conscious of their disproportionately powerful roles within the network. However, at the Dhaka conference in 2004, movement delegates unanimously approved the continued existence of this group and, in the first step to devolve the group from Europe, its expansion to include a Thai activist, based in Thailand. By 2007, two of the Europeans had left the group, and the AoP had yet to ratify their participation as a Southeast Asian convenor (an issue we discuss later in this chapter).

7   The first conference was held in 2000.

8   These were gender, privatisation and exploitation of resources, labour conditions and migration in Asia, indigenous rights, peasant rights and food sovereignty, war and militarism, and biodiversity, sustainability and biopiracy.

9   We are grateful to Sara Koopman for insights into the issue of language interpretation.

10 For a fuller discussion on what some have termed the 'new farmer's movements' in India, see Brass (1995).

11 Routledge's networking activities in Bangladesh in 2002 contributed to providing links in the network by carrying information across the network from group to group and building personal relationships with those whom he visited, especially key activists and movement leaders. He acted to inform people about PGA and its processes and initiatives, promoting its ideas, reinforcing the beliefs of participants, encouraging them to action, educating them regarding initiatives elsewhere in the world, etc. Such meetings helped to vitalise the movements in various ways, and carried ideas to and fro within and between them, including the writing up of reports of such trips which then entered the flow of communication within and between the participants of the convergence. For example, during work with the BKF, Routledge's speaking at community-based meetings of grassroots activists helped the BKF in its own organising practices by highlighting the movement's international dimension in peoples' imaginations (interviews, Dhaka, Bangladesh, 2004), and contributed to the BKF's decision to host the Dhaka conference.

12 Until this time, BKF activities had been coordinated out of the movement's general secretary's home.

13 The India caravan visited struggles of tribal peoples, fisherfolk and rubber workers in southern India. It included activists from various countries who had attended the PGA international conference in Bangalore.

14 Indeed, Routledge conducted such visits as part of his participant observation of the network.

15 The *Iban Pagan* are one of the *Dayak* indigenous communities of Sarawak, Borneo.

6

International Federation for Chemical, Energy, Mine and General Workers: labour internationalism as vertical networking?

ICEM (International Federation for Chemical, Energy, Mine and General Workers) is one of the ten Global Union Federations (GUFs), formerly known as International Trade Secretariats, set up to represent and coordinate worldwide labour interests. It unites workplace-based branches of 408 trade unions in its sectors (essentially chemicals, oil, energy and mining) on all continents. It receives its core funding to carry out its operations through affiliation fees from national affiliates, so exists in a dependency relationship, particular to the more powerful national union centres. It is also dependent at the national level for funding for particular projects. It is heavily male-dominated, reflecting its origins in traditional industries, and has tended to be driven by the interests of European affiliates who provide the majority of financial resources, although its membership is increasingly diverse. All together, ICEM represents some 20 million workers in 125 countries. Its head office is located in Brussels and until late 2004 ICEM had five further regional offices in Latin America, Asia, Eastern Europe, Africa and North America. A first point to note therefore is that ICEM, in contrast to PGA Asia, has a substantial organisational presence with considerable potential as a network with global reach.

ICEM is also a much longer established network than PGA Asia with a history that dates back to 1907. Since its inception, it has mutated numerous times, due to political and economic changes, mergers and reorganisations within the union movement itself. In its current form, it represents the merger – in 1995 – of the International Chemical and Energy Federation (ICEF) with the MIF (the International

Mining Federation). In its founding declaration, ICEM commits itself to a 'focus on achieving practical results and gains for its members. Strength is its sinew, service its duty, action its day-to-day business. Solidarity in practice, permanently renewed and strengthened, the ICEM's driving force' (ICEM, 1995). As a global union network, its collective vision is one of developing trade union and workers' rights, tackling poverty, exploitation and poor working conditions. This involves a shared commitment to addressing the current imbalance of the global economy towards MNCs by creating united global labour organisations.

In common with other GUFs, ICEM is industry-based and dedicated to developing practical forms of solidarity that are identifiable with the material interests of its members. As a convergence space, ICEM represents a coalition of different labour interests, perspectives and ideologies, ranging from a moderate European social democracy – particularly in the influential German and Nordic affiliates – to more Marxist-inspired movements (the French CGT and many of the affiliates from the Global South, especially South Africa) and autonomous/syndicalist traditions (in elements of British, French and Australian unions). The merger in 1995 created further tensions between a chemicals section, which has tended to have a more global orientation, reflecting the industrial context, and a mining section which, with the withdrawal of the British NUM (National Union of Miners) in the late 1980s to join the Communist international federation, became dominated by more conservative unions with a more restricted internationalism.

Operational logics, network imagineers and relational dynamics

In terms of operational logics, a major contrast can be drawn with PGA Asia in terms of the way the network functions. ICEM can be understood first and foremost as operating through a 'verticalist' logic, displaying a conventional hierarchical structure, centred upon powerful national affiliates, with a leadership, mass membership and social relations based on delegation and formal organisational processes. Because the ICEM and its affiliates have a paying membership with full-time officials and elected delegates, this clearly creates a principal-agent relationship that does not exist in more horizontalist social movements. The delegate structures also mean that most of the international work is carried out by professional officers and elected officials at the national and international scales to the extent that the grassroots membership is largely passive and excluded. These network imagineers are critical in developing ICEM's global vision and strategy, translating the network's goals for the wider constituency and conform to Tarrow's notion of 'rooted cosmopolitans' (2005), as actors who emerge out of particular national contexts to shape international activities. This relational topography – of key social relations that work across scales – is critical to understanding how particular nationally embedded perspectives influence the global imaginery of ICEM.

ICEM imagineers emerge predominantly from European and North American unions, whose dominance over international activity reflects both a higher level of resources and greater access to and influence over government and corporate actors. The powerful German *Industriegewerkschaft Bergbau, Chemie, Energie* (IG-BCE) is the largest contributor to the ICEM, although its contribution in mining has been declining in recent years.[1] The second most important affiliate, in terms of members, is the US union PAICE (Paper and Allied Industries, Chemical and Energy Union). Whilst not being particularly active at the international level in the past, these two national union centres – along with key Japanese affiliates which dominate the Asia Pacific network – retain considerable power to block initiatives if they are perceived as contrary to national union interests (authors' interviews). Outside the Global North, the South African miners union is the most powerful in terms of members and influence. Several union officials that we spoke to suggested that some individual unions declare more members than they have on their books and subsequently pay higher fees to the federation as a strategy to obtain more voting power, although conversely some may declare less to reduce their fee.

It is also important to note that many affiliates are involved in more than one GUF, so that ICEM is not always the most important global network within which national unions are embedded. Many of the more traditional industrial unions are also affiliated to the International Metalworkers Federation, whilst those in the energy sectors that have interests in electricity and gas, where battles against privatisation have been a major focus of concern, are plugged into the international public sector federation, Public Services International. The extreme case is the British Transport and General Workers Union (TGWU) which is affiliated to nine GUFs. What this means in practice is that national affiliate unions are themselves differentially embedded in transnational union networks, further empowering particular imagineers against more spatially restricted actors.

ICEM operates primarily through four main mechanisms, or 'moments' of translation, through which the network is operationalised. As discussed in Chapters 3 and 5, these mechanisms problematise network functions (in order to effect solutions that enable the network to act more productively); they attempt to designate networked roles for actors (e.g. by allotting key tasks for participant union members and materials); they work to enrol other unions and materials into the network; and they work to mobilise all enrolled entities (e.g. through conferences). Through these relational processes, individuals, movements, materials and places are incorporated into the ICEM network (Murdoch, 1997a). The durability of these networked relations, continually performed over time and mobility through space (the materials and processes of communication which enable acting at a distance) constitute the key 'strategies' of network translation within ICEM (Law, 1992).

The most obvious translation mechanism is through regular meetings and assemblies of delegates. Primacy is given to the World Congress, described as 'the supreme authority' (ICEM, 2003a: 7), which takes place every four years and is where policy is decided and voted on. It also has a ruling 'Presidium' of 16 members (14 Vice Presidents, plus President and General Secretary) that meets twice per year, and an 80-member Executive Committee that meets once yearly and is effectively a policy-making apparatus between conferences. Appointments to these committees are through national affiliates, reflecting membership numbers with varying degrees of democracy, but there is a built-in bias towards areas with established union presence in Western

Europe and the Nordic countries and against 'developing' areas in Africa, Latin America and Southeast Asia especially (Table 6.1).

Candidates for Vice President are elected by the Congress, although this takes place after the allocation by region has been taken, which in turn is based on numbers of paid-up members (ICEM, 2003a: 10). Hierarchy within ICEM institutions is further reinforced by the statute that 'Only persons holding a post in an affiliated trade union shall qualify for an elected position' (ibid: 8), thus excluding many grassroots members. Each affiliate union is entitled to one vote for every 5,000 members (ibid: 8), again reinforcing the domination of the larger European affiliates.

Second, the Brussels headquarters acts as an important hub for network operations. It both carries out the day-to-day operations of the network, through the actions of its professional staff, and acts as an intermediary in facilitating the establishment of bilateral relationships between affiliate unions. It also coordinates campaigns to support union building initiatives in countries such as Iraq, or intervenes directly in protesting against worker abuse or in supporting particular movements in selected countries such as China and Colombia. Because of its long-established presence, and

Table 6.1 Membership of the Presidium by World Region, 2003

Region	Number of Vice Presidents	Countries represented
Western Europe	4	Belgium, Netherlands, Italy, Germany
Nordic Countries	2	Sweden, Denmark
North America	2	United States (2)
Asia/Pacific	2	Japan (2)
Central Europe	1	Slovakia
Eastern Europe, Central Asia and Trans-Caucasus	1	Ukraine
Africa	1	South Africa
Latin America	1	Brazil

Source: ICEM, 2003a; 2003b

subsequent connections to corporate and state actors, ICEM is able to play a global role in attacking human and labour rights abuses beyond anything that PGA Asia, as a newer and less stable network, can currently envisage. It is especially effective in spotting opportunities to assert labour rights, where other political and geopolitical agendas mean that particular government regimes or corporations have been under the media spotlight. One example involved protecting the rights of Turkish workers against their own government by mobilising European governments and OECD contacts in the context of Turkey's application to join the EU:

> We're involved with our affiliates very much in Turkey. We used the leverage of the army and the government's denial of trade unions rights to our rubber and cement affiliates and also our mining affiliates just in terms of labour disputes that they've been going through over the last year. And then in terms of Turkey trying to get into the EU. So we use that with Reinhard (EMCEF[2] General Secretary) to broadcast some of the 'labour ills' around various ministers and whatever in Turkey. And we find that once we do that the government backs off the unions. So a lot of what we do is just finding certain kinds of leverage. We work with TUAC (Trade Union Advisory Committee) which is an agency of the OECD. (interview with ICEM official, Brussels, Belgium, 2004)

ICEM is at its most effective when it can mobilise this kind of spatially extensive coalition for particular forms of solidarity, and such 'moments' are the main forms of network action that can support local and grassroots union initiatives.

Third, ICEM produces newsletters and information briefs diffused through its website (www.icem.org) and via electronic correspondence – two of its immutable mobiles. In this sense, the Internet acts more as a disseminator of information from the headquarters outwards, rather than the more horizontal and participatory fora for communication and debate said to characterise more informal social movement networks (McDonald, 2002). The ICEM website provides information and expertise on topics ranging from collective bargaining to health and safety standards, to ongoing campaigns, providing an important resource for national affiliates and local union branches. Critically though, the Internet has not fundamentally shifted the

operational or geographical logics of ICEM operation, reinforcing Lee's (2004) point about its undeveloped social and
political potential. Whilst the Internet has become an
important resource in permitting transnational communication, particularly in terms of developing solidarity campaigns
against local employer exploitation, decision-making power
resides in the interactions between key actors at ICEM in
Brussels and at the headquarters of key national affiliates.

The three mechanisms discussed thus far work as
'globalising' rather than 'grassrooting' vectors, in the sense
that network activities operate primarily through national
and transnational arenas and spaces that largely exclude
grassroots activists. A fourth mechanism – the attempt to
create global union networks within multinational corporations (MNCs) – has greater potential in this respect, though
so far progress here has been limited. Two different types
of strategy have been pursued to date: Global Company
Networks (GCNs) and Global Frame Agreements (GFAs).
GCNs were established through ICEM's second Congress in
1999, the principle being to provide a decentralised communication and information exchange mechanism for shop
stewards from different countries. Since ICEM does not have
the capacity to administer more than a very small number
of networks, the Executive Committee decided that it
should be the responsibility of affiliates to take on the role
of administering any network prior to it being established.
As of May 2007, ICEM has created 12 global company
networks including Bridgestone/Firestone in Japan and Rio
Tinto in the UK and Australia (see Sadler, 2004 for an
overview of the campaign against Rio Tinto) and, perhaps
most significantly, one inside Exxon Mobil bringing together
workers from 18 countries in both the Global North and
South (interview, ICEM official, Brussels, Belgium, 2004).

GFAs are voluntary agreements signed with multinational
companies, which pledge to respect a set of principles on
labour and trade union rights, based on ILO core conventions,
typically including the rights for unions to organise and
equality of conditions between genders and ethnic groups.
The first such agreement was signed in 1999 with Statoil, a
Norwegian oil company and in the meantime another ten
have been signed, the latest with French multinational
Rhodia in January 2005 (*Table 6.2*). In fact, ICEM is regarded

Table 6.2 Global Frame Agreements signed by ICEM and affiliates

Company	Employees	Country	Sector	Year
Statoil	16,000	Norway	Oil	1998
Freudenberg	27,500	Germany	Chemical	2000
Endesa	13,600	Spain	Power	2002
Norske Skog	11,000	Norway	Paper	2002
AngloGold	64,900	South Africa	Mining	2002
ENI	70,000	Italy	Energy	2002
SCA	46,000	Sweden	Paper	2004
Lukoil	150,000	Russia	Oil	2004
Electricite de France	167,000	France	Energy	2005
Rhodia	20,000	France	Chemical	2005

Source: Gibb, 2005

as having played a pioneering role and acquired particular strength with regard to GFAs. Among the GUFs, this makes ICEM less confrontational and more willing to bargain with multinational corporations compared to others such as the International Union of Food and Agricultural Workers (IUF) or the International Transport Workers' Federation (ITF). We return to a discussion of the role of GFAs in developing global solidarity below.

An across-the-board decline in union membership at the national scale – particularly in the core sectors of mining and chemicals – over the past 25 years has resulted in diminishing affiliation fees and less resources to commit to transnational activities at a time when 'there has been [. . .] a gradual increase in demands on the ICEM from our affiliates' (ICEM Congress Report, 2003a: 4). For example, British affiliates, which have traditionally played a very active role in international union structures, are finding it increasingly difficult to commit independent resources to international work in the face of declining membership numbers (authors' interviews). The consequence is that some of the affiliates from smaller European countries, such as the Nordic countries and the Netherlands, where membership levels have been more robust, have more resources to devote to international activity (authors' interviews). As one French union official noted:

> The Norwegians are loaded with money so they can feed in. Even if they do nothing, they give the money and it's the others who act. So as a result, it is possible to implement projects that are financed by others. (interview, Paris, France, 2005)

However, power over strategy ultimately rests with the union affiliates that command the largest block votes at the major congresses, principally those in the larger European states (especially Germany), the United States and Japan. Without the support of these national affiliates, it is difficult to forge effective international strategy, a reality that became self-evident during the 1990s (see below). The dominance of larger players is likely to increase as union affiliates respond to shrinking membership by merging at the national level. To provide three examples from our case study affiliates: in France, the *Confédération Française démocratique du travail* (CFDT) merged its chemical and energy federation as far back as 1993; in the UK, the merger between the two ICEM affiliates, TGWU and Amicus (engineering union) in May 2007, created the UK's largest union, Unite, with almost 2 million members; whilst, on a smaller scale, the Norwegian Chemical Workers union (NKIF) merged with the Norwegian oil workers, *Norsk Olje og Petrokjemisk Fagforbund* (NOPEF) in 2006, to create a union of 46,000 members. Such mergers may reduce divisive internecine conflicts and help to achieve scale efficiencies, but only at the risk of distancing union leaderships and growing bureaucracies from the grassroots.

Whilst the ICEM has a fundamentally different, and arguably opposing, set of operational and organisational logics to PGA Asia, it faces common problems in developing and sustaining genuine and effective forms of international solidarity and collective action across the global network. The advantage of a more bureaucratic and permanent set of organisational structures is that it has more regular and routine transnational activity, meaning that the network itself functions more systematically than PGA Asia, which remains reliant upon sporadic developments around key imagineers. Annual, biennial and, in the case of World Congresses, triennial conferences, alongside frequent workshops dedicated to particular issues (e.g. organising, AIDs/

HIV, the oil industry) provide important reflective material spaces for transnational strategies to develop, mitigating against the biodegradable processes that commonly afflict more decentred activist networks (Plows, 2004). Such meetings allow both the scaling up of particular local campaigns and actions to the wider global network and the ongoing development of global strategy and tactics. Of course, such structures can also encourage institutional inertia and an attachment to outmoded practices, particularly limiting the ability to respond quickly and effectively to broader economic and political processes.

However, in a similar fashion to PGA Asia, the key processes that sustain the network, on a day-to-day basis, reside in the actions and practices of a number of key individuals and organisational actors, or imagineers as noted above, and networking largely by-passes the grassroots members of the movement, through the globalising vectors of meetings and ICEM spaces. Because of the 'verticalist' nature of the federation, the critical 'relational networking processes' are between particular national affiliates; who either provide the finance for international activities or have the organisational power (see above); and the ICEM secretariat in Brussels. Geographically, therefore, national and international headquarters (in Western Europe and North America) are important nodes through which the ICEM network is territorialised and where imagineers operate from, in debating and developing strategy. Effectively, the network operates through what are often close-knit and longstanding personal relationships between individuals from similar national, ethnic and socio-cultural backgrounds operating at the interface between the national representative level and the international scale. The largest union affiliate, the German IG-BCE, has close links with the French CFDT, which together are the main axes in forging European level policies, and between them have considerable power to block broader global strategies without being particularly active. Another set of key relationships is between national officials of the British affiliate unions (especially the TGWU) and the ICEM secretariat, which is dominated by English-speaking officials and elected officers; the last two General Secretaries, Vic Thorpe and Fred Higgs, have been British.[3] Fred Higgs in particular rose to become General Secretary from the shopfloor, having started off as a union shop steward in the oil industry, rising to become the national officer of the TGWU's oil industry section. This in itself was significant as Higgs was, in the words of one respondent: 'the first General Secretary to come from the base' (authors' interviews, Blackpool, UK, 2005).

Another important organisational actor in recent years, 'punching above its weight' (Cumbers, 2004) has been the NOPEF. It is a relatively small affiliate in membership terms, with around 20,000 members whose leader for over two decades (until his retirement in 2000) was Lars Myrhe. As President of the Oil Industry section of ICEM in the 1990s, and as the General Secretary of one of the richest national affiliates in funding international activity, Myrhe has been a key 'imagineer' within ICEM's oil section and was instrumental in the setting up of the first Global Frame Agreement with the Norwegian state-run oil company, Statoil (Table 7.2). Operating from a relatively secure domestic base, with close political and often personal relationships with national politicians and businesses, Myrhe and NOPEF have been in a position to exercise considerable discursive power in promoting and projecting a Nordic model of social democracy and partnership onto the global level.[4] In his own words:

> We are in permanent discussion with the government and oil companies. If you compare the development of oil in our country with others, we have been very successful. They listen to us and we listen to them. When we need something, we go to the Labour Party. We also have very good relationships with Statoil and Norsk Hydro [the two main Norwegian oil companies]. (interview, Norway, 2005)

Myrhe forged a close relationship with Fred Higgs and the 'Statoil model' became instrumental in the development of ICEM's global strategy towards MNCs in the early 2000s (see below). Overall though, it is important to stress the role of these key relationships in not only shaping the discourses and developing strategies through which global activity takes place, but also being an effect of the network itself, in the sense that their power both produces and is reproduced through the structures and practices of ICEM (Riles, 2001; Juris, 2004a). This can be exclusionary if new union affiliates do not fit with the strategy and philosophy of the imagineers.

A case in point is the Norwegian oil union, *Sammen-slutningen av Fagorganiserte i Energisektoren* (SAFE), which has always been a rival for members in Norway with NOPEF. SAFE is an 'independent' union, as one not affiliated to the LO, the main national trade union umbrella body recognised by the state in employment regulation. It also rejects partnership and sees itself as a grassroots organisation with a rotating leadership, all with experience of working in the North Sea. SAFE's application to join ICEM in the early 1990s was blocked by Myrhe who, together with LO officials, actively dissuaded other European ICEM affiliates from developing collaborative ties with SAFE. However, this failed in the case of the French CGT, where as one SAFE member told us wryly:

> Myrhe is working internationally, and we saw that when we tried to work internationally and went into Europe to make contact with unions in Spain and Portugal and all that, he was calling them and warning them about OFS (now SAFE). 'Do not talk to them.' But, for example, in France, the CGT, they think 'OFS, what's that? They must be a good union since LO are warning us against them. (interview, Norway, 2005)

Through Myrhe, ICEM has also warned other organisa-tions from establishing relations with SAFE, in one case threatening to cut ICEM travel support to two formerly imprisoned Nigerian oil workers if they attended a SAFE conference in Stavanger (*ibid*). Apart from protecting his union's own domestic interests, the main rationale for this action appears to be protecting his – and ICEM's – inter-national partnership discourse. Even the slightest possibility that the oil workers would present an unflattering picture of the national oil union, Statoil's operations in Nigeria, at a meeting that would have included senior Norwegian politicians, was perceived as an unacceptable threat to the projection of a national corporatist discourse to the global scale.

In this way, power within ICEM is held by key imagineers such as Myrhe and other officials operating at the interface between national politics and transnational institutions. These union bureaucrats also owe their power as imagineers to participation in other networks outside of ICEM such as other GUFs, as well as governance institutions operating at different geographical scales (e.g. UN, EU, national governments) and relations with domestic corporate actors. Whilst local union activists and officials are drawn into and enlisted for particular projects and programmes, they have little role in shaping such struggles and, indeed as the SAFE example illustrates, can be frozen out if their presence is likely to challenge entrenched interests. For some grassroots activists, there are concerns that the social distance between the workplace and union elite is growing as a new generation of bureaucrats with university degrees, language skills and often a background in NGO work is replacing an older working-class generation in carrying out international work (authors' interviews).

Entangled powers and spatial dynamics

The legacy of verticalism within the international trade union movement and difficulties of transcending this to empower workers at the local level in global networking operation can be illustrated through the case study of an attempt to reform ICEM structures in the 1990s. The case also highlights the problems that occur within convergence spaces when opposing political positions (cf. Juris, 2004a) and very different scalar perspectives come into conflict. The period following the merger in 1995 was a particularly fraught time with diverse perspectives producing a stalemate in the ICEM leadership.

One condition of the merger was a split leadership with a General Secretary from the energy section and a Deputy from mining. The outcome was increasing tension between the General Secretary of the merged federation, Vic Thorpe (who came from a chemicals background as the former Deputy General Secretary of ICEF) and his new Deputy, from the mining section of the German union IG-BCE.

As a trade unionist, Thorpe was part of what one long-term union activist referred to as: a 'post-1968 New Left generation' (author's interview, Manchester, UK, 2004) that came into positions of power in the global union federations in the 1990s. Thorpe had been ahead of his time in arguing for transnational union activism and structures to counter the threat of MNCs in the 1970s. As a researcher in the ICEF he was the 'ghost-writer' for two influential books authored by the then General Secretary, Charles Levinson, in the 1970s, *Capital, Inflation and the Multinationals* (1971) and *International Trade Unionism* (1972).[5]

The ICEF was one of the few union internationals to attempt to create World Company Councils in the 1970s, although these proved to be short-lived. When Thorpe became General Secretary in 1992 he attempted to pursue the strategy of creating independent worker networks at the local level within individual MNCs, in opposition to many within the international trade union movement who were arguing for partnership and dialogue in setting international labour standards with governments and MNCs (see Gumbrell-McCormick, 2004). ICEF and its US affiliate, the USWA (United Steelworkers of America) were also innovative in launching the first successful 'cyber-picket' against the US tyre maker Bridgestone/Firestone in 1994. When the company fired over 2,000 of its unionised workforce at 5 of its US plants, the unions were able to use the Internet to develop a global protest network which both allowed the rapid transmission of information about the dispute and allowed activists worldwide to protest to the company and its customers itself (Herod, 2001: 149). The global pressure brought to bear on the company led to the reinstatement of all the sacked workers and was hailed by many union activists and academics as a foretaste of the new networked internationalism that was possible in age of the Internet (Lee, 1999).

Thorpe's commitment to a decentred and horizontalist networking strategy was clearly enunciated in a pamphlet produced by ICEM in 1996 that was once again far-sighted in recognising some of the problems facing unions from globalisation. Emphasis was placed upon shifting away from a 'top-down' strategy towards an international solidarity network of decentralised decision-making and 'locally owned' labour action (ICEM, 1996: 56). At the root of this strategy was a sophisticated analysis – reflecting the emerging tendencies in the wider resistance to neoliberalism – about the need to develop a new oppositional politics to global capital, less wedded to the dominant post-war model of trade union politics and pursuing power through the state and the vehicle of national party politics, but was about networking and empowering local unionists at the level of everyday struggles within individual MNCs. As Thorpe put it in an interview:

> [. . .] the union movement is not actually structured to deal with multinational issues. It is too wed to its own national politics and relationships and hasn't followed the economic logic over the last thirty years as it should have done and therefore it's losing out [. . .] For me the issue has always been to try to get the international more widely networked, to break away from the dominance of the major unions . . . To bring together people at plant level operating in different companies. The difficulty was, they always had somebody from national office – a minder sitting alongside them. (interview with Vic Thorpe, Paris, France, 2005)

One of Thorpe's key initiatives in this respect was to implement an international levy – similar to that operated by the Canadian Auto Workers Union (Gindin, 1998), direct from members at the local level to global workplace networks independent of national control. In particular, the idea was:

> To escape from the resource squeeze of the international and spend time and our efforts in developing these as pools of power in their own right, but every time the idea of the levy was raised there was a scream because people knew exactly what was going on. The national officers knew that we were trying to float these things away from their grasping hands and it was always a tension and we never got through to being able to raise a levy. (*ibid*)

The idea of the levy drew particularly strong opposition from the German IG-BCE, which was wary of surrendering any power to the shopfloor. A further and related Thorpe initiative was the establishment of GCNs as independent union networks that operated within companies at plant level. Critically, from Thorpe's international syndicalist perspective, the intention was that GCNs would also operate independently of existing national structures, adding a layer of horizontal relations into the ICEM federation that would diffuse power away from the union bureaucrats and their entrenched interests. The first such network was with BASF and was developed by using the existing works council which was controlled by local shop stewards at the company's headquarters in Ludwigshafen, Germany:

> We did a good job on BASF ironically, despite the Germans, because we had good relations with BASF at the heart in

Ludwigshafen at the level of the works council. We did networking in Latin America and within Asia. We brought them together with the Europeans and formed a fairly solid BASF network. I don't know what's happened since. (*ibid*)

Despite this early success, Thorpe and the 'new left' leadership were constantly being undermined by the German affiliate. As he noted wryly: 'We were unlucky in that we had the German mining and chemical unions which were on the right of the German trade union movement. Had we had IG Metall or somebody like that, we may have been in a much better position' (*ibid*).

The internal politics of IG-BCE itself did not help the situation with a weak mining section – having been reduced to less than 40,000 members out of a total of 500,000 (authors' interviews) – being allocated the 'international' (i.e. non-European porfolio) with the more powerful chemical section becoming dominant in the European parallel, but independent, organisation, EMCEF. What is also important here is the underlying culture and structure of the IG-BCE, which tends to be extremely hierarchical and bureaucratic with the leadership extremely remote from the grassroots. As one French trade unionist noted:

> The General Secretary of the IG BCE, Hubertus Schmoldt, whom I know well and who's an adviser to Schröder (ex German Chancellor), he's unable to say 'I know this or that union secretary in Ludwigshafen, in Bochum, etc.' (interview, Paris, France, 2005)

Leaders and officials in many of the major European affiliates tend to have closer social and personal ties to senior politicians and business leaders at the national level than they do to local union activists. As another ex-ICEM union official told us: 'the idea of multinational company networks is the right one but it's still somewhat stymied by national interests – relationships between unions and at national level, big employers and their own national governments' (authors' interviews, France, 2005).

Ultimately, the tensions between Thorpe and the German affiliate reflected very different political and geographical imaginaries in responding to neoliberalism and globalisation. Thorpe's emphasis upon committing scarce resources to independent networked local labour action at the global scale

(Waterman, 1998), ran contrary to the dominant approach being enunciated by German and other European Union leaderships, which was to scale up the best models of national labour regulation to the European level as part of the market integration process. As part of this, the more moderate unions in Western Europe (such as the British Amalgamated Engineering and Electricians Union (AEEU), French CFDT and German IC-BCE) were committed to continuing dialogue and partnership with employers and the state at the national scale, whilst simultaneously lobbying for legislative change through the institutions of the EU. The transfer of resources to the local scale on a global basis, promoting initiatives that would both empower 'rank-and-file' workers at the expense of regional and national officials and potentially create a more militant unionism, were clearly out of step with the dominant mood among the elites of the European labour movement.

The balance was tipped even further by the election of Labour and Social Democratic governments in Germany, the UK and France in the second half of the 1990s, which further stimulated a belief in the vision of social partnership and the scaling up of national models of corporatism to European and global scales as a means of dealing with multinational capital. Indeed, the trade union umbrella body, the European Trades Union Congress (ETUC), continues to push a 'Social Europe' agenda,[6] whereby the aspiration is to use regulatory structures and existing collaborative institutions such as the European Works Councils to promote worker rights with the aspiration of achieving European wide collective bargaining.

Thus far, however, there is little evidence of any tangible gains to workers and trade unions from this more moderate state-centric strategy at national or European level (Ramsay, 1997; Weston and Lucio, 1997; Gibb, 2005) with the possible exception of the British Government's 1998 Employment Relations Act that introduced new rights for trade union recognition.[7] Importantly, on the broader canvas of forging transnational solidarity across continents and between Global North and South, the continued emphasis upon influencing regulation through the EU institutions has also mitigated against a more expansive and progressive inter-nationalism, leading many unions in the Global South to point to a continuing 'Fortress Europe' mentality among their European counterparts. The same charge has been levelled at key US affiliates, though not necessarily those in ICEM, of having a restricted internationalist vision which is defensive and primarily regionalist in the sense of a focus upon cross-border solidarity in the wake of NAFTA (Burgoon and Jacoby, 2004).

Because of the inability to drive through the desired changes, Thorpe quit the Federation in 1999. Although he had the support of American, British, South African and Scandinavian trade unions for his strategy, the Germans and the Japanese were opposed. Thorpe could have won a vote, but only at the expense of a divided 'international'. The scalar constraints of ICEM's organisational geography, the need to forge a consensus between powerful affiliates protecting perceived national interests and the innate conservatism this ultimately produces became self-evident. As part of his resignation deal, Thorpe was able to persuade the Federation to end the dual leadership system, with the appointment of Fred Higgs as General Secretary alongside the progressive Australian miners' union leader, John Maitland, in the less hands-on role of President. From a grassroots perspective, Higgs came with impeccable credentials. A local organiser who had risen through the ranks, Higgs developed a reputation as a tough negotiator in his dealings with oil companies. He himself had seen the ICEM post as a chance to escape the straitjacket of UK national union politics where the link between key movement leaders and the 'New Labour' Government, notably the close friendship and political affiliation between Higgs's boss, TGWU leader Bill Morris, and Finance Minister Gordon Brown (now Prime Minister), were stifling attempts to establish more innovative union strategies that might conflict with the emerging neoliberal line within the Labour Party hierarchy (interview with Fred Higgs, UK, 2005).[8]

Because of his background, there were hopes that Higgs would continue the Thorpe strategy of decentralisation and local democracy. However, the evidence since Higgs's appointment suggests a more top-down strategy in which the ICEM has operated through existing structures at national and international levels, rather than attempting to organise independent global networks of the sort envisaged by Thorpe. In part, some have hinted that this may be Higgs's personal autocratic style which has resulted in a haemorrhaging of officials from the Brussels office since 2000 (authors' interviews), but undoubtedly it also reflects a more general failure within the organisation of the need for change.

As part of the Higgs strategy, ICEM also appears to be promoting greater dialogue and cooperation with MNCs, a strategy that is unpopular with some of the more radical affiliates (authors' interviews). Tellingly, in a telephone conversation with an ICEM official, one of our research team was told that the Federation 'did not see itself as a "resistance network", but as an organisation interested in promoting social justice, workers' rights and achieving this through negotiation and bargaining with employers (authors' interviews, January 2002). Higgs was also involved – as the union representative on the five-person Advisory Committee – in the UN's Global Compact, a voluntary code set up in 2000 and signed by 1,800 leading MNCs to agree to respect basic human, labour and environmental rights. Reflecting the shift towards a more pragmatic approach, we were also informed that the ICEM were not interested in collaborating with academics as they had limited resources and could not see how we could provide practical help to them in their work.[9]

The most obvious manifestation of the change in direction was Higgs's controversial 2004 decision to close ICEM's five regional offices, centralising the federation's staff and organisation in Brussels, which now carries out all the international work. The decision was taken because of perceived corruption and mismanagement in some of the regional offices, particularly a lack of visibility in the use of funds and evidence of nepotism in appointments (authors' interviews). As one French respondent noted, important issues of effectiveness and communication were resolved by reorganisation:

> And so Fred Higgs said – after a meeting held in the executive committee, which caused some stirs as South Africa didn't agree – that instead of having dispersed offices that nobody knows what they're doing, we would have a contact person for that region in Brussels [. . .] They can only be more effective than before. When we used to call the Rio de Janeiro office, most of the time there wasn't anyone to answer. When we were sending an email, we would only get a reply a week later. The person who deals with the regional office from Brussels now, she's rarely in Brussels but she's in her region and it is more efficient. And in terms of costs, it doesn't cost us more. And there is some

control because now he has to account to the general secretary who is actually there on the spot. (interview, Paris, France, 2005)

With shrinking resources, Higgs decided that it would be best to centralise operations, defending the decision in terms of building a better team and collective ethos (interview, 2005). Whilst most of our respondents from a range of different countries and political positions tend to support Higgs (authors' interviews), the restructuring has only reinforced accusations of European 'colonialism' among affiliates in the Global South (see Waterman, 1998), and prompted the resignation of the ICEM President, John Maitland. In his resignation statement, Maitland makes it clear that although he supported some restructuring, he opposed both the way the process occurred – without consultation of the regional offices and affiliates in the Global South – and the outcome of centralising employment in Brussels (Maitland, 2005). As one national officer, who sympathised with Higgs in terms of the corruption issue but also disagreed with the centralisation of all ICEM operations in Brussels, put it memorably: 'An organisation should look like its members. It shouldn't all be pale male and stale.' (interview, Blackpool, UK, 2005).

Forging mutual solidarity: Global Frame Agreements

The central plank of ICEM strategy under Higgs has been the setting up of GFAs, with 10 of the 11 signed since he took office in 1998. It is important to note that they are not collective bargaining agreements and have no legal sanction, either in national or international law. Typically, they involve the rights of workers to organise, the agreement that the company will provide the time and space for union representatives and guarantees of decent local living wages and equal rights in the workplace. The ICEM is second only to the IMF in the number it has signed (Gibb, 2005).

There is considerable ambiguity in the trade union movement about the role of GFAs in forging transnational solidarity and developing global labour networks. On the one hand, there is scepticism from labour activists and academics, who feel that at their worst they provide a 'tick box' corporate social responsibility for multinationals without any legally binding commitment to better workers rights (Gibb, 2005). Certainly, GFAs are no panacea for tackling all labour's ills at the hands of MNCs. Neither GFAs nor the Global Compact have had much impact, thus far, upon the more flagrant abuses of employees and labour activists in the Global South. As one French trade unionist, who was opposed to the whole global partnership agenda, put it succinctly in an interview:

> About the existence of codes of conduct, I think that it is first and foremost an American trend to give oneself a good conscience. I have just met with a Colombian who told me that in his union, there are now something like 125 members who've been killed. Are we not capable today of stopping this kind of thing? Don't we have the material, physical and even political means to stop that? Because today it is obviously companies like BP and TOTAL that control paramilitary groups since security is not being controlled by the state – something which ought to be one of its primary tasks – but it is the petrol companies that pay the paramilitary groups themselves. So you can write all the codes of conducts you like but you are not getting to the heart of the problem. (interview, Paris, France, 2005)

It is no accident that the majority of GFAs signed thus far have been between Northern European MNCs where more often than not they have developed out of existing European Works Councils. In this respect, they share the same drawback as being reliant upon company-centred and controlled networks to monitor and police them, being open to the same abuses (Wills, 2000). Furthermore, because GFAs are voluntary codes, there is little sanction against corporate mistreatment of workers in practice, other than through public relations exposes. Spatially, a feeling among some activists is that they represent the naïve exportation (on the part of union leaders and well often well-intentioned managers) of a relatively consensual Northern European model of employment relations to more hostile anti-union environments:

> Norwegian trade unionists do not act critically when abroad. They go on company visits, to places like Latin America and so on and they just go to events and meetings organised for them. They don't put their critical glasses on. It's partly the result of the strong consensus [with business] at home. (interview, Norwegian labour activist/academic, Oslo, Norway, 2005)

Ironically, it was a similar criticism – of an 'evolutionary optimism' (Ramsay, 1999: 195) – in scaling up a European model of employment relations to the global level, that was blamed for the failure of World Company Councils (a Levinson and Thorpe initiative) to make any headway in the 1970s (Webster *et al.*, 2008). Learning from this experience, Thorpe had explicitly made the change from 'council' to 'network', symbolising the shift towards a more horizontalist and grassrooted approach:

> When I got back in as general secretary [early 1990s] later down the road, I changed the idea of company councils to the idea of networks to loosen it up again and that's really where we stand and that's a lot of what the internationals are now pursuing, the idea of multinational company networks but it's still somewhat stymied by national interests – relationships between unions and at national level big employers and their own national governments.' (interview, France, 2005)

Critical to this is that transnational connections are built from the ground level up through the development of genuine mutual affinities between workers that can only emerge from an ongoing dialogue and exchange of experiences. Without being firmly embedded in the particular places of work through which MNCs and their supply chains operate, GFAs will be relatively superficial networks that, at the same time, because of their place of origin, reinforce the impression of an imposition of European and North American practices on unions in the Global South.

Despite these concerns, GFAs do offer considerable potential for creating genuine networks of transnational labour solidarity. Critically, as Gibb (2005: 15) maintains, 'they open the space for workers to organise and bargain collectively' (see also Bendt, 2003). If used properly by unions they provide the framework for creating global labour networks, rather than being finalised global collective agreements *per se*. In this sense, GFAs work best where they are developed multi-laterally, with the greatest number of local union partners being involved in the negotiation of an agreement from the outset. As Dan Gallin, ex-General Secretary of the IUF, notes, 'the main condition for the successful implementation of an IFA (GFA) is union strength on the ground, i.e. the presence of unions capable of monitoring the implementation of the agreement locally' (cited in Gibb, 2005). GFAs, in this sense, can act as convergence spaces (Routledge, 2003a, Cumbers *et al.*, 2008) for the coming together of different union experiences and traditions, but their effectiveness will be contingent upon the manner in which they have been set up, the process through which agreements operate, and the internal power relations that run through them.

From this perspective, evidence from the ICEM's existing GFAs suggests a varied picture. The ICEM-Statoil agreement has already been used to support unions in struggles with employers in Nigeria, Poland and the United States as well as helping to build new local union organisations in Azerbaijan (Cumbers, 2004; Gibb, 2005), although SAFE representatives challenge the independence of this union from state and corporate interests (author's interview, August, 2005). In addition, the recent agreement with French company, Rhodia, is innovative in proposing the involvement of NGOs, recognising that they are often more locally embedded and therefore better placed to monitor labour standards. However, evidence of success in building local union strength in new areas, particularly the Global South, is thin on the ground. Significantly, in Gibb's (*ibid*) overview of GFAs, it is the International Metalworkers Federation and the International Federation of Building and Wood Workers (IFBWW) who are setting the pace in developing local union presence in new regions and within subcontractors rather than ICEM. Where the relationships between global union federation, national affiliate and local activists are carefully constructed to provide support and an enabling framework for grassroots network building, such a spatially extensive strategy can be effective.

From our interviews, it is clear that in some cases, the ICEM leadership in Brussels is attempting to control, impose and administer GFAs rather than encouraging a greater dispersal of power to the local level. This is exemplified by the setting up of the *Norske Skog* Agreement in 2002, which involved the Norwegian affiliate, *Fellesforbundet* (a general workers union). Research by the Norwegian LO revealed that local union organisers in Norway and elsewhere had largely been excluded from the initial negotiations, which had been concluded through the Brussels office of ICEM:

> *Norske Skog* has a Global Agreement. We looked at the *Norske Skog* agreement through some research in Brazil and the local

unionists were a bit frustrated . . . not the fact that they didn't have the agreement . . . because they love it, but they were frustrated that they were not drawn in on the consultation when they were making the Global Agreement. When I asked the shop steward in Norway, 'Why didn't you involve them?' He said 'To be honest, I wasn't very involved either.' The project was between Mr Fred Higgs and the company with some representation from the union in Norway. But it was very much a Brussels-based deal and it was not popular with the Brazilians that they were not informed when it was formalised. When I criticised ICEM on this, they said 'We couldn't . . . it is difficult. . . it is not something we can inform anybody about until it is finalised.' But I don't believe that. I believe it is possible to pull in more local people so that they feel ownership. They do not feel any ownership because they feel it belongs to Brussels and isn't theirs. (interview, International Officer, LO, Oslo, Norway, 2005)

The failure to involve local union activists in agreements is a growing problem within ICEM and is leading to considerable friction. This is leading some of the more progressive national affiliates to organise new agreements through more established channels such as global works councils, where they exist. In the *Norske Skog* case, for example, a new global network has been established through the existing works council, much to the chagrin of the ICEM leadership:

The global works council agreement was different because that was actually worked out between the shop stewards in Norway and the company . . . and Higgs came in later . . . and they felt more happy about that. It was their deal and not Fred Higgs's deal [. . .] and when I was in a meeting in Bonn last year and I met one of the colleagues from ICEM and I told everybody about the new agreement with *Norske Skog*, she was very upset, because she said, 'That's not the principle of the ICEM, we shouldn't have global agreements through works councils, we don't believe in that. So, how can you sign something like that. So, there was a big scandal . . . and everybody had to make phone calls. In the end she calmed down because the comrades from *Norsk Skog* here said: 'Well, we will just resign. We don't want to be part of ICEM anymore if that's a problem for them.' So it was sorted out in the end. But, I find there is a problem around the process of Global Agreements. (*ibid*)

The positive aspect of this case is the growing confidence of some local union organisers to develop their own transnational networks, developed through a growing sense of shared affinities with other workers. There is arguably more potential in these networks to generate mutual solidarity because power relations are likely to be more equal, connections and communication more open and respectful of local context and difference (Holloway and Pelaez, 1998; Olesen, 2005).

Ultimately, as a growing number of national affiliates are beginning to understand, for GFAs to achieve even the modest aim of monitoring global labour standards in individual MNCs and their supplier networks, local activists will need to be more empowered than at present. A lack of resources in most cases means that the national and international offices that sign GFAs are in no position to monitor or enforce them. It is only through local activists and shop-stewards and workplace-based networks that they can function effectively:

> We don't have the resources to go around to every factory in every country that is operating from Norway. We're totally dependent on our local shop stewards who are able to carry out overseas visits on company time. (Vice President, Norwegian affiliate, commenting on their recently signed GFA, interview, Oslo, Norway, 2005)

In the words of one Norwegian trade unionist they are 'the beginning of the process, not the end point' (interview, Oslo, Norway, 2005). GFAs are thus more likely to be successful where the national affiliate involved has an existing culture of decentralisation and local autonomy that is itself projected up to the global scale. Our four case studies suggest that this varies within countries between unions, reflecting different class, industrial and ideological perspectives, and even the size of unions involved. It is an irony that the reality of organising on the ground may propel the ICEM and other GUFs back towards the philosophy of grassroots networks espoused originally by Vic Thorpe. Unfortunately, so far, the ICEM leadership does not seem to have absorbed these lessons. In his opening remarks to the 2003 ICEM World Congress, Fred Higgs suggested that: 'we continue to support the formation of Global Company Networks... [but] Global Networks can complement or assist in the establishment of Global Agreements' (ICEM 2003b: 6). If anything, the logic needs to be the other way around.

Grassrooting the global imaginary in the ICEM network

From our interviews, it is clear that the ICEM as a whole has had limited success in inculcating a more 'global imaginary' among the grassroots union members, unable for the most part to make the 'relational' link between their workers' employment and conditions at home with broader international activities and structures (Massey, 2005). In this respect, many ICEM affiliates are caught on the horns of a dilemma, between trying to protect the pay and conditions of a shrinking national membership, which often comes as the result of global outsourcing by domestic MNCs, and finding money for international activities and campaigns. For one international officer of a British trade union, the difficulties were in persuading his comrades of the importance of international work:

> If you try and do something, say if I wanted to tie up with rural workers in Thailand and they're using my chemicals: very difficult. I could only do it through the International Food Workers' or ICEM. It would be virtually impossible to do anything through my union. There's just not the structures, there's not the budgets [. . .] If I say 'hold on, there's been a big petrol agreement with Venezuela and I think they're forming a Latin American cartel and doing the refineries in Cuba,' I can see a role for my union 'cause we're the oil worker's union. But nothing's gonna happen. I can't do it. I physically couldn't do it. Even if I was to prioritise it, I'd still be under pressure from the members [. . .] what happens is somebody says 'why is he fucking about with Cuba when we've got members down in Darlington. Can't you get an officer to go down and see them? They're getting the sack in Darlington and he's buggering about in Cuba.' So you're caught in a dilemma. And remember: when it comes to the top as it will, there'll be people resisting it. And no matter what else is coming to the top 'cause there's a new left leadership in this union and they'll pick on it. If we form an international department, they'll say 'why are you forming an international department with five people in it when we need more people in health and safety.' (authors' interviews, Blackpool, UK, 2005)

The resistance from within the union often comes from regional and national officials, as much as ordinary members. Where international work is prioritised it is often defensive, responsive to particular plant closures, or is geographically proximate, aimed at extending union reach within regional blocs such as the EU or NAFTA. However, as capital as a whole becomes more global, it becomes impossible to develop a national strategy that does not have a global component. As one General Secretary of a UK ICEM affiliate puts it:

> The forces influencing the working lives of Amicus members now extend far beyond the borders of the UK and Ireland. Developments and decisions taken are at an international level, often by multinational companies, and these have a serious impact on our international members. Amicus can no longer effectively represent members' interests without being active on the international stage. (Derek Simpson, General Secretary of Amicus, Foreword to the Guide to Amicus International Work, May 2005, www.amicustheunion.org, last accessed July 2006)

This is particularly the case in core ICEM sectors such as oil and chemicals, where MNCs are long established and workers at the grassroots are often only too aware of the importance of building transnational support networks to counter the actions of corporations. At a focus group of 12 workforce convenors for the UK oil refining industry (held in November 2005), participants described how local managers would hide behind 'globalisation' to attempt to drive through cost-cutting or job-shedding initiatives.

Critically, for these workers, it was national level networks and, in particular, regular meetings with other UK counterparts that were more important for sharing and disseminating information and countering local management's attempts to offload the blame for unpopular and exploitative measures to decisions made elsewhere. In our discussion, workers displayed considerable awareness of the importance of the global and voiced the need to upscale such networks to European and even global levels, particularly with US workers (Focus Group discussion, London, 2005), but expressed frustration with existing structures such as work councils and ICEM networks:

> The other part of your questions there was, what kind of contact do we have internationally? I would say, it's basically zero. And, I have been a steward for about 12 years or so, I got invited once to an ICEM conference in Brussels. I know Mark has recently been to Rome for an ICEM meeting. I mean, we get all the . . . As branch secretary you get all the paperwork about Colombia

and Iraq and whatever, but there's no other, apart from the literature, there's no other. (interview, London, UK, 2005)

Unlike many PGA Asia grassroots activists, a local shop steward within an ICEM affiliate is likely to receive a considerable amount of information about global labour issues and campaigns, through newsletters and other union literature. Access to the Internet is also more widespread among local union activists, allowing the potential for more communication. However, as the above quote highlights, the information flow is largely one-way with little opportunity for shop stewards themselves to contribute to broader European or global agendas.

The one established forum for regular dialogue between grassroots workers within ICEM, European Works Councils (EWCs), do not allow for the informal exchanges that allow trust to be built for mutual affinities to develop. Most EWCs remain formal company-based networks that were found to be particularly useless at building trust and genuine affinities (see also Wills, 2000). A recurring problem was a lack of information about, and therefore a suspicion of, some of labour representatives from other countries. One UK oil worker tells of meeting an unelected women representative from southern Europe who was there 'because her boss had asked her to attend' whilst another discovered that what he thought were union representatives from Eastern Europe were actually Human Resource managers (authors' interviews). In one extreme case, the Exxon European Works Council, meetings were held at Brussels airport on a single day with return flights booked over a restricted time period of a few hours that left little freedom at all for interaction beyond the formal timetable of meetings (*ibid*).

There was also the feeling that if more global networks were developed, through the auspices of ICEM, or independently through union affiliates, 'It would not be us going along to these, but someone higher up from head office' (*ibid*). Two of the ten shop stewards on our focus group had been to ICEM events but only one in each case, and these were dedicated sector specific one-off conferences, reinforcing the overall impression of a severe disjuncture between transnational networking and local workforce practice. In this sense, attempts to bring 'rank-and-file' workers together on a global basis remain few and far between.

The more sustained and horizontal forms of transnational solidarity between grassroots union members are, more often than not, created through the work of national affiliates, although this happens unevenly, reflecting the different geographical contexts that we have alluded to above. Transnational solidarity is not achieved overnight and our evidence suggests that much of the more effective interactions have developed over a long time period through relations between individual unions or workers. For French and British unions, international connections between unionists often reflect their respective countries' colonial past and attendant global connections of their domestic oil MNCs. Thus, British unions will often have continuing links (though a lack of funding) with union movements in Africa and the Middle East, whilst French unions will have international connections spanning North and West Africa and Vietnam. The German affiliates appear to have the lowest levels of bilateral cooperation outside Europe, whilst Norwegian unions tend to be developing links wherever their own MNCs are locating.

Despite the funding difficulties of the British unions, the TGWU has provided one of the most innovative examples of grassroots networking in recent years, through a recent joint project with the International Federation of Workers Educational Associations, funded by the UK's Department for International Development. The International Study Circles programme (WEA, 2000) uses the Internet to bring together groups of workers around common global themes. These have included: 'Transnational Corporations', 'Migrant Workers in the global economy', 'Women workers in the global food industry' and 'Globalisation and the responses of trade unions in Asia' and have involved workers from the UK, Finland, Hungary, Peru, Philippines, South Africa, Barbados, Estonia, Bulgaria, Germany and Sweden.[10]

Elsewhere, the Norwegian affiliates have the greatest level of resources committed to local union building activities, particularly in Africa and Southeast Asia. This happens through a complex spatially extensive set of relations, whereby the funding for international activities tends to come from the *Landsorganisasjonen* (LO) in partnership often with Norwegian civil society groups (Cumbers, 2004), but because the focus is always on a Norwegian MNC, projects are usually coordinated by the affiliate union with its company-based shop stewards and union representatives. In best case scenarios, such projects allow the opportunity for the build-up of strong inter-personal trust relations at the local level, with funding to allow workers from Norway to spend months at a time in other countries, interacting with local workers and vice versa (*ibid*). However, the dangers in such a strategy are that, without detailed local knowledge of the host region, unions may end up in partnerships with state or business-centred unions that have little interest in developing independent worker organisations. A particularly controversial project, ongoing since 1997, is the development of links with Chinese workers through the state-controlled All China Federation of Trade Unions (ACFTU). Defending the link on the basis of a pragmatic attempt to forge connections with local workers and deal with what exists rather than the ideal, one LO official told us:

> The reality is that we have to have some kind of relationship. But that's one of the reasons why we in LO thought it was good that the chemical workers and other unions could have relations on a sectoral level. Because then, maybe we reach more people. I'm not sure we do [laughs] . . . but at least we don't just have the political communication at the top level between the ACFTU – Beijing and LO Norway here. But we get more sectoral, more people are involved. We have a relationship with someone in Shanghai at the plant level. (interview, Oslo, Norway, 2005)

As the quote suggests, there are considerable limitations and dangers to this kind of initiative which may actually work against genuinely independent groups gaining more international recognition. Whatever the merits of this link-up, there is no disputing that it has allowed the development of more genuinely horizontalist relations, with exchange visits between China and Norway having taken place over a considerable time period. Norwegian unions have a long history of such bilateral international work and, in common with some French unions, have built up strong relationships with union organisations in former communist countries such as Vietnam and Russia, and continuing anti-capitalist regimes such as Cuba and Venezuela as a result. Once again, however, the degree of independence of local union actors in these situations is a moot point.

A final but important point to note here is that some of the most impressive grassroots solidarity-building initiatives in the oil and chemicals sectors happen through unions outside the ICEM network altogether, such as SAFE in Norway and various CGT federations in France, which have more decentralised union structures at the national level and therefore greater local autonomy (author's interviews). The FNME-CGT (mining federation), for example, which is now affiliated to EMCEF but not ICEM, has been running bilateral twinning arrangements between local union branches in France and unions in Africa, South America and Asia for over 20 years to the extent that over 20 local branches are now involved (interview, Paris, France, 2005). Undoubtedly, the strong historical culture of socialist internationalism among its own grassroots activists, allied to its own organisation, where the affiliation structure is such that local branches collect fees and send an amount to the centre, are critical factors here and mean that deep and well-established transnational links and personal connections exist that go back four decades in some cases (ibid). FNME-CGT also participates with NGOs in much of its overseas work and tends, wherever possible, to develop links through the provision of practical support (e.g. providing water or electrification for union localities in the Global South) whereby its own members are actively involved overseas, rather than simply providing funding for projects. The CGT was instrumental in setting up the International Mining Organisation (IMO) in the 1980s as an independent alternative to ICEM and to Soviet-dominated trade unions. IMO provides international networking opportunities for many African unions that cannot afford to pay an affiliate fee to ICEM.[11]

Network durability and limitations

As a GJN, ICEM represents the strengths and weaknesses of the GUFs and the international trade union movement more generally. On the one hand, as a long-established convergence space with dense transnational connections and linkages, it has the strong interpersonal ties that provide the basis for the construction of collective identities and collective action (Bosco, 2001). Drawing upon long-established relations between its national affiliates, and connections to other social actors in government, business and broader civil society, ICEM is involved in a considerable amount of international solidarity activity, both on the issue of labour rights and, more broadly, in developing a global social justice agenda through participation in initiatives such as its AIDs programme in southern Africa.

Through its organisational structures and practices, it is also a network that operates on a more sustained and effective basis than a grassroots network such as PGA Asia, with the ability – albeit uneven – to generate resources to enforce its objectives. In this respect, ICEM can intervene at key moments to support local union action and protest against instances of exploitation and abuse. Permanent offices in Brussels and in key national affiliates, and dedicated staff, allow the network to be realised on an ongoing basis, rather than through episodic moments. Whilst conferences and seminars are important 'moments of translation' for ICEM, the key mechanisms (or vectors) through which the network is operationalised are the channels between the ICEM headquarters and key union imagineers operating between national and transnational scales. Where ICEM operates as a 'hub' in helping to generate mutual exchanges between affiliates and providing informational resources for local action, it can also provide a spur to grassroots organising.

On the other hand, however, ICEM remains a network that is heavily 'verticalist' in its operation (Tormey, 2004a), ultimately dependent upon key national affiliates who provide both the material and discursive resources for its activities. This became most evident in the 1990s when the efforts by the Thorpe leadership to devolve more power to the local level were thwarted by entrenched national interests. As a convergence space, its operation reveals the unequal power relations between trade union actors and the dominance of those from the Global North over the South (Waterman, 1998). Its global imaginary has been constructed largely by dominant imagineers in key European unions where a more moderate and corporatist approach to employment relations has been scaled up to the global level, most notably through the emphasis upon GFAs.

ICEM also highlights the limitations of traditional forms of global labour networking, where a top-down model of transnational solidarity persists, and where grassroots activists are largely excluded from the main vectors through which global collective visions are enacted and practised. However, the evidence here has highlighted the contradictions of verticalism in an increasingly global economy where national and international union elites are seeing their discursive and material power reduced, where strategies can only be realised through strong local union organisation. Developing more effective forms of transnational solidarity in the future requires inculcating more horizontalist, democratic and participatory practices into their operation.

Notes

1 Though it has not been possible to get a complete breakdown of voting numbers, figures given during an interview provide some indication of relative voting strengths with the German affiliate having the largest bloc of 140, as against 80 for the Japanese affiliates and 60 for UK unions (authors' interviews).

2 An independent but parallel European trade union network that also covers chemical and energy. Most ICEM national affiliates are also members of European Mine Chemical and Energy Workers Federation (EMCEF), although there are some from the latter (often formerly Communist affiliates) that are not members of ICEM.

3 It is worth remarking on the influence of the British trade union movement on the international trade union network. In the early 2000s, 11 of the 14 global union federations had British General Secretaries. At a more superficial level, this reflected the dominance of English as the global *lingua franca*, but it also reflected a pivotal role that British unions played in holding international networks together in the face of warring factions. However, this influence as office holders should not be mistaken for power, which ultimately resided in more powerful national union affiliates in the United States in particular. In the context of Cold War geopolitics, British trade unionists were often seen as 'honest brokers' (interview with international trade union activist, Manchester, 2004) between more powerful opposing ideological camps. The same did not apply to the international department of the TUC which was staffed by bureaucrats and regarded by many as an arm of the Government's Foreign Office (Cumbers, 2004).

4 In common with the other Nordic countries, Norwegian trade unions have considerable representative rights within the state and economy akin to codetermination, which remains legally enshrined in the constitution, despite the exposure to neoliberalism and globalisation. These include the continuation of national collective bargaining, despite attempts by employers to decentralise employment relations, and the requirement that one third of all board members of Norwegian corporations are elected by employees. The 'official' Norwegian union movement is thus embedded within state and corporate structures, providing it with a more powerful national base than many of its larger

counterparts in other countries. This presence has been particularly important in the development of the Norwegian oil industry since the discovery of North Sea oil in the 1960s, and as Norwegian MNCs have become important global players is translated into considerable potential for international solidarity.

5   Eric Lee has termed Levinson the 'Jules Verne of Labour Telematics' (1999: 229) because he was already advocating the linking up of company databases by telex in the early 1970s before the Internet had come into existence (ibid).

6   The tensions within the EU movement were thrown into sharp relief by the opposing positions taken on the recent debate over the new Constitution. Whilst most on the left of the movement and among grassroots activists were against it, including most of the left-leaning unions in France and the UK, the German union establishment, the French CFDT and the ETUC General Secretary John Monks were fully behind it.

7   Though even here, gains have been minimal reflecting both government unwillingness to repeal the most anti-union laws passed by previous Conservative administrations and the continued lack of commitment by trade unions to grassroots democracy (see Cumbers, 2005).

8   One consequence was the failure of Morris and the national leadership to back the Liverpool Dockers, despite global support from other unions, in their struggle against their employer from 1995 onwards for fear that it would damage the electoral prospects of the Labour Party (Castree, 2000; Kennedy and Lavalette, 2004; authors' interviews).

9   This position contrasts dramatically with other union federations, for example, with that of the ITF, which has been engaged in considerable dialogue and even partnership – through sponsoring research and even doctoral dissertations – with the academic community.

10 For a report on these activities, see: www.ifwea.org/, last accessed 6 June 2007.

11 New affiliates to ICEM have to pay fees after a five-year period.

7

Social Forums as convergence spaces

The emergence of the World Social Forum (WSF), and its associated regional and local fora, is the most significant process of convergence for the diverse movements that have emerged to contest neoliberal globalisation. Beyond individual days of action, such as protests against G8, WTO, WB or IMF meetings, the establishment of the WSF signalled a step-change in the resistance to neoliberalism (Wallerstein, 2004), representing the transformation of a growing global protest movement into a forum to envisage alternatives, manifested in the slogan 'Another World is Possible'. Critically, with the decline of alternative positions within mainstream politics, and the hegemony of neoliberal thinking across the political spectrum, social fora have grown in importance for those still committed to pursuing a more egalitarian and social justice agenda.

The first meeting of the WSF in Porto Alegre, Brazil in 2001 attracted over 20,000 people, primarily from Latin America, but with some activists from Western Europe and to a lesser extent North America. Subsequent fora have seen numbers increase until in 2005 over 155,000 participants attended with 6,873 organisations represented and over 2,500 events organised (Bramble, 2006: 289–290). Reflecting awareness among the organisers of the importance of geography – particularly the need to diffuse the WSF process away from its dominant Brazilian/Latin American origins, and inculcate a global consciousness on other continents, especially in the Global South – the 2004 Forum was held in Mumbai. The 2005 Forum returned to Porto Alegre before the decision to hold a decentred fora in Mali, Pakistan and Venezuela in 2006. The 2007 Forum was held in Nairobi and drew around 75,000 participants (see http://wsf2007.org/, last accessed 28 June 2007). The next WSF is planned for 2009 with a global week of action scheduled for January 2008.

More than any other development, the WSF process has come to embody the new democratic and participatory ideals of the broader international resistance against neoliberalism with its aspiration to provide an open and enabling space for debate about alternative(s) to neoliberalism. The call for tolerance, diversity and openness, are for many observers the distinguishing features that sets the 'forum' and its constituents apart from earlier revolutionary (especially Marxist) political movements (Sen, 2004; Smith, 2004; Wallerstein, 2004). It is, in short, the example *par excellence* of a convergence space, providing an arena for differentially placed movements to create links and networks. Communication, information-sharing, solidarity, coordination and resource mobilisation are all evident in its operation, as we shall illustrate. Yet the WSF is not without its problems and contradictions. Like PGA and ICEM, it is prone to the same kinds of problems associated with uneven power relations, entangled geographies and differentially placed politics (Cumbers *et al.*, 2008). Whilst its form – as a theoretically inclusive space that is open to anyone to organise a session or workshop – is horizontalist in aspiration, the process and structures through which the WSF have emerged have been accused by some of being exclusive and hierarchical with a small number of individuals and groups (who constitute the social forum 'imagineers'), setting and controlling the agenda (Juris, 2004a; 2005c; Smith, 2004, Dowling, 2005, Bramble, 2006). In short, the issues confronting the WSF go to the heart of the wider dilemmas facing those concerned with building effective networks of global solidarity and justice.

Social Forums as spaces of interaction and communication

The WSF emerged as a direct response to the World Economic Forum (WEF), the meeting of world political and business leaders, held every year in January at the Swiss ski resort of Davos. The purpose of the gathering was initially to protest against the WEF as a symbol of the hegemony of neoliberal thinking and policymaking in the global economy, and to discuss and present concrete alternatives to it (Houtart and Polet, 2001; Cassen, 2003). It was originally conceived following a discussion between Cassen, one of the founders of the French social movement ATTAC,[1] and two Brazilians, Oded Grajew, an entrepreneur, and Chico Whitaker of the Commission on Justice and Peace of the Council of Brazilian Bishops (Cassen, 2003; see also Juris, 2004a; 2005c). These people could be characterised as the nascent imagineers of the forum process.

The intention of the WSF was to create an alternative transnational space of dialogue, reflection and the exchange of experiences, ideas and strategies between groups engaged in resistance to neoliberalism (see Juris, 2004a; 2005c). The participants include diverse social movements, NGOs, trade unions, solidarity committees and farmers' networks from the five non-polar continents (see Sen *et al.*, 2004). In this respect, the WSF represents a transnational political initiative of variation and flux, where the links between actors (activists) and various intermediaries tend to be in process and are contestable. Subsequently, the WSF has mushroomed out into a multi-scalar process with associated (but independent) fora springing up at regional (Europe, Asia), national and even local scales, with various city fora now operating (Teivainen, 2002). The most significant of these is the European Social Forum, held for the first time in Florence in 2002, followed by subsequent meetings in Paris (2003), London (2004) and Athens (2006). The first US Social Forum was in Atlanta in 2007. There have also been thematic fora, such as those on neoliberalism in Argentina (2002) and 'Drugs, Human Rights and Democracy' in Cartagena, Colombia (2003).

The collective visions of the WSF are enshrined in its slogan 'Another World is Possible' and its Charter of Principles. Among the key principles are the following:

- The WSF is an open space for the democratic and free exchange of ideas and experiences and the formulation of proposals between civil society groups and movements.
- The alternatives proposed at the WSF respect universal human rights . . . and will rest on democratic international systems and institutions at the service of social justice, equality and the sovereignty of peoples.

- The WSF is a plural, diversified, non-confessional, non-governmental and non-party context that, in a decentralized fashion, interrelates organisations and movements engaged in concrete action at levels from the local to the international to build another world.
- The WSF will always be a forum open to pluralism and to the diversity of genders, ethnicities, cultures, generations and physical capacities, providing they abide by this Charter of Principles. Neither party representations nor military organisations shall participate in the Forum. Government leaders and members of legislatures who accept the commitments of this Charter may be invited to participate in a personal capacity.
- As a context for interrelations, the WSF seeks to strengthen and create new national and international links among organizations and movements.

(from Sen *et al.*, 2004: 70–71)

First and foremost, the WSF is perceived by its founders as a social and political process of convergence, rather than merely a series of meeting places for debate: 'The World Social Forum is a permanent political and social process of networking inside organized civil society across the world, punctuated with forum events' (www.wsfprocess.net, last accessed 28 June 2007). The Charter of Principles articulate certain unifying values that create common ground to enable debate to take place, but allow for the diversity of (local) alternatives, projects, tactics, etc. since no single agenda could contain the different 'militant particularisms' (Harvey, 1996) of such a multiplicity of participants. But inevitably, the unanimity of the principles conceals various contested social relations, as we explore below.

The formal decision-making process of the WSF is dominated by the Organising Committee (OC), consisting of the Central Trade Union Confederation, the Movement of Landless Rural Workers and six smaller Brazilian civil society organisations. The members of the OC comprise the primary imagineers of the WSF process. The other main organ of the WSF is the International Council (IC), which consists of 113 organisations (including the OC), the majority of whom come from the Americas and Western Europe (Teivainen, 2002), but which has far less decision-making power than the OC. The WSF is organised in part through the Internet via its website (www.forumsocialmundial. org.br). The WSF website is translated into four languages and provides information about the history of the network; WSF international and regional conferences; various actions and initiatives that the WSF has organised; and upcoming events, etc. However, the primary process of interaction in the WSF are the international and regional conferences and meetings that provide material spaces within which representatives of participant movements can converge, and discuss issues that relate to the functioning of the network (Juris, 2004a). Such conferences and meetings also enable strategies to be developed and enable deeper interpersonal ties to be established between different activists from different cultural spaces and struggles.

The social forum process operates through certain mechanisms, or 'moments' of translation through which the social forum network is operationalised, in particular through working to enroll other political actors and materials into the process, and to mobilise all enrolled entities (e.g. through world and regional social fora). Through these relational processes, individuals, movements, materials and places are incorporated into the social forum process (Murdoch, 1997a). As noted in Chapters 5 and 6, the durability of these networked relations, continually performed over time, and mobility through space (the materials and processes of communication which enable acting at a distance, such as the Internet) constitute the key 'strategies' of network translation within the social forum process (Law, 1992).

While the WSF and regional fora represent transnational collective rituals *par excellence* (Juris, 2004a), they have also facilitated other events, such as global days of action, elsewhere. For example, the WSF and the 2002 ESF in Florence played important roles in building global opinion against the 2003 War in Iraq by providing arenas where anti-war activists could meet, discuss and plan transnational collective action (Sen, 2004a). As a result, in part, of this process there were global protests against the war on 15 February 2003 (amounting to as many as 30 million people worldwide). The WSF has also played an important role in more 'local' interventions with some of its constituent movements, particularly ATTAC and radical trade unions, being critical to the 'No' votes against the EU Constitution in France and the Netherlands in 2005 (Cassen, 2005).

Spatial dynamics

Places have been used strategically to sustain the WSF. The identification with particular places can be of strategic importance for the mobilisation strategies of particular movements and networks. These can contribute to the construction of strategic network ties with other movements/ networks in other localities, helping to mobilise others along common interests and concerns (Bosco, 2001). Hence, Porto Alegre was chosen for the first meeting, as a symbol of a more democratic alternative politics, through its much celebrated participatory budgeting process, which has been imitated by radical local authorities and activists elsewhere (see Wainwright, 2003). It is also a city with a strong radical tradition as a centre of left resistance during the long years of Brazil's military rule, based upon vibrant neighbourhood associations that had strong links to the Workers Party (*Partido dos Trabalhadores*, PT). Indeed the city was one of the PT's strongholds, having been governed by the party since 1988. As such it became an 'articulated moment' in the enactment of the WSF, where opposition to neoliberalism as well as alternative visions could be voiced. Critically, some activists have pointed to the WSF venue as being geographically significant as a site of global resistance: challenging the ideological hegemony of northern social movements and unions by being rooted in 'Liberation Theology' and a particular Latin American revolutionary consciousness (Olivers, 2004; Santos, 2004).

Geographically, it is important to recognise the significance of social fora as providing critical spaces of transnational dialogue, activism and resistance. The impressive degree of participation from left and centre-left politicians, social movements, NGOs and trade unions suggests that they already hold important symbolic value for those aspiring to spatially extend their activities beyond their local and national arenas of action: building broader transnational support networks and coalitions to help in their locally based struggles and campaigns. At the WSF we attended in Porto Alegre, 2005, there was ample evidence of this kind of convergence taking place, particularly in the smaller workshops and seminars, which allowed for local movements and groups to both create and build upon existing transnational solidarity networks around specific themes and issues.

A good example was a workshop entitled 'Informationalisation, Subcontracting and Business Process Outsourcing: Challenges for International Trade Unionism'. This was organised by WSF India and the Indian Trade Union Congress and involved speakers from Confederation of South African Trade Unions (COSATU) in South Africa, Indonesian trade unions and a representative from the International Transport Federation (a GUF). Interventions were then made from the floor by a couple of Indian trade unionists (including a female activist), a Moroccan trade unionist, a British academic and trade unionist, a policy officer from a Washington-based NGO and a delegate from a Belgian (Christian affiliated) trade union. Despite this heterogeneity, the session was heavily male-dominated, with no female speaker, although there were women in the audience who made interventions during the discussion. But, in reiterating the point made above, the session was driven by Southern-based activists, in contrast to most other global union initiatives (Chapter 6).

Although the workshop was about the sharing of information and the building of common understandings about MNC restructuring and outsourcing, as the discussion developed it became evident that activists in the 'South' were becoming increasingly empowered, through being able to impart knowledge of the most recent changes to the outsourcing strategies of global capital. For example, the Indonesian and Indian speakers drew attention to patterns of recent spatial restructuring in the garment sector within the Global South, whereby successive waves of relocation in search of low wages and cheaper regulation were driving jobs from India to Indonesia to the central Asian republics of the former Soviet Union.

In another workshop, a lawyer from South Africa reported upon the transnational network that had been established through the NGO, Jubilee South Africa, to challenge European and American banks still claiming debt repayment from the apartheid regime. The emphasis of the campaign has been on bringing prosecution cases in the banks' home countries, particularly in the United States where corporations can be liable if profits have been made through human rights abuses. The focus of another smaller meeting that we attended was on the campaign organised by Mexican tyre workers against the closure of a local plant by the German multinational, Continental. One of the main themes was the failure of US and German trade unions to provide solidarity to the Mexican workers' strike and an interesting discussion followed between the Mexican workers and grassroots activists from the German unions concerned.

What is apparent from such examples is the way the WSF acts as a key opportunity space for campaigns and movements in the 'South' that lack the networking capacity in their everyday activities of more established and powerful actors in the Global North. The ability to both inform and incorporate other actors into local campaigns can in this way help to subvert dominant power hierarchies. Hence, as an opportunity space, the WSF helps to redress existing spatial disparities in discursive power and material resources, providing at least temporary opportunities for movements to escape their normal spatial constraints.

In addition, the WSF can provide alternative channels of communication, whereby particular voices that are suppressed in their own society may find articulation and their concerns projected and amplified to more spatially extensive audiences. The Mumbai WSF has been celebrated for the way local movements and actors imposed their own distinctive imprint, particularly in giving voice to lower caste groups normally excluded from transnational networks (Conway, 2004). Similarly, the Nairobi Forum was seen as critical in helping to support the growing, though still relatively weak, African attendance at WSF events (Smith, 2004).

Moreover, the WSF can provide momentum for dialogue and the development of solidarities between movements and actors with diverse and hitherto opposing identities (Smith, 2004). The Mumbai WSF, for example, played a useful role in enhancing dialogue and understanding between social actors from India and Pakistan with a delegation from the later being honoured by the hosts (*ibid*). More generally, by hosting transnational movements with avowedly participatory practices, local actors are forced to confront their own exclusionary and hierarchical organisational structures. In this sense, convergence at fora has topographical and topological dimensions, both facilitating collaboration and communication across space and potentially generating a more reflective and relational consciousness in grassroots communities, when activists in particular places are exposed to the practices and beliefs of others active in broader spatial networks.

Operational logics and relational dynamics

While purportedly a relatively open space of diverse opinion sharing, the WSF has been critiqued by many participants and commentators. The OC has drawn criticism because of its hierarchical organisation and lack of transparency in decision making (regarding who the decision makers actually are, who gets to speak at the Forum, the allocation of spaces and resources at the Forum for different groups, etc) (cf. Juris, 2004a; 2005c). In addition, the Forum as a process has been criticised because of the special treatment and privilege allotted to celebrity speakers, and the privileging and co-optation of the Forum by institutionalised political struc-tures, political parties, trade unions and mainstream NGOs (Osterweil, 2004). At the WSF in Porto Alegre in 2005, for example, two state premiers, Luiz Inácio Lula da Silva from Brazil and Hugo Chávez from Venezuela, were invited speakers despite the barring of formal political parties and the eschewing of hierarchy, whilst suspicions have also been aired about the underlying role of the Brazilian PT in Porto Alegre, and the Indian Communists in Mumbai. Critics of the ESF have also pointed to the dominant, though implicit, roles played by traditional left organisations in controlling the organisation and shaping agendas in Florence (Italian Communists), Paris (CGT trade union and Socialist mayor, Delanoe) and London (Mayor Ken Livingston and Socialist Workers Party) (cf. Juris, 2005c).

Other critics have highlighted the geographical and social unevenness of the WSF in the groups and actors that are included and dominant in shaping the process. The WSF is far from being a genuinely 'world' representative body (Huish, 2006: 2): even the 'South' perspective remains predominantly Latin American and Brazilian in character, with African and Asian influence only emerging when the social forum process takes place in those continents. Politically, the 'non-violent' emphasis of the WSF has been used to exclude some radical movements – such as the Zapatistas or Nepalese Maoists (Smith, 2004).

Despite almost half of WSF participants being women, the Forum remains an initiative dominated by middle-class, and middle- and upper-caste men (Sen, 2004: 218). In addition, certain 'key' events taking place at the WSF are privileged over all of the others – their presenters stay in better accommodation than most participants, and the space and resources allotted to these events are disproportionately greater than the other events (Albert, 2004). Moreover, all of the space allocated to the media has been occupied by mainstream media leaving no space available for alternative or independent media such as Indymedia (Adamovsky and George, 2004). The WSF is also a space where various inter-state agencies such as the UN have access or upon which they exercise influence. Certain state-dependent funding agencies and private US foundations have supported the WSF itself or various selected NGOs influential within it. The organisational space of the WSF is dominated by the official programme, which has been conceived without notable discussion beyond the governing bodies. Many small or radical groups and events are marginalised geographically and politically (Waterman, 2004: 156).

The discursive dominance that individuals have in relation to communication flows and inter-connections is because different groups and individuals are placed in more or less powerful ways in relation to such flows. Generally speaking, it is the leaders of movements, rather than grassroots activists that travel trans-continentally to participate at WSF, reflecting existing hierarchies in place-based struggles. As the PGA chapter shows, awareness of global networks is often lacking among grassroots activists in the Global South, which only serves to reinforce the elite position of those mobile 'global' activists or 'imagineers', discussed in Chapters 5 and 6. Hence, the 'decentralisation' of the WSF (e.g. to Asia and Africa) is essential in nurturing greater grassroots participation (Huish, 2006). The Mumbai WSF was regarded as particularly successful in this respect as it provided opportunities for local grassroots activists from unions and social movements to publicise their struggles to broader 'global' networks and develop new affinities with other activists (Conway, 2004; Smith, 2004). However, the costs of international travel, and organisational difficulties such as obtaining visas, etc., are likely to continue to bias larger and more established social actors such as NGOs and trade unions over smaller and more fledgling organisations, with the added likelihood that this may privilege more moderate positions over more radical ones.

There is greater potential for grassroots involvement in local and regional fora where transport costs are less and there is more opportunity for groups and individuals to travel together as a collective. The 2007 US Forum, for example, was notable for the way that southern US based initiatives were developed to reach out to constituencies that were not normally part of activist circuits (Uhlenbeck, 2007). These included: the 'South by Southwest Freedom Caravan' which spanned five states and brought together nearly 1,000 people from New Mexico, Texas, Louisiana, Mississippi, Alabama and Georgia; four bus loads of community workers and activists from the Mississippi Workers Center and Mississippi Immigrant Rights Alliance (MIRA); and the Southern Rural Black Women's Initiative which brought over 200 members from Mississippi and Alabama (ibid).

A noticeable split has emerged between the more autonomous groupings that are increasingly critical of the way the WSF and other fora are organised and the more vertically-structured traditional left parties and NGOs (Tormey, 2004a; Dowling, 2005; Juris, 2005c). For example, at the 2002 WSF in Porto Alegre, the 'Intergalactika Laboratory of Disobedience' was established, undertaking direct action against the official forum (Juris, 2005). Its main aim was to pose questions of organisational practice, rather than being against the Forum per se. At the Mumbai WSF in 2004, various activist and autonomous groups were critical of the way powerful actors such as the trade unions and Communist parties were able to dominate proceedings. As a result, a parallel Mumbai Resistance meeting was organised between those who argued that the WSF's critique of capitalism was become muted (Smith, 2004). Criticisms also extend to the dominance of plenary sessions with celebrity speakers over more informal workshops, although this was supposedly being addressed at the fora from 2005 onwards (Smith, 2004). As a result, an International Youth Camp was established in Mumbai, providing an autonomous space for thousand of non-affiliated activists, although it was incorporated into the mainstream space of the WSF in 2005.

Furthermore, many of those involved in the organisation of the London ESF protested at the covert and undemocratic organising process that went against the spirit of the WSF (Dowling, 2005; Sullivan, 2005). Key British organising bodies were the Mayor of London, Ken Livingston's Office,[2] (that provided much of the funding for the debate and influenced the agenda through a 'shadow' organisation know as Socialist Action); the Socialist Workers Party (SWP) and key trade unions such as the Rail Maritime and Transport union (RMT) (Dowling, 2005; Sullivan, 2005). It was argued by some social forum participants that this lead to the dominance of more planned, traditional forms of meeting and the dominance of key themes – such as the Iraq war and racism/fascism – that were desired by dominant organising groups (interviews, London, England, 2004). In the lead-up to the event, differences over organisational tactics led the Italian and French delegates on the organising committee to protest at the undemocratic way decisions were being reached, and to accusations of bullying and 'macho' tactics by dominant actors (Dowling, 2005). This, in part, resulted in the setting up of alternative fora or meetings outside the main process, by groups such as the Wombles[2] and Indymedia.

Moreover, in contrast to the Paris ESF, the London ESF was organised on a 'professional' (i.e. commercial) basis. Much of the work behind the Forum was subcontracted out through competitive tendering, organised directly by the Greater London Authority (effectively the London municipal government) and adhered to economic, rather than social, principles. One anecdotal example of this difference was that the catering at the London ESF contained the usual multinational brands (e.g. Mars, Coca Cola, Nestlé) – including many that were themselves the focus of resistance by many participants – whereas in Paris the food was determinedly localist and non-corporate in origin, some being provided by local farmers' cooperatives. However, unlike Porto Alegre – symbolically associated with economic and political radicalism – the London and Paris ESFs represent primary world cities at the heart of contemporary capitalism, key locations of global 'command and control' (Massey, 2004).

Juris describes a divide emerging between 'network' and 'command' logics (2005c: 254) that reflects the key divide in the wider movement between verticalist and hortizontalist perspectives (Juris, 2004a, b; Tormey, 2004a). Dowling suggests a division between those who aspire to democratic and participatory principles in the organisation of events compared to those whose mantra is either about 'getting the job done' or delegated to the vanguard that 'knows best'. Yet, critically, as Dowling notes, such issues are not trivial but go to the heart of what the broader movement is about: 'how to change the world' (2005: 207): 'the way the event is organised – how decision-making processes are conducted and what thematic content is given to the forum – is intricately bound up with its politics' (ibid). As with PGA Asia and ICEM, the social forum process can be understood as a convergence space which contains contested social and power relations, wherein unequal discursive and material power relations exist, resulting from the differential control of resources and placing of actors within decision-making processes. The social forum process involves entangled power relations, where relations of domination and resistance are entwined, creating spaces of resistance/domination (Sharp et al., 2000).

The Social Forum process has also been criticised for the sheer size that it has attained. Whilst the size, on the one hand, reflects its success, it does, on the other, lead to problems of coherence with a growing concern among some participants and commentators that it has become too all-embracing with the result that the critique of capitalism becomes diluted (Tormey, 2004b; Waterman, 2006). At a more practical level, and as we have found in our own attendance of various World and European fora, participants can be bewildered by the vast array of events and issues that are represented (interviews, London, England, 2004; Porto Alegre, Brazil 2005). For those attending a meeting of this kind for the first time – particularly grassroots activists with limited linguistic abilities – fora can be intimidating and alien spaces, rather than enabling and embracing (Smith, 2004).

Such exclusions can be exacerbated by the physical layout of the fora. Whereas the 2005 WSF in Porto Alegre was largely centred on one venue, stretching along the coast, both the London and Paris ESF[4] were spread out across different sites, making it difficult logistically for participants to travel between locations (cf. Juris, 2004a; 2005c). This was in contrast to Florence where the event was far more centred and coherent, evoking a special atmosphere and collective affinity for those that attended (Tormey, 2004b). The organisational geography of the London ESF involved a subtle segregation of events with the plenaries and larger sessions located at the main venue, Alexandra Palace, with the smaller workshops taking place in Bloomsbury or, in the case of some of the alternative autonomous events, further north on the outskirts of London at Middlesex University. This meant that the many attendees would gravitate towards the set-piece events and celebrity speakers and miss out on some of the more innovative and participatory workshops held elsewhere (interviews, London, England, 2004).

However, despite these critiques, the social forum process represents a considerable achievement in providing a novel and important space for transnational convergence against neoliberal globalisation, where there is a continued commitment to a degree of horizontalism and openness in its operation (Juris, 2005). The manner of this convergence and the future direction of the social forum process are issues that we explore further in the final two sections of this chapter.

Mutual solidarity: the 2004 European Social Forum

An important claim about the WSF is that it has brought together hitherto diverse and often conflicting actors and movements in dialogue that has initiated a new moment in the resistance to neoliberalism. In this way, the Forum is represented as a process building upon the solidarity supposedly achieved at the WTO protest in Seattle in 1999 between trade unionists, green campaigners, human rights activists and global development campaigners, encapsulated in the phrase 'Teamsters and turtles, together at last' (St Clair, 1999). However, the extent of genuine convergence and mutual solidarity between disparate groups, aside from pragmatic temporary coalitions, is open to debate.

In exploring some of these issues, we will draw upon our own research carried out at the European Social Forum (ESF) in London in 2004. We interviewed 103 people using a structured questionnaire at the various locations of the ESF: registration at Conway Hall in central London; Alexandra Palace, the main venue in north London; and on the streets at the closing demonstration. Most of the interviews were conducted in English, although some were also conducted in French and German. Our sample size was small, relative to the 20,000 undertaking the event, so was not representative. Instead, we undertook purposeful sampling designed to obtain a mix of views from the different nationalities, gender and age groups with the primary aim of obtaining data that would illustrate the thematic concerns of participants. The interviews in this sense allowed a 'detailed elucidation of the interplay among strategy, history and circumstances' (Schoenberger, 1991: 184). Alongside the interviews, we also carried out some participant observational research through attending seminars, workshops and the main set-piece demonstration on the last day of the forum. Attendance at the forum – and indeed at other fora in 2003 (ESF, Paris) and 2005 (WSF, Porto Alegre) – enabled a more ethnographic and indeed activist approach to the research, situating ourselves within key meetings and processes.

What was immediately notable about the social characteristics of the London ESF participants interviewed was the absence of traditional working-class groups, or those from mainstream British society ('middle England') and the high preponderance of students and academics (including teachers), that accounted for over 40 per cent of the people interviewed. Other white collar professionals (including accountants, union representatives, NGO workers, lawyers, civil servants, health and social workers) comprised another 20 per cent of those interviewed. Whilst there was a lot of trade union involvement, with just under a half of the respondents in our interviews being (middle-class) trade union members, what was striking was the degree to which there was a marked schism between union membership and that of NGO groups. Only 8 out of 28 NGO members in our interviews were also trade unionists and even less – only

4 – were members of political parties. This contrasts, in part, with the findings of della Porta *et al.* (2006: 45) in their study of the Florence ESF in 2002. Of the participants they interviewed, significant numbers were members of political parties (42.4 per cent), trade unions (44.3 per cent), NGOs (52.9 per cent) and student collectives (58.5 per cent).

What was interesting in our study was the surprisingly low level of multiple memberships of different participants. Twenty per cent of people interviewed were not members of any group, although when asked about this several respondents suggested that not being affiliated allowed a more polyvalent identity, creating the kinds of fluidity and mobility identified by McDonald (2002). Reflecting on the audience for the set-piece debate between Alex Callinicos and Toni Negri, entitled 'Working Class or Multitude' at the Paris ESF, Tormey noted:[5]

> [. . .] one looked around in vain for someone who appeared vaguely 'working class' as opposed to being part of the 'multitude'. If there were any horny-handed 'toilers' present, then they were lost in a sea of Peruvian hand-knitted woollen hats, carefully coiffed dreads and 'combat' threads. (Tormey, 2004: 152)

This was also a key failing identified by our respondents. One mentioned the need to 'reach the average people' (interview, London, England, 2004). The idea of outreach to others was also formulated in terms of 'reaching out into the middle class' to break out of the image of the 'stereotypical activist' (interviews, London, England, 2004). Others were in favour of 'educating the masses' so as to raise consciousness (interviews, London, England, 2004). There was also a particular demographic dimension to the London Forum with the relative dominance of those in their twenties and the absence of people with children and older generations (especially pensioners). As one interviewee told us: 'it tends to be a movement of fairly young people up to their mid-thirties. In a way it seems to appeal to a certain group of people. It would be great if your seventy-year-old neighbour got involved as well rather than just hippy activists' (interview, London, England, 2004). Others remarked upon the Forum's inaccessibility for many segments of the population, particularly those in regular employment or with children.[6] As a consequence, the only opportunity for some people to participate was the march on the Saturday morning (interviews, London, England, 2004).

However, there was the degree of convergence on certain issues among delegates. For example, while a range of political issues were considered important – such as social rights (i.e. equality issues), social justice, the environment and resisting neoliberalism – the issue of the war in Iraq was top of most people's concerns, reflecting the ongoing British involvement and the primacy given to the issue in the WSF the year before. Convergence was also apparent in the attitude of some respondents who stressed the importance of the forum for taking themselves out of their everyday realities to experience new thinking and refresh their radicalism. For example, a French civil servant with a municipal authority had experienced: 'refreshing perspectives which is not easy in the environment I usually work in' (interview, London, England, 2004). A retired German schoolteacher stressed that: 'it's important that events like these should happen so people can exchange ideas. Each country has to organise so as to take on its own ruling class and we must support each other', whilst another participant argued that: 'the exchange of ideas is the most important. Perhaps nothing concrete comes out of it but ideas can be shared. Each person can reinforce their own personal convictions' (interviews, London, England, 2004). An important theme that characterised most respondents was the need to learn and share ideas rather than impose a particular dominant party line. Like the PGA Asia conference in Dhaka, the social fora can provide the spaces for myriad informal networking conversations and opportunities between different activists. Such communication can enable the creation of common ground between activists from different backgrounds and struggles as a precursor to mutual solidarity

Anand has coined the term 'multivalent citizenship' (2004: 143) to emphasise the fluid nature in which WSF participants move through the physical spaces and ideas of the forum. However, from our research we found that in the operation of the actual debates and workshops, there appeared to be little coming together of activists from different types of movements. What was significant was the continued fragmentation of forum sessions into single-issue groups or narrow communities of interest with little evidence of cross-sectoral solidarity. A similar situation has been remarked upon concerning the Mumbai WSF:

> At Mumbai the flipside of the WSF's extraordinary diversity, the striking displays of music, dance and street theatre, the strong presence of Dalits, tribals, women's groups and trade unions – was the fact that political awareness was more limited and sectoral in character. Neither leaders nor ordinary members of any of the large movements or groups gathered there showed much interest or involvement in the conferences, seminars and workshops lying outside their specific areas of concern. (Vanaik, 2004: 59)

This was also our experience in attending the London ESF. For example, a set-piece debate on 'Oil Addiction' that we attended did not have a single union representative speaking, but was dominated by environmental groups and activists, where the emphasis for action was lifestyle and consumer politics in tackling the social and environmental consequences of oil dominance. Only one speaker from the floor raised the subject of how oil workers might also be involved in the struggle against oil multinationals. Conversely, a plenary session on 'globalisation', whilst composed of an impressive geographical range of speakers (from Colombia, Switzerland, Italy, UK, Iraq and Romania) was, with the exception of a single speaker from the development NGO War on Want, dominated by male trade unionists.

Another example was that trade union-sponsored debates – concerned with issues, such as defending the welfare state (particularly against the European Union Constitution and further attempts to deepen market integration) and the need to forge new European level alliances to defend worker rights – were largely exclusive union affairs where the audience was primarily males over 50 years of age, with few speakers from outside the union movement. However, in contrast, dialogues and campaigns are taking place between Global North and South activists. There were reports at the London ESF of a number of campaigns in which 'Northern' unions and NGOs are engaged in solidarity campaigns with 'Southern' groups, such as the Colombia Solidarity Campaign to provide support and publicity for Colombian oil workers. One theme that appears to have huge potential to become a genuinely transnational cause that can forge mutual solidarity between different groups is the campaign against privatisation, particularly in the water, energy and other utilities sectors, which are common issues facing NGOs, trade unions and other social movements that cut across national borders. The Global Union Federation, Union Network International (UNI), for example, is coordinating a global campaign against privatisation in the water industry.

Certainly, the ESF does play a role at the level of individual movements in bringing like-minded groups together to share information, exchange ideas and develop strategies. For the European trade union movement, it has clearly become an important space for more activist and left-leaning union officials to congregate and discuss alternative agendas to the more corporatist approach being pursued by the European trade union elites (see Chapter 6). Similarly, it is an important convergence space for anti-war activists to develop strategy and discuss tactics for ongoing campaigns against the war in Iraq and nuclear proliferation. It is also, despite the attempts of some 'verticalists', an important site for autonomous groups to come together and develop future agendas for collective action – although increasingly in opposition to the main forum process.

The impression both from the ESF and the WSF processes is that the more genuine affinities and convergences occur within networks that are already operative, and in which the fora have now become important 'networking vectors' for the transmission of recent events, exchange of information about strategy, and communication about future directions and targets. In this way, fora play a role in strengthening and mobilising existing relationships as well as providing the opportunity for other movements to join such networks. Undoubtedly the WSF process has effected some changes in the way social relations operate within the wider resistance to neoliberalism. The WSF can clearly be seen as playing a 'performative function in the sense that it aims to embody what it is calling forth' (Olivers, 2004: 182; see also Juris, 2004a). Certainly convergence at fora has produced the kind of 'contamination' in confronting established political identities with the imperative to be respectful of different identities and visions (della Porta, 2005). While this process is creating new 'tolerant identities' (della Porta, 2005: 178) that place a positive emphasis on the diversity of political actors resisting neoliberalism, the cross-fertilisation of ideas between such actors, and the development of certain common campaigns between different movements, the experience of the London event raises an important caveat. For some groups, social relations and practices continue to be underpinned by traditional vertical and vanguardist perspectives on power, that tend to be exclusionary rather than inclusive in character. This also reflects some of the critiques about how the WSF has been organised, as we have discussed earlier.

Beyond convergence?

As early as 2002, criticisms of the direction of the WSF were emerging (see Juris, 2004a; 2005c). For more autonomous and anti-capitalist grassroots movements, fora were becoming too corporate and aligned with state and establishment actors.[7] For others, as we have seen, the fora have not lived up to the 'open space' ideals, with familiar and insidious verticalist politics reasserting itself through the back-door control of the events by political parties. From another direction, the growth of the forum is leading to a dilution of its politics; with the tolerance of increasingly diverse perspectives leading to a *pot-pourri* assemblage ranging from introspective lifestyle themes such as yoga and stress relief to the more urgent imperatives of changing the world (Tormey, 2004b). At a prosaic but perhaps more urgent level, questions remain as to the actual political effects of the social forum process, and whether the process is becoming genuinely global in character (Bourgeois, 2006).

Regarding the latter, the decision to hold polycentric regional fora in 2006 and have a global event on a biennial basis was seen as step towards creating new spaces of resistance and convergence (Bourgeois, 2006). Whilst successful in the sense of achieving this aim, with two parallel fora in Mali and Venzuela, the disparities between the two events served only to highlight the uneven geographies of the WSF process and the groups that participate in it. At the Mali Forum in Bamako between 15–20,000 people participated, primarily drawn from West Africa, reflecting the transport costs and lack of resources of African 'civil society' and the lack of connection between movements (*ibid*: 10).

In contrast, more than 75,000 people from 170 countries were present in Caracas, many drawn to Chavez's Bolivarian revolution (*ibid*).

Beyond the continuing realities of its uneven geographies, for some of the original 'imagineers' of the forum, such as the former ATTAC convenor, Bernard Cassen, the WSF has been at an impasse since the mid-2000s (Tormey, 2004b). Having successfully become a space for debate and dialogue between disparate traditions and perspectives, those occupying a more traditional left socialist perspective are increasingly frustrated by the failure to develop a more coherent political strategy. Cassen and others[8] were behind an initiative launched at the 2005 WSF, the Porto Alegre Manifesto. The Manifesto represented an attempt to put forward a broad alternative programme and involved 12 main proposals, including the cancellation of debt in the Global South; the implementation of the Tobin Tax; and the reform and democratisation of global institutions.[9]

Many of these principles would have been acceptable to the majority of movements taking part in the WSF – to both 'verticals' and 'horizontals' and would have conformed to a collective vision. However, the Manifesto was voted down by the Assembly of Movements, the main voting body of the forum, and has been subsequently discarded. It has been followed by the Bamako Appeal, an attempt to re-launch it at the Mali strand of the polycentric forum in 2006.[10]

Whilst the content may have been unacceptable for some, the key problem for many activists was the manner in which the Manifesto was set out, which smacked of 'vanguardism', by an exclusive group of predominantly white male intellectuals, and the attempt to impose a particular alternative vision on the forum (Waterman, 2006). In this sense, the debate over the Manifesto revealed a key and continuing fault-line within the forum process between the different operational logics that we have discussed in earlier chapters. One logic seeks to develop a centralised policy and agenda for achieving power, and an opposing perspective eschews both the notion of achieving and holding power in a way that replicates existing capitalist structures, and the attempt to pose a singular alternative or model of anti-capitalism (Juris, 2004a; Tormey, 2004a; 2005). It thus brings to the surface the tensions and entangled politics at the heart of the WSF process.

Beyond these binaries between reform and revolution and 'verticals' and 'horizontals', it is critical to reflect upon what as a convergence space, the forum process has so far achieved in terms of forging transnational solidarity and developing resistance to neoliberal globalisation. Given the increasingly parlous state of global geopolitics, the growing global divisions between rich and poor, the seemingly limitless power of global capital and the acceleration of ecological destruction, the frustration of some at the 'talking shop' element of the forum is understandable. Yet, this, as various commentators have noted (e.g. Juris, 2005; Tormey, 2005) is to misunderstand the nature of the forum and its achievements. The fact that it exists at all, as a space that brings together disparate and geographically dispersed actors *en masse* serves a warning to global capitalism of the forces arraigned against it and of their degree of connection. As Tormey (2004b) notes, the fact that this has occurred in a relatively disorganised and unstructured fashion is testimony to the networked and horizontalist reality of the broader resistance to neoliberalism. Ultimately, however, returning to the main theme of our book, its future significance is likely to depend upon its ability to continue to generate useful forms of communication and support for the territorially based actors in their local and national struggles.

Notes

1 ATTAC stands for *Association pour la Taxation des Transactions Financieres pour l'aide aux Citoyens* and was originally created by French journalists from the radical periodical *Le Monde Diplomatique* in 1998. Subsequently it has become an international network of around 30,000 activists in over 30 countries, campaigning specifically for a global tax on international currency speculation to be used to fund development in the 'Global South', but more generally against neoliberalism.

2 While Livingston has been an arch critic of the Iraq war and western foreign policy in the Middle East, as Mayor of London (since 2000), he has pursued a 'boosterist' and largely neoliberal economic agenda aimed at maintaining London's competitive advantage as a financial centre.

3 For example, the Wombles meeting at the London ESF was titled: 'Beyond ESF: 5 Days and Nights of Anti-AUTHORITARIAN Ideas and

Actions'. On its website, it offered: 'a radically different alternative to the Official ESF. No government sponsorships (GLA and Mayor of London) and no political parties. There will be no 'leading activists', 'big name speakers' or entrance fee. [The fee for the London event was £30 for an individual]. However, there will be thousands of people from groups and collectives from around Europe – sharing their experiences in taking back their lives.' (www.wombles.org.uk, last accessed December 2004).

4 Paris was particularly bad in this respect with the Forum organised in five suburbs in a concentric ring around the city. Despite the generally excellent transport network, it could take over an hour to travel between meetings, often with the result that you missed the event that you wanted to attend, or in many cases, arrived to find that venues were full (author's field diary, November 2003).

5 When waiting in vain to be admitted to this session, Andy Cumbers overheard an SWP activist in the queue shouting 'Who's swarming now Toni?'

6 There were no crèche facilities.

7 In his articulate critique of the ESF, Tormey anticipated the growing corporatisation of the Forum in London when he said: 'Where better to promote the social forum as commodity-spectacle than at the UK home of the alter-commodity?' (2004b: 153).

8 The Manifesto was signed by 19 'leftist intellectuals and activists' (Bourgeois, 2006: 8), including leading figures such as Samir Amin, Immanuel Wallerstein, Ignacio Ramonet and Frei Betto.

9 The full list of proposals are: 1. The cancellation of the debt of countries in the global south; 2. Implementation of the Tobin Tax on financial speculation; 3. The dismantling of tax havens; 4. The implementation of basic rights to employment, welfare and a decent pension and equality in this regard for men and women; 5. Rejection of free trade and implementation of fair trade and environmentally sound trade principles; 6. Guarantees of national sovereignty over agricultural production, rural development and food policy; 7. Outlawing knowledge patenting on living organisms and privatisation of common goods especially water; 8. Fight by means of public policies against all kinds of discrimination, sexism, xenophobia, anti-semitism and racism; 9. Urgent action to address climate change, including the development of an alternative model for energy efficiency and democratic control of natural resources; 10. Dismantling of foreign military bases except those under UN supervision; 11. Freedom of information for individuals, the creation of a more democratic media and controls on the operation of major conglomerates; 12. Reform and democratisation of global institutions incorporating institutions such as the WB and IMF under the control of the UN.

10 There is not the space for a detailed critique of these proposals. See instead the recent papers by Waterman, 2006 and Bourgeois, 2006.

8

Geographies of transnational solidarity

> Solidarity is not a matter of altruism. Solidarity comes from the inability to tolerate the affront to our own integrity of passive or active collaboration in the oppression of others, and from the deep recognition of our most expansive self-interest. From the recognition that, like it or not, our liberation is bound up with that of every other being on the planet, and that politically, spiritually, in our heart of hearts we know anything else is unaffordable. (Morales, 1998: 125)[1]

Our concern in this book has been to go beyond the simplistic and superficial gloss on the growing resistance to neoliberal globalisation as an emergent global civil society. In the preceding chapters we have done this by critiquing existing discourses and developing our own conceptual-isation of Global Justice Networks (GJNs) which we have then grounded through three case studies: PGA (Asia), ICEM and the Social Forum process. We consider each of these examples of GJNs, comprising differentially-placed and resourced social movements, trade unions, NGOs and other political actors working together to articulate demands for social, economic and environmental justice. GJNs comprise a series of overlapping, interacting, competing and resourced networks (Juris, 2004a). In this book, we have specifically conceived of GJNs as 'convergence spaces': associations of differentially-placed actors and resources which are put into circulation in a continual effort to make political actions durable through time and mobile across space. Each GJN that we have studied in this book is an example of attempts made by different actors – peasant movements, trade unions, NGOs, etc. – to forge collective visions and mutual solidarities.

Moving away from the more abstract claims about networks and topological relations made in the literature, an important element of our analysis has been to highlight the importance of geography to understanding their operation. We have conceptualised GJNs as convergence spaces: geographically dispersed social coalitions that: (i) are composed of place-based, but not necessarily place-restricted movements; (ii) articulate collective visions; (iii) involve a practical relational politics of solidarity; (iv) facilitate spatially-extensive political action; (v) require 'networking vectors'; (vi) are characterised by horizontal and vertical networking logics; and (vii) comprise sites of contested social and power relations.

By considering GJNs as convergence spaces we have attempted to spatialise the everyday workings of networks so as to determine their characteristics, their operational logics and strategies, and their spatial dynamics. As we noted in Chapter 4, an understanding of the spatiality of GJNs provides insights into the geographical context in which they operate (e.g. the conditions, opportunities and constraints that they face) and the strategies that they employ – how myriad ongoing connections are generated that combine different parts of the world together (by connecting different place-based social movements) and how, in turn, these are constituted through, and constitute, particular sites and places (Featherstone *et al.*, 2007). Thus, whilst we have highlighted the issues of convergence within GJNs – around certain common visions and especially shared resistance to neoliberal capitalism – we have also highlighted the tensions and fault lines that exist when movements embedded within particular place-based struggles seek to become part of much broader networks of collective action.

We would argue that much recent literature on transnational activism (e.g. della Porta, 2005; Tarrow, 2005) neglects the spatial practices of transnational political activity, and presents a singular notion of what constitutes networks (della Porta and Mosca, 2007; but see Juris, 2004a; 2005c, for notable exceptions). As we have shown, a GJN may possess common enemies but not necessarily common understandings between its participants. For example, despite the collective visions of PGA Asia, there remain fundamental differences (of political practice) and a plurality of place-specific political identities between the participant movements. In this sense, alliances are not the products of a singular network but rather the coming together of different dynamic trajectories of political activity, articulated through the practices of different place-based movements. Therefore, in this chapter, our purpose is to draw together the key findings and in doing so examine the future prospects for generating meaningful and sustained transnational (mutual) solidarity in ways that may begin to advance a global justice agenda.

Global justice networks

GJNs are networks and flows of communication, action, and experience. We have conceived of them as products of hybridities, overlappings, competitions and juxtapostions whereby different place-based political actors such as social movements, trade unions and NGOs, become connected to more spatially extensive coalitions with a shared interest in articulating demands for greater, social, economic and environmental justice. Although convergence spaces are rooted in particular place-based struggles, they are not necessarily local. What also gets diffused and organised across space is the 'common ground' shared by different groups, often the result of groups' entangled interests (Routledge, 2003a). PGA Asia participants tend to hold common collective visions, enshrined in the network's hallmarks. However, contradictions persist. For example, commitments within the hallmarks to decentralisation and non-discrimination are undermined by hierarchical operational logics and caste and gender discriminations within certain movements (e.g. see Eschle and Maiguashca, 2007).

Whilst ICEM affiliates all hold to a core set of collective visions related to basic labour rights; to unionise, to decent wages, to decent forms of work; they do at the same time attach different meanings to global solidarity and how this can be achieved. Most notably, there is a basic schism in the tactics to deal with corporate and state actors, between dialogue/partnership and militancy/independence. In comparison with the other two GJNs, what marks out the Social

Forum process – alongside a more general resistance to the excesses of global capitalism – is a set of practices that commit its participants to open, democratic debate and dialogue, though even here there are tensions that reflect different political and ideological positions, and power and gender inequalities.

Through their operation, GJNs can be perceived as significant in helping to constitute 'transnational counterpublics' (Olesen, 2005): 'open spaces for the self-organised production and circulation of oppositional identities, discourses, and practices' (Juris, 2004a: 401). However, whilst this may represent a 'scale shift' in the resistance to neoliberalism and capitalist globalisation (Tarrow, 2005), this does not constitute the global civil society – or even the beginnings of one – envisaged by some commentators (Kaldor, 2003; Keane, 2003)

Space and place are critical in understanding the operation of GJNs and their potential to contribute to an alternative global politics. Spatially, the global linkages of GJNs can be seen as creating spatial configurations that connect places (and the movements that operate therein) with each other in opposition to neoliberalism. Whether it is trade unions within a global network seeking to raise employment standards within a particular commodity chain, or peasant movements exchanging tactics in battles against land appropriation, the key element is a forging of a wider spatial consciousness. But, whilst there has been a spatial extension of solidarity, we have also shown that GJNs are fraught with tensions. We have shown that particular places and movements become empowered whilst others remain marginal within the operations of GJNs. A range of place-specific conditions enable or constrain movements in their capacity to organise their struggles and participate within GJNs. Within ICEM, for example, particular national union affiliates from the Global North dominate the agenda both through greater resources and stronger positions nationally vis-à-vis their own corporations. Within PGA Asia, certain Indian farmers' movements have had considerable influence within the network owing to their ability to mobilise large memberships, or their access to greater resource bases (interviews, Dhaka, Bangladesh, 2004; Kathmandu, Nepal, 2004). The WSF process itself emerged from the particular spatial context of Porto Alegre, where favourable local political conditions were important in providing both material and symbolic support. Whilst progressive, in the sense of subverting dominant actors from the Global North, the WSF continues to be uneven in its effects, struggling to broaden its participation beyond Latin America, Western Europe and parts of Asia (particularly India).

An important finding is that transnational alliances are more likely to be facilitated and sustained when movements possess significant mobilisation capacities already; when they have the capacity for regular communication with other movements; and when each organisation's members take some responsibility for brokering bonds of solidarity (Bandy and Smith, 2005). In addition, the ability of movements to participate in transnational alliances is also shaped by the actions, policies, limitations and challenges posed by the governments of the states in which they are located and their relationship to the state (Burawoy *et al.*, 2000; Glassman, 2001; Rai, 2003). In these ways, networks are both influenced by and replicate, the existing 'power geometries' (Massey, 1999) that distinguish connections between places under economic globalisation. In addition, as we have shown in this book, networks evolve unevenly over space with some groups, movements and actors within them able to develop relatively more global connections and associations whereas others remain relatively more localised. Therefore potential conflicts arise from such complex geographies, which only become evident through analysing the specific operation and evolution of different networks.

For example, our analysis of ICEM suggests that power and resources reside with the national affiliates who provide the funding for projects and delegates to ICEM committees. The decline in union membership has led to a considerable degree of merger activity within some of the national union movements (notably the UK, Germany and USA) so that a few key players – with massive voting blocks – can wield considerable power in ICEM elections. However, there is a spatial disjuncture within the ICEM because the most powerful affiliates are not always the most active at the international level. For example, whilst British affiliate unions are often over-represented on ICEM committees, their decline domestically has meant that they have struggled to find finance for international work in recent years (authors' interviews, see also Cumbers, 2004).

Our research suggests considerable differences in the way the three networks are organised and operate through space, although these should not be exaggerated. ICEM operates in a more structured, hierarchical and centralised fashion than PGA Asia (although many of PGA Asia's participant movements have verticalist operational logics) while the WSF, despite its horizontalist aspirations, displays elements of verticalism in the way certain key decisions are made.

For the PGA Asia and ICEM networks, the national scale remains important for the mobilisation of resources and development of international agendas. Movements and unions have to respond primarily to local/national realities (as Tarrow, 2005 has argued contra Hardt and Negri's (2004) optimistic view of the multitude). For example, in Nepal, ANPA has had much of its organisational work and resources consumed by responding to the Royal Military coup of 2005 (and similarly for the AoP in Thailand after the military coup of 2006). The continuing importance of local and national scales poses critical issues in particular for sustaining effective ongoing transnational solidarity beyond momentary connection, an issue that we will return to below.

We have shown that GJNs are fragile entities that can be disrupted by a range of different issues, including securing funding to provide key resources, and the problem of movements potentially leaving the network or joining other networks. In PGA Asia, each movement is involved in numerous other networks for their own specific political and campaign-oriented purposes. Hence nearly all of the movements involved with PGA Asia are also participants in the international farmers' network *La Via Campesina* (e.g. KRRS, BKU, ANPA, BKF, MONLAR); Indian movements also participate in the national social movement network, the Indian Coordinating Committee (e.g. KRRS, BKU, NBA); many of the South Asian movements are also participants in the Asian Peasants Coalition (e.g. BKU, ANPA, BKF, MONLAR); yet other movements are involved in the Pesticide Action Network (e.g. ANPA); the International Rivers Network (e.g. NBA), etc. Whether these networks are issue-specific (e.g. concerning the impacts of large dam construction, as in the case of the International Rivers

Network) or sector-specific (e.g. concerning the rights of farmers as in the case of *La Via Campesina*), they nevertheless tend to compete with each other for resources – be they funds or, at times, particular movements' levels of participation. Moreover, some of the participants within GJNs are themselves networks of different movements. For example, the AoP in Thailand – a network of anti-dam, peasant, student and labour movements – has in the words of one Thai activist 'factionalised into separate movements with little coordination between them and no-one taking responsibility for the network' (interview, Bangkok, Thailand, 2006). As a result there has been a failure of horizontal coordination. For example, at the PGA Asia conference in Dhaka in 2004, participants agreed that the AoP should act as the Southeast Asia regional convenor for the network. This decision remains to be ratified by the AoP network. Indeed, as one activist commented:

> Each movement in the Assembly acts separately and is organised by separate NGOs. Different movements participate in different global events and do not communicate their experiences with the rest of the network. No-one has a clear overall picture of global resistance realities. (interview, Bangkok, Thailand 2006)

Similar issues face the ICEM affiliates, many of whom have links to more than one global union federation (GUF) although, in theory, the affiliation of all GUFs to the umbrella trade union body, the ICFTU (International Confederation of Free Trade Unions), should make it possible to avoid unnecessary duplication of time, personnel and resources and allow for greater future cooperation. Certainly, compared with PGA Asia, ICEM and the broader union movement should have the capacity for more sustained solidarity activities.

Within networks (both national and international) and within movements there are competing personalities, jealousies, turf wars, strategies and claims on time and resources. These are further problematised by the (in)effectiveness of the communication, linguistic translation and operational links between a GJN's participant movements. Few activists in grassroots communities in PGA Asia have English language skills, and thus there is a danger that, at conferences, interpretation ghettos can emerge where folks barely communicate outside of their language group. Moreover, it is the imagineers in the network – the movement leaders and key organisers – who have the necessary language skills for transnational communication. The linguistic dimension is echoed by affiliates of ICEM, particularly the French who, whilst aware that they are lagging behind in terms of language training, complain that the hegemony of the English language in conferences and meetings gives rise not only to communication problems, but also to asymmetric power relationships (see also Stirling and Tully, (2004), for an overview of a similar debate in European Works Councils). Several officials we spoke to argued that language differences can be used to the advantage of certain affiliates to the detriment of others. Moreover, whilst there are interpretation facilities in international congresses, the lack of linguistic abilities can hamper the establishment of bilateral links. As a result, partnerships tend to be forged according to linguistic affinities. Thus the Nordics are more likely to cooperate with the British and the French with the Belgians. Within the Social Forum process, an elite group of left intellectuals – a 'Third Worldist' cadre that includes Samir Amin – has formed which some have accused of vanguardism for putting forward the Bamako Appeal (Waterman, 2006).

Another important issue is that tensions arise between developing more horizontalist networks that facilitate democracy and grassroots participation, and the need to develop structures that can relay a global consciousness to local activists. For the three networks, these tensions are manifested in different ways. PGA Asia is facing tensions between the principles of a decentred politics that can be fully understood and participated in by grassroots activists, and establishing more formal structures at a national level to mediate between local and global action. This is exacerbated by power differences due to caste and gender inequalities between movement leaders and grassroots activists.

Conversely, ICEM has become too reliant upon top-down initiatives that, without effective local activism, are unlikely to generate lasting improvements in workers' conditions. For example, Global Frame Agreements (GFAs) are signed by the ICEM General Secretary, and national officials from affiliate unions. Because of its limited resources, ICEM is dependent upon its national affiliates for both the establishment of GFAs and the development of Global Company Networks (GCNs). However, this ensures that campaigns are devolved down to the national level with affiliate unions being responsible for the administration of networks. But it also means that effective networking has to be undertaken at the local level, facilitating transnational connections between grassroots workers within corporations. The WSF meanwhile is fraught with tension between horizontals and verticals over: how meetings are organised and who is invited/ excluded; who sets the agenda and how; the future of the process; whether it should continue to be a space for dialogue and engagement or become a more formal political force (Juris, 2004a; 2005c).

Making effective connections

As we have argued, understanding the dynamics of network operational logics entails thinking about power relations across space and not necessarily in any one place. This relational perspective focuses on the effectiveness of connections (e.g. communication and operational links) between the actors in the network (Latour, 1992; Massey, 1994). Agency is a relational effect generated by interaction and connectivity within the network (Juris, 2004a), while power becomes the ability to enroll others on terms that allow key actors to 'represent' the others (Castree, 2002). Owing to differential access to (financial, temporal) resources and network flows, differential material and discursive power relations exist (see Routledge, 2003a).

A particularly crucial issue is that of leadership. Self-organising networks of relatively independent, loosely connected actors have been seen in much of the literature as increasingly important (e.g. Klein, 2002; Notes from Nowhere, 2003; Starr, 2005). However, as we have argued in this book, this obscures very real hierarchies of power that exist within GJNs; the lack of transparency; and the 'tyranny of structurelessness' (Freeman, 1970; cf. Juris, 2004a) embodied in the existence of the imagineers. The reality remains that for peasant movements in the Global South, and for trade unions in the Global North and South, leaders are required who can inspire and empower individuals and groups to engage in difficult realities; work through conflicts; and participate in the hard and long-term work of resistance to neoliberalism.

Transnational solidarity and leadership both require a politics of trust: a collective commitment to balancing within a convergence, coherence and pluralism, unity and diversity. This requires the transparency and accountability of active leadership and facilitation rather than the pretence that no 'leaders' (or imagineers, key catalysts or organisers) exist (as claimed, amongst others, by Klein, 2002; McDonald, 2002). Of course, this is related to the specific organisational logics of the movements, unions and GJNs in question. However, even vertical operational logics take many divergent forms: some leaders are very open, nurture active mass participation and only embody the collective decisions of members. Other leaders remain corrupt and bureaucratic (Raskin *et al.*, 2002).

In each of the networks, and irrespective of stated aims about organising principles, the reality is that much international work at present devolves to a small number of key actors who sustain networks through their own inter-action and personal communication – what we have termed imagineers (see also Juris 2004a). They conduct much of the routine (international) organisational work of GJNs helping to organise conferences, mobilise resources and facilitate communication and information flows between movements and between movement offices and grassroots communities. They also attempt to 'ground' the concept or imaginary of the network (what it is, how it works, what it is attempting to achieve) within grassroots communities who comprise the membership of the participant movements. In PGA Asia, it is the interpersonal relations between key movement leaders and support group activists that enable the network to function. Within ICEM, it is General Secretaries of affiliates and professional officers who undertake most international work. In the Social Forums, it is a mix of movement leaders and officials and some more independent activists, though usually middle-class and educated elites.

Within the three GJNs, these imagineers – because of their structural positions, communication skills and experience

in activism and meeting facilitation – tend to wield disproportionate power and influence within the networks. There
is an over-reliance upon the imagineers to instigate events,
raise funds, etc. It is frequently they who participate in the
different networks since they are the key nodes within a
movement who are responsible for international networking.
Therefore, there is the danger of a growing social distance,
measured in terms of culture, politics and ideology between
those who network globally and those engaged in day-to-
day struggles in their workplaces. However, as we have
also shown, grassroots activists will often defer authority to
imagineers and let them get on with the work of international networking, leaving activists free to concentrate on
local issues and organising (see also Routledge *et al.*, 2006).
This can sometimes be due to place- and organisationally-
specific understandings of authority, or because of an
inability of grassroots activists to visualise what a network
really is, and how it works (interviews, Bangkok, Thailand,
2004; Dhaka, Bangladesh, 2004).

Moreover, imagineers can also act as the key links or
facilitators in overlapping networks. For example, one of
PGA Asia's imagineers is also an activist in the Thai Labour
Campaign and has worked with Fred Higgs, General
Secretary of ICEM, and with Thai jewellery workers in their
campaign to join ICEM and has worked with ICEM member
unions in Thailand. This activist commented:

> It is important to work at local, national, regional and global
> levels to look for alliances at all scales. It is important to get
> global actors to help because they are so powerful. ICEM can
> mobilise twenty million workers worldwide. They have the
> strength of the boycott. Global union people have the power to
> exert pressure on companies in Thailand. (interview, Bangkok,
> Thailand 2006)

Therefore, for both PGA Asia and ICEM, a key issue is
how the network's imaginary is visualised and developed at
the grassroots. The emergence of a transnational activist
elite is perhaps inevitable – and even a necessity – if GJNs
are to be sustained for reasons that we have discussed in
earlier chapters. But, although some forms of leadership are
required, the operation of GJNs must be such that they
remain accountable to their grassroots members, and their
operational logics remain as far as possible open, democratic

and participatory. The dominance of certain ICEM affiliates through the network's hierarchical voting structures – which favours established over newer affiliates – is certainly not a model to follow in this respect.

Mutual solidarity

Mutual solidarities are co-produced with the constitution of networks, forged out of the collective articulations of different struggles and constituted as (often messy, problematic, always negotiated) interconnections that mediate in the heterogeneous associations between humans and nonhumans in networks (Featherstone, 2005). They are part of the ongoing connections, social and material relations and articulations between places. As we have shown, this process is far from smooth: GJNs are fraught with political determinations and contested social relations, because different groups articulate a variety of potentially conflicting goals, ideologies and strategies.

Solidarities can become articulated in contested ways within and between movements and not just subordinated into a general resistance to neoliberalism. They are shaped through the ongoing and contested negotiation of spatially stretched power relations (Featherstone, 2008). They are dynamic and situated interventions in the geographies of GJNs.

The different ways that unequal geographies of power are contested is constitutive of different political identities. Such resistant identities may articulate very different 'maps of grievance' (Featherstone, 2003) that might involve exclusionary nationalisms, localisms or gender practices. This can have significant impacts on the conduct of mutual solidarities. For example, according to an Indian activist, in PGA Asia, the Indian farmers' movements (e.g. BKU, KRRS) control the GJN process and others (e.g. NBA) feel marginalised (interview, Kathmandu, Nepal, 2006). Similarly, a particular Eurocentric view currently prevails in ICEM, favouring the construction of global partnerships with multinationals over more independent worker networks.

The three GJNs display considerable variation in both the extent and nature of their international solidarity activities.

Because it has permanent structures in place in the form of offices, professional staff and regular conferences, ICEM is able to pursue a number of strategies and campaigns in a more concerted and sustained manner than PGA Asia, which lacks permanent organisational structures and is still developing its transnational connections and associations.

Two strategies in particular have been prioritised by ICEM in recent years: GFAs and GCNs (Interview, ICEM General Secretary). GFAs are collective agreements signed between a global union federation and a multinational corporation (MNC) whereby the MNC pledges to respect a set of principles on trade union rights, health, safety and environmental practices in all its global operations. Eleven have been signed to date. GCNs are independent union networks that operate within companies often hostile to trade unions, with the aim being to foster communication between grassroots workers. Of the eight established, the most significant GCN has been inside Exxon-Mobil, historically anti-union in its activities. Originally it was set up in 2003 in 11 countries, both in the Global North and South (Belgium, Canada, Italy, Japan, Malaysia, Nigeria, Singapore, Spain, Thailand, United Kingdom and the USA) but has subsequently expanded to 18 countries.

For PGA Asia, its regional conferences provide important spaces within which representatives of participant movements can converge and discuss issues that pertain to the functioning of the network (cf. Juris, 2004a). As one PGA Asia imagineer stated:

> The purpose of such conferences is to develop solidarity through the development of deeper interpersonal ties between activists from different struggles, the coordination of joint actions and resources, the development of political strategies, the enrolment of new movements into the network, and the construction of economic and political alternatives to neoliberalism. (interview, Kathmandu, Nepal, 2004)

Practical support and forms of solidarity, where they have so far been developed, tend to be bilateral.

The WSF has succeeded primarily in opening up a global dialogue between hitherto disparate movements although, as we noted in the previous chapter, it is perhaps most effective in helping to strengthen existing connections. It has also undoubtedly provided a greater voice for movements from the Global South and, for the first time since the end of the Cold War, begun to articulate a set of alternative political imaginations.

In all three networks, gatherings (such as the Dhaka conference for PGA Asia, the union congresses and assemblies for ICEM, the international and regional social fora) provide performative spaces that play a vital role in face-to-face communication and exchange of experience, strategies and ideas, and generate collective energy and sense of identity (Juris, 2004a). They all – in different ways – help in what Juris (*ibid*) characterises as the production and reproduction of 'transnational counterpublics' (Olesen, 2005).

For ICEM, congresses and meetings are subservient to the everyday actions of its professional staff in Brussels who work on strategy and campaigns. The Brussels office acts as an intermediate to facilitate the establishment of bilateral relationships; helps build unions in countries such as Iraq or China; facilitates joint campaigns between affiliate members; or intervenes directly towards particular struggles in selected countries such as Columbia (interview, Brussels, Belgium, 2005).

The differences between the three networks reflect the reality of very different forms of convergence space. ICEM is a fixed network with durable structures within which socio-spatial interaction takes place on a regular and even daily basis. In contrast, PGA Asia is a network in process that is materialised through particular moments in particular places, although more frequent, if uneven, e-mail contact takes place between network imagineers. The ICEM network also appears to be more successful than PGA Asia in generating practical support and aid for movements engaged in local struggles. However, it should also be recognised that ICEM operates less as a space for mutual exchange and collective solidarity-building, but more a space of unequal power relations, where powerful actors are able to mobilise across scales from one part of the network to support more vulnerable and often place-constrained movements in another. In contrast, PGA Asia does represent a more egalitarian solidarity politics where there is less of a scalar imbalance between the constituent movements. The Social Forum process, despite its horizontalist aspirations, is open to domination by particular groups, as the experience of the London ESF demonstrated.

However, transnational solidarity (and by extension the emergence of a global civil society) continues to be compromised by a range of place-specific issues concerning the realities of everyday struggle and resource availability; as well as the organisational logics of GJN participant movements, and the role of the imagineers. While solidarities are forged to challenge unequal power relations (manifested locally, nationally, globally), in practice the operational processes of GJNs frequently involve power differences due to differences in resource access between activists (Rai, 2003; Eschle and Maiguashca, 2007), exemplified by the imagineers. As one Indian PGA Asia activist commented:

> Movements in South Asia have a limited resource capacity to fully engage in global solidarity, things like time, money, language skills and computer skills. Hence most Indian movements are not really ready to fully participate in a global movement, to commit to it full time, or to fully involve and engage the grassroots in it. Most movements in India are leader based and many of these leaders have neither computer skills nor English language skills and thus they profess to be uninterested in global organising since they so not possess the necessary skills for it. Most folk who do global organising primarily like to travel and enjoy the benefits of conference hotels – they aren't serious about global solidarity. The language of many movement leaders is influenced by NGO discourse and not by the language of the grassroots. We need to return to the grassroots since most global work is too much in the air. (interview, Kathmandu, Nepal, 2006)

Similar sentiments were expressed by attendees at the ESF about connecting with ordinary working people. In another conversation, a Norwegian trade union international officer lamented the difficulties of engaging grassroots members, not because of their ignorance of broader networks, but rather because of their concern with day-to-day struggles:

> That is the dilemma. International work is becoming more and more important for trade union movements and I think that our union has to be involved more and more in international work than we do today but when membership is declining, the ordinary member or shop steward says, 'The issue is here and now. It's in our plant. It's the Norwegian problems with the industry. It is here that we have to use the resources and the

people.' And to get the understanding of the bigger picture, and to see these things not as separate issues, I think it's quite a challenge. (interview, Oslo, Norway, 2005)

In addition, many networks and their campaigns have been based on temporary, turbulent alliances that fragment (see della Porta *et al.*, 2006). Particular struggles remain too dispersed, diffused and small-scale to systematically transform the current trends of neoliberal globalisation. This is exacerbated by the active opposition of entrenched powers to social movement and GJN demands, the limited access to the media enjoyed by GJNs and the extension of global consumer culture that nurtures cynicism, resignation and apathy among many (Raskin *et al.*, 2002). Under such circumstances, it becomes all the more important for GJNs to nurture the full participation of grassroots communities. However, the problem remains as to how to construct senses of shared (or 'tolerant') identities (della Porta, 2005) among very different place-based communities: the co-recognition and internalisation of others' struggles as our own in a global community. In part this must be based on shared values and principles concerning economic and political justice and ecological sustainability. These, in turn, require the internal motivation of shared dreams or, as we have termed them, collective visions. In addition, this will also require the grounding of network imaginaries in grassroots communities, a process that will need to be attentive to the place-specificity of each movement (and its struggle) that comprise a particular GJN. This will also require plural solutions (that also take account of place-specific conditions and movement contexts) within such broader, shared, collective visions (Eschle and Maiguashca, 2007). However, as our research infers, trade unions are able to mobilise workers across geographic space within the same industry, for example in opposition to a particular TNC. In contrast, social movements do not necessarily have the same strong common grounds upon which to mobilise.

The great strength of the WSF has been its commitment to maintaining itself as a forum refusing to articulate an official platform or resolutions that would endorse specific policy recommendations, despite emergent tensions. By limiting the gathering to the exchange of ideas and information, the broadest range of civil society actors are able to participate. However, as we have seen, the process is slow and flawed, and the leadership is mired in ideological divides and factional power struggles. There is also a lack of transparency in the process and a lack of full democratic mechanisms that could hold the leadership accountable to the interests of the participants.

International solidarity needs to inspire local struggles in local communities. These require not so much a reactive or defensive politics but rather a politics of hope (see R. Solnit, 2004) embodied in proactive, positive interventions and initiatives that produce what Sparke (2007) terms 'geographies of repossession'. This will take on different forms, depending upon the specific features of class struggle present in different places. For peasants and farmers' movements in the Global South it is a battle against primitive accumulation or accumulation by dispossession (Harvey, 2003), but for workers in the Global North it is the struggle against accumulation in production. In either case, it is critical to remember the common enemy: the struggle against commodification and the rule of capital (Cleaver, 2000; Holloway, 2005).

GJNs and geographies of transnational solidarity

> Is it possible to envisage a domain of counter-power to neoliberal globalisation that is conscious of itself and that seeks to deepen connections across, organisations and networks? (Chesters, 2003: 50)

> The constituent power of the multitude has matured to such an extent that it is becoming able, through its networks of communication and cooperation, through its production of the common, to sustain an alternative democratic society on its own. (Hardt and Negri, 2004: 357)

We opened this book by questioning certain claims that have been made concerning what we termed 'the irresistible rise of resistance to neoliberalism'. We questioned (*contra* della Porta *et al.*, 2006) both the existence of a global movement against neoliberal capitalism and claims made about global civil society. The two quotes above are representative of one of the key questions of our time, and an over-optimistic and premature answer to this question.

By analysing three case studies in depth, we have sought to ask a range of questions that attempt to answer the first quote and question the veracity of the second. Do conferences, global days of action, global frame agreements and social fora constitute the emergence of such a global civil society? Are grassroots peasant movements, trade unions or NGOs best equipped, or best represent, such a global civil society? Is such a heterogeneous assemblage unified, or unifiable, and would we want it to be? What are the most appropriate mechanisms for translating informal deliberative moments (e.g. conferences) into more permanent mutual engagements between political actors?

Though we would agree with Hardt and Negri's (2004) general analysis of the emergence of a multitude in its relation to global capital, they present a singular account of the network which is experienced in the same way by different movements and groups. Diverse movements with different trajectories are collapsed into the same structure of commonality. This avoids a consideration of the practices of articulation through which solidarities and alliances are constituted: the constitutive differences, antagonisms, striations, inequalities that cross cut solidarities and collective identities formed through GJNs (cf. Juris 2004a). Their multitude is constituted through smooth space, not situated in particular places. This ignores the diverse and generative connections that make up struggles and transnational networks (Featherstone, 2008). Places are the key sites through which GJNs are made and remade. Moreover, Hardt and Negri project a consciousness as an established fact rather than something which remains to be constructed. As we have tried to show in this book, through a consideration of the convergence spaces of the three different GJNs, the reality on the grounds of struggle is more complex and problematic, and raises a series of issues that shed light upon the difficulties and potentials of constructing transnational solidarity.

For example, in PGA Asia, activists rarely see a connection between the realities of their daily lives and the network. The PGA imaginary remains abstract to many grassroots activists, for whom the networking logic of PGA Asia is unfamiliar, and for whom the immediacy of place-based concerns takes precedent. As one Indian movement leader commented:

> Activists in the villages are often happy to depend upon me to organise the international side of the movement, because they do not see a link between their movement and their daily lives and struggles, and PGA. (interview, Kathmandu, Nepal, 2004)

The idea of grassrooting the imaginaries of global labour struggles is felt as being a major challenge by the union officials interviewed in Europe – the difficulty being the creation of fraternal bonds and shared imaginaries with distant fellow workers, particularly in the new Member States of the EU. The Social Forum process clearly does inculcate a more global consciousness among its participants, but both its sustainability and its wider influence in the mainstream of economic and social life remain open to question.

Understanding the potential for GJNs to develop a sustainable politics of international solidarity involves not just understanding the way that the local is enmeshed in wider spatial relations but also, and perhaps more critically, assessing how the 'global' in invoked in struggles that take place nationally and locally. Overall, our evidence here leads us to be suspicious (*contra* della Porta *et al.*, 2006) of analyses that invoke an emergent global civil society, but instead to draw attention to the entangled operational logics, differential power relations and dilemmas surrounding the grassrooting of network imaginaries that characterise the convergence spaces of GJNs. The emergence of GJNs has not resulted in the finished construction of a global civil society but instead represents an ongoing, uneven process in which continuous effort is required by imagineers to link locally based struggles with a broader global consciousness (Juris, 2004a).

The resonances produced by spectacular global days of action in the media, social science analyses and specific political contexts also shape the self-perception of the movements' actors (Brand and Wissen, 2006). The geographical focus of most of these global days of action occurred in those places where the targets of the actions (e.g. the G8, WTO, etc.) were meeting, namely in North America (e.g. Seattle, 1999; Washington, 2001) or Europe (e.g. Prague, 2000; Genoa,

2001). Hence, it is perhaps unsurprising that is has been European and North American activists and academics who have argued with the most hubris about the emergence of a global movement and a global civil society. As Tarrow (2005) notes, most such global days of action have been characterised by primarily *national* participation. Indeed, most activists in the Global North and South are more closely linked to the local, national and regional movements in which their struggles are embedded than to any global civil society (Glassman, 2001; Eschle and Maiguashca, 2007). Moreover, many movements in the Global South see defence of their local spaces and opposition to national governments (pursuing neoliberal policies) as their most appropriate scales of political action (Mertes, 2002). Even where international campaigns are organised, local and national scales of action continue to be important (Herod, 2001). Indeed, though global events and networks are important, arguably more time and resources should be spent on networking locally and nationally (e.g. constructing more effective *grounded* resistance to the neoliberal project).

Many of the quotidian workings of GJNs (e.g. *certain* conferences, e-mails, even global days of action) constitute 'weak ties' between the network's participant movements. Indeed, it has been argued that too much time is devoted to events, especially conferences, and not enough time on collective actions or in strengthening the more mundane everyday resistance to capital (Ettlinger, 2002; Tormey, 2004b).[2] While conferences are necessary and important networking vectors, they are not sufficient in themselves for the generation of grounded and durable mutual solidarity. GJNs might be able to forge networks of horizontal social solidarities, but these consist of hierarchies of power (within movements, unions and social fora). Therefore, the generation of a genuinely open and transnational public sphere where deepened democracy (Appadurai, 2006) can be practised, and mutual solidarity in resistance to neoliberal globalisation nurtured, is always in process, and is constantly negotiating the geographical dilemmas inherent in movements/'unions' political actors embeddedness in national realities where the state remains a powerful influence (Chesters, 2003).

Therefore, we need to acknowledge the different class and class-fractional positions of various constituencies of Global Northern and Southern movements, for examples, the differential powers of certain Global Northern trade unions in key industries as compared to Global Southern peasant farmers' organisations. Moreover, there are profound situational differences of different militant groups' relationships to the regional and national movements in which they are embedded (Glassman, 2001).

Rather than conceiving of a global civil society, our geographical understandings lead us to reverse the spatial logic in deciphering the significance of GJNs and their potential to develop alternatives to neoliberalism. Where they can be effective is in strengthening local struggles that have the potential to form an alternative politics from the grassroots up. For example, Thai activists who do participate in GJNs do so to gain access to resources (expert testimony, logistical support, international media exposure, etc.) that can be used in struggles for democracy and labour rights within their national civil society (interviews, Bangkok, Thailand, 2004). The same is largely true of the Zapatistas: they used international solidarity networks to bid for national reforms and autonomy within Mexico (Olesen, 2005).

The notion of a global civil society can itself be regarded as another form of top-down politics, although usually cast in liberal rather than revolutionary tones. It is for this reason that we reject it along with other failed vanguard projects of the twentieth century. The 'global' in global civil society remains abstract, and beyond the everyday reach for most activists, even as the effects of a globalising neoliberalism impinge upon their lives. Radicalism ultimately emerges from the grassroots itself out of the experience of repression. The great difference today, compared with movements in the nineteenth or early twentieth centuries, is the potential that exists to connect up these struggles and the ways that this is beginning to happen. However, any discussion of possibilities of transnational solidarity must confront, and then negotiate, a range of messy place-specific 'ground realities'. In other words, sociology and political science must seriously engage with geography. Through exploring the operational dynamics and convergence spaces of three GJNs we have attempted to shed light on the political potential of an emerging global civil society. Our findings suggest that GJNs provide important communicative and coordinative tools to enable geographically scattered political actors (e.g. social movements, NGOs, trade unions) who are, to greater or lesser degrees, locally-based, to extend their spatial reach in order to generate connections with resisting others. In so doing, complex, contradictory and contested spaces of convergence are generated. Certainly, embodied and articu-lated moments of convergence (i.e. conferences and fora), while temporary, enable activists to generate interpersonal relations and affective connections, and exchange ideas, resources, strategies and practices (Juris, 2004a; Eschle and Maiguashca, 2007).

However, looking to the longer term, the sustainability of such networks and their ability to develop a credible alternative politics to neoliberal globalisation will depend, in part, on the extent to which network imaginaries are grounded successfully, and meaningfully, in grassroots communities and workplaces. This will depend, in part, on 'imaginative geographies of connection, composed of sympathies and affinities' (Featherstone, et al., 2007: 388). In this sense, local and national scales remain important in both constraining and facilitating global solidarity. Clearly, resistance to neoliberalism should be neither totally 'local' (see Hines 2000), nor wholly globalised at the level of a world parliament (see Monbiot 2003). Rather, solidarity entails joint articulations between different place-based struggles, opposition to neoliberalism being located at the intersection of different routes of resistance (Featherstone, 2008).

Geographies of protest are uneven. Depending upon their goals and outcomes, struggles against the colonisation of the lifeworld that neoliberalism represents, may be ruptural, involving the revolutionary takeover of the state and the economy; interstitial, involving social empowerment in the niches and margins of society which may have the potential to overtake, displace or ignore capital; or symbiotic, involving institutional reform and the democratisation of the state (Wright, 2006). However, while it is important to celebrate successes when and where they take place, we would argue that it is crucial to attend to the limitations, as well as the liberatory potentials of movements, trade unions, etc. and their convergence in GJNs. This is to caution against ascribing them more than they are capable of achieving, or indeed being (see Brand and Wissen, 2006). Nevertheless, transnational solidarity remains a 'work in progress'; something that remains to be fought for, constructed, defended, sustained and expanded. It is the acknowledgement of the same hope that lives in all of us, and that fuels our anger, inspires our passion and love, and nurtures our pursuit of economic, political and environmental justice.

Notes

1   Many thanks to Sara Koopman for making us aware of this quote.
2   Although see Riles (2001) and McDonald (2006) on the importance of 'events'.

References

Adamovsky, E. and S. George, 'What is the Point of Porto Alegre?', in J. Sen, A. Anand, A., A. Escobar and P. Waterman (eds), *World Social Forum: Challenging Empires* (New Delhi: The Viveka Foundation, 2004), pp. 130–135.

Agrikoliansky, E., O. Fillieule and N. Mayer, *L'Altermondialisme en France: La Longue Histoire d'une Nouvelle Cause* (Paris, Flammarion, 2005).

Albert, M., 'WSF: Where to Now?', in J. Sen, A. Anand, A. Escobar and P. Waterman (eds), *World Social Forum: Challenging Empires* (New Delhi: The Viveka Foundation, 2004), pp. 323–328.

Alvarez, S., E. Dagnino and A. Escobar, 'Introduction', in S. Alvarez, E. Dagnino, and A. Escobar (eds), *Cultures of Politics, Politics of Cultures* (Boulder: Westview Press, 1998), pp. 1–32.

Amin, A., 'Spatialities of globalization', *Environment and Planning A*, 34 (2002), 385–399.

Amin, A., 'Regions unbound: towards a new politics and place', *Geografiska Annaler B*, 86:1 (2004), 31–42.

Amoore, L. and P. Langley, 'Ambiguities of global civil society', *Review of International Studies*, 30 (2004), 89–110.

Anand, A., 'Bound to Mobility? Identity and Purpose at the WSF', in J. Sen, A. Anand, A. Escobar and P. Waterman (eds), *World Social Forum: Challenging Empires* (New Delhi: The Viveka Foundation, 2004), pp. 140–147.

Anheier, H. and H. Katz, 'Network approaches to global civil society', in H. Anheier, M. Kaldor and M. Glasius (eds) *Global Civil Society Year Book 2005/6*. (London, Sage, 2005), pp. 206–221.

Anheier, H., M. Glasius and M. Kaldor, 'Introducing Global Civil Society', in H. Anheier, M. Glasius and M. Kaldor (eds), *Global Civil Society 2001* (Oxford: Oxford University Press, 2001), pp. 1–22.

Anheier, H. and N. Themudo, 'Organisational forms of global civil society: implications of going global', in H. Anheier, M. Glasius and M. Kaldor (eds), *Global Civil Society 2002* (Oxford: Oxford University Press, 2002), pp. 191–216.

Appadurai, A., 'Grassroots Globalization and the Research Imagination', *Public Culture*, 12:1 (2000), pp. 1–19.

Appadurai, A., *Fear of Small Numbers* (Durham, NC: Duke University Press, 2006).

Arquilla, J. and D. Ronfeldt (eds), *Networks and Netwars: The Future of Terror, Crime, and Militancy* (New York: Rand, 2001).

Auyero, J., 'Spaces and places as sites and objects of politics', www. sunysb.edu/sociology/faculty/Auyero/SPACESCONTENTION2.pdf, accessed 1 April 2005, in R. Goodin and C. Tilly (eds), *Oxford Handbook of Contextual Political Analysis* (Oxford: Oxford University Press, 2005).

Ayres, J. M., 'Global Civil Society and International Protest', in G. Laxer and S. Halperin, (eds), *Global Civil Society and Its Limits* (New York: Palgrave, 2003).

Bandy, J. and J. Smith (eds), *Coalitions Across Borders* (Oxford: Rowman and Littlefield, 2005).

Barvosa-Carter, E., 'Multiple Identity and Coalition-Building: How Identity Differences within Us enable Radical Alliances among Us' in J. Bystydzienski and S. Schacht (eds), *Forging Radical Alliances across Difference: Coalition Politics for the New Millennium*, (Lanham, MD: Rowman and Littlefield, 2001), pp. 21–34.

Baschet, J., *La rébellion Zapatiste* (Paris: Champs Flammarion, 2005).

Beaumont, J. and W. Nicholls, 'Between Relationality and Territoriality: investigating the geographies of justice movements in The Netherlands and the United States', *Environment and Planning A.*, 39 (11) (2007), 2554–2574.

Bendt, H., *Worldwild Solidarity: The Activities of the Global Union in the Era of Globilisation* (Bonn: Frierich Ebert Stiftung).

Bennett, W. L., 'Communicating Global Activism', *Information, Communication and Society*, 6:2 (2003), 143–168.

Bey, H., *Temporary Autonomous Zone*, (Brooklyn: Autonomedia, 1991).

Bircham, E. and J. Charlton (eds), *Anti-Capitalism: A Guide to the Movement* (London: Bookmarks, 2001).

Blum, W., *Rogue State* (Monroe, ME: Common Courage Press, 2000).

Bob, C., 'Marketing rebellion: insurgent groups, international media, and NGO support', *International Politics*, 38:3 (2001), 311–334.

Böhm, S., S. Sullivan and O. Reyes, 'Editorial: The Organisation and Politics of Social Forums', *Ephemera*, 5:2 (2005), 98–101.

Bosco, F., 'Place, space, networks, and the sustainability of collective action: the *Madres de Plaza de Mayo*', *Global Networks*, 1:4 (2001), 307–329.

Bosco, F., 'The *Madres de Plaza de Mayo* and Three Decades of Human Rights' Activism: Embeddedness, Emotions, and Social Movements', *Annals of the Association of American Geographers*, 96:2 (2006), 342–357.

Bourgeois, F., *The World Social Forum at a Crossroads* (Geneva, CASIN, 2006).

Bové, J. and F. Dufour, *The World is not for sale* (London: Verso, 2001).

Bramble, T., 'Another world is possible: a study of participants at Australian alter-globalization social forums', *Journal of Sociology* 42:3 (2006), 289–311.

Brand, U. and M. Wissen, 'Neoliberal Globalisation and the Internationalisation of Protest: A European Perspective', *Antipode*, 37:1 (2006), 9–17.

Brandt, J., Geopoetics: *The Politics of Mimesis in Poststructuralist French Poetry and Theory* (Stanford: Stanford University Press, 1997).

Brass, T., *New Farmer's Movements in India* (London: Routledge, 1995).

Braun, B. and L. Disch, 'Radical democracy's "modern Constitution"' *Environment and Planning D: Society and Space*, 20 (2002), 505–511.

Brecher, J. and T. Costello, *Global Village or Global Pillage* (Boston: South End Press, 1994).

Brecher, J., T. Costello and B. Smith, *Globalization from Below* (Boston: South End Press, 2000).

Brown, D. and J. Fox 'Accountability within Transnational Coalitions', in J. Fox and L. Brown (eds), *The Struggle for Accountability: The World Bank, NGOs, and Grassroots Movements* (Cambridge, MA: MIT Press, 1998), pp. 439–484.

Burawoy, M., J. A. Blum, S. George, *et al.* (eds), *Global Ethnography: Forces, Connections and Imaginations in a Postmodern World* (London: University of California Press, 2000).

Burawoy, M., 'For a Sociological Marxism: The Complementary Convergence of Antonio Gramsci and Karl Polanyi', *Politics and Society*, 31:2 (2003), 193–261.

Burgoon, B. and W. Jacoby, 'Patch-work solidarity: describing and explaining US and European labour internationalism', *Review of International Political Economy*, 11:5 (2004), 849–879.

Callinicos, A., *An Anti-Capitalist Manifesto* (Cambridge: Polity Press, 2003).

Callon, M., 'Some Elements For A Sociology of Translation: Domestication of the Scallops and the Fishermen of St-Brieuc Bay', in J. Law (ed.), *Power, Action and Belief : a New Sociology of Knowledge?* (London, Sociological Review Monograph: Routledge and Kegan Paul, 1986).

Callon, M., 'The dynamics of techno-economic networks', in R. Coombs, P. Saviotti and V. Walsh (eds), *Technological change and company strategies: economic and sociological perspectives* (London: Harcourt Brace Jovanovich, 1992), pp. 77–102.

Cardon, D. and F. Granjon, 'Peut-on libérer des formats médiatiques ? Le mouvement alter-mondialisation et l'Internet', *Mouvements*, 25 (2003), 67–73.

Carter, J. and D. Morland, 'Are we all Anarchists now?' in J. Carter, and D. Morland (eds), *Anti-Capitalist Britain* (New Clarion Press: Cheltenham, 2004), pp. 8–28.

Cassen, B., 'On the Attack', *New Left Review*, 19 (2003), 41–60.

Cassen, B., 'Attac against the Treaty', *New Left Review*, 33, (2005), 27–33.

Castells, M., *The Rise of the Network Society* (Oxford: Blackwell, 1996).

Castells, M., *The Power of Identity* (Oxford: Blackwell, 1997).

Castells, M., *End of Millennium* (Oxford: Blackwell, 1998).

Castoriadis, C., *Philosophy, Politics, Autonomy: Essays in Political Philosophy* (Oxford: Oxford University Press, 1991).

Castree, N., 'Geographic Scale and Grassroots Internationalism The Liverpool Dock Dispute 1995–1998', *Economic Geography*, 76:3 (2000), 272–292.

Castree, N., 'False Antitheses? Marxism, Nature and Actor-Networks', *Antipode*, 34:1 (2002), 111–146.

Cecena, A., 'The subversions of historical knowledge of the struggle: Zapatistas in the 21st century', *Antipode* 36, (2004), 361–370.

Chari, S., 'The Vicissitudes of Marxism in "Postmodern" Times' *Antipode*, 35:1 (2003), 178–183.

Chesters, G., 'Shape shifting: Civil Society, complexity and social movements', *Anarchist Studies*, 11:1 (2003), 42–65.

Chin, C. and J. Mittelman, 'Conceptualising Resistance to Globalisation', *New Political Economy*, 2:1 (1997), 25–37.

Cleaver, H., 'Computer-linked Social Movements and the Global Threat to capitalism', http://polnet.html atwww.ecoutexas.edu (1999).

Cleaver, H., *Reading Capital Politically* (Leeds, AK Press, Second Edition, 2000).

J. Cohen and A. Arato, *Civil Society and Political Theory* (Cambridge: MIT Press, 1992).

Cohen, R. and S. M. Rai, (eds), *Global Social Movements* (London: The Athlone Press, 2000).

Cohen, S. and K. Moody, 'Unions, strikes and class consciousness today', in L. Panitch and C. Leys (eds), *Socialist Register* (London, Merlin Press, 1998), pp. 102–123.

Coleman, J., 'Social Capital in the Creation of Human Capital', *The American Journal of Sociology*, 94 (1988), 95–120.

Coleman, M., 'Geopolitics as Social Movement: The Causal Primacy of Ideas', *Geopolitics*, 9:2 (2004), 484–491.

Collins, R., *Interaction Ritual Chains* (Princeton: Princeton University Press, 2004).

Comaroff, J., *Body of Power Spirit of Resistance* (Chicago: University of Chicago Press, 1985).

Comaroff, J. and J. L. Comaroff, 'Introduction', in J. Comaroff, and J. L. Comaroff, (eds), *Civil Society and the Political Imagination in Africa* (Chicago: University of Chicago Press, 1999).

Commons, J. R., 'Institutional Economics', *American Economic Review*, 21 (1931), 648–657.

Conway, J., 'Place Matters: India's Challenge to Brazil at the World Social Forum', *Antipode* 34 (2004), 357–360.

Corbridge, S. and J. Harriss, *Reinventing India* (Cambridge: Polity Press, 2000).

Corbridge, S., 'Countering Empire' *Antipode*, 35:1 (2003), 184–190.

Cresswell, T., 'Embodiment, power and the politics of mobility: the case of female tramps and hobos', *Transactions of the Institute of British Geographers*, 24:2 (1999), 175–192.

Crossley, N., 'The Global Anti-Corporate Movement A Preliminary Analysis', paper presented at the Seventh International Conference on Alternative Futures and Popular Protest Manchester Metropolitan University (2001).

Cumbers, A., 'Embedded internationalisms: building transnational solidarity in the British and Norwegian trade union movements' *Antipode*, 36:6 (2004), 829–850.

Cumbers, A., 'Genuine renewal or pyrrhic victory? The scale politics of trade union recognition in the UK', *Antipode*, 37:1 (2005), 116–138.

Cumbers, A., P. Routledge and C. Nativel, 'The entangled geographies of Global Justice Networks', *Progress in Human Geography*, 32:2 (2008), 179–197.

D'Arcus, B., *Boundaries of Dissent: Protest and State Power in the Media Age* (London: Routledge, 2005).

De Angelis, M., 'Globalization New Internationalism and the Zapatistas', *Capital and Class*, 70 (2000), 9–35.

Debord, G., *La société du spectacle* (Paris: Gallimard, 1967).

De Landa, M., 'Meshworks, Hierarchies and Interfaces' www.t0.or.at/delanda/meshwork.htm, site accessed June 2007.

della Porta, D., 'Multiple Belongings, Tolerant Identities, and the Construction of 'Another Politics': Between the European Social Forum and the Local Social Fora', in della Porta, D. and S. Tarrow (eds), *Transnational Protest and Global Activism* (Lanham, MD: Rowman and Littlefield Publishers, 2005), pp. 175–202.

della Porta, D. and M. Diani, *Social Movements: An Introduciton* (Oxford: Blackwell Publishers, 1999).

della Porta, D. and S. Tarrow 'Transnational Processes and Social Activism: An Introduction', in D. della Porta and S. Tarrow (eds), *Transnational Protest and Global Activism* (Lanham, MD: Rowman and Littlefield Publishers, 2005), pp. 1–17.

della Porta, D. and S. Tarrow (eds), *Transnational Protest and Global Activism* (Lanham, MD: Rowman and Littlefield Publishers, 2005).

della Porta, D., M. Andretta, L. Mosca *et al.*, *Globalization From Below* (London: University of Minnesota Press, 2006).

della Porta, D. and L. Mosca, '*In movimento*: "contamination" in action in the Italian Global Justice Movement', *Global Networks*, 7:1 (2007), 1–27.

Delueze, G. and F. Guatarri, *A Thousand Plateaus* (Minneapolis: University of Minnesota Press, 1987).

Diani, M., *Green Networks* (Edinburgh: Edinburgh University Press, 1995).

Diani, M., 'Social Movements and Social Capital: A Network Perspective on Movement Outcomes', *Mobilizations*, 2:2 (1997), 129–147.

Diani, M. and D. McAdam (eds), *Social Movements and Networks: Relational Approaches to Collective Action* (New York: Oxford University Press, 2002).

Dicken, P., *Global Shift* (London: Sage, 2006).

Dicken, P., P. F. Kelly, K. Olds *et al.*, 'Chains and networks, territories and scales: towards a relational framework for analysing the global economy', *Global Networks*, 1:2 (2001), 89–112.

Dikeç, M., 'Two Decades of French Urban Policy: From Social Development of Neighbourhoods to the Republican Penal State', *Antipode*, 38:1 (2006), 59–81.

Doherty, B., 'Friends of the Earth International: Negotiating a Transnational Identity', *Environmental Politics*, 15:5 (2006), 860–880.

Dowling, E., 'The Ethics of Engagement Revisited: Remembering the ESF 2004', *Ephemera* 5:2 (2005), 205–215.

Doyle, T. and B. Doherty, 'Green Public Spheres and the Green Governance State: the Politics of Emancipation and Ecological Conditionality', *Environmental Politics*, 15:5 (2006), 881–892.

Drainville, A., *Contesting Globalization: Place and Space in the World Economy* (London and New York: Routledge, 2004).

Eschle, C., *Globalizing Civil Society? Globalization and Social Movements* (New York: Palgrave, 2001).

Eschle, C. and B. Maiguashca, 'Rethinking Globalised Resistance: Feminist Activism and Critical Theorising in International Relations', *BJPIR*, 9 (2007), 284–301.

Escobar, A., 'Culture sits in places: reflections on globalism and subaltern strategies of localization', *Political Geography*, 20:2 (2001), 139–174.

Ettlinger, N., 'The Difference that Difference Makes in the Mobilization of Workers', *International Journal of Urban and Regional Research*, 26:4 (2002), 834–843.

Ettlinger, N. and F. Bosco, 'Thinking Through Networks and Their Spatiality: A Critique of the US (Public) War on Terrorism and its Geographic Discourse', *Antipode*, 36:2 (2004), 249–271.

Fagan, A., 'Neither "North" nor "South": The Environment and Civil Society in Post-conflict Bosnia-Herzegovina', *Environmental Politics*, 15:5 (2006), 787–802.

Falk, R. A., 'The State System and Contemporary Social Movements', in S. Mendlovitz and R. Walker, (eds), *Towards a Just World Peace: Perspectives from Social Movements* (London: Butterworths, 1987), pp. 15–48.

Fantasia, R., *Cultures of Solidarity: Consciousness, Action and Contemporary American Workers* (Stanford: University of California Press, 1988).

Featherstone, D., 'Spatialities of transnational resistance to globalization: the maps of grievance of the Inter-Continental Caravan', *Transaction of the Institute of British Geographers*, 28:4 (2003), 404–421.

Featherstone, D., 'Towards the Relational Construction of Militant Particularisms: Or Why the Geographies of Past Struggles Matter for Resistance to Neoliberal Globalisation', *Antipode*, 37:2 (2005), 250–271.

Featherstone, D., R. Phillips and J. Waters, 'Introduction: spatialities of transnational networks', *Global Networks*, 7:4 (2007), 383–391.

Featherstone, D., *Resistance, Space and Political Identities. The Making of Counter-Global Networks*, RGS–IBC Book Series (Oxford: Wiley-Blackwell, 2008).

Fisher, W. F. and T. Ponniah (eds), *Another World is Possible* (London: Zed, 2003).

Foot, P., *The Vote* (London: Penguin, 2005).

Foucault, M., 'Of Other Spaces', *Diacritics*, 16 (1986), 22–27.

Foucault, M., *Power* (London: Penguin Books, 2001).

Fraser, N., *Justice Interruptus: Critical Reflections on the "Postsocialist" Condition* (New York: Routledge, 1997).

Freeman, J., 'The Tyranny of Structurelessness', http://flag.blackened.net/revolt/hist_texts/structurelessness.html, site accessed June 2004 (originally published 1970).

Fukuyama, F., *The End of History and the Last Man* (London: Penguin, 1992).

Gerhards, J. and D. Rucht, 'Mesomobilization Organizing and Framing in Two Protest Campaigns in West Germany', *American Journal of Sociology*, 98:3 (1992), 555–596.

Gibb, E., *International Framework Agreements: Increasing the Effectiveness of Core Labour Standards* (Geneva, ILO Working Paper, 2005). Available at: www.global-labour.org/euan_gibb.htm, last accessed 14 August 2007.

Giddens, A., *The Consequences of Modernity* (Cambridge: Polity Press, 1990).

Gill, S., 'Towards a Postmodern Prince? The Battle of Seattle as a Moment in the New Politics of Globalisation', *Millennium*, 29:1 (2000), 131–140.

Gindin, S., 'Notes on labor at the end of the century: starting over?', in E. Meiskins Wood, P. Meiskins and M. Yates (eds), *Rising from the Ashes? Labor in the Age of Global Capitalism* (New York: Monthly Review Press, 1998), pp. 190–202.

Glassman, J., 'From Seattle (and Ubon) to Bangkok: the scales of resistance to corporate globalization', *Environment and Planning D: Society and Space*, 20:5 (2001), 513–533.

Gordon, N. and P. Chatterton, *Taking Back Control: a journey through Argentina's popular uprising* (Leeds: School of Geography, University of Leeds, 2004).

Graeber, D., 'The New Anarchists', *New Left Review*, 13 (2002), 61–73.

Gramsci, A., *Prison Notebooks* (New York: International Publishers, 1971).

Granovetter, M., 'The Strength of Weak Ties: A Network Theory Revisted', *Sociological Theory*, 1 (1983), 201–233.

Gumbrell-McCormick, R., 'The ICFTU and the World Economy: a Historical Perspective', in R. Munck (ed), *Labour and Globalization* (Liverpool: Liverpool University Press, 2004).

Gunnell, B. and D. Timms, *After Seattle: Globalisation and its Discontents* (London: Catalyst, 2000).

Gupta, A., *Postcolonial Developments* (Durham: Duke University Press, 1998).

Gupta, A. and J. Ferguson, 'Spatializing States', *American Ethnologist*, 29:4 (2002), 981–1002.

Hardt, M., 'Today's Bandung?', *New Left Review*, 14 (2002), 112–118.

Hardt, M. and A. Negri, *Empire* (Cambridge, Massachusetts: Harvard University Press, 2000).

Hardt, M. and A. Negri, *Multitude* (Cambridge, Massachusetts: Harvard University Press, 2004).

Harman, C., 'Anti-capitalism: theory and practice', *International Socialism*, 88, 2000 http://pubs.socialistreviewindex.org.uk/isj88/harman.htm, site accessed May 2006.

Harvey, D., *The Condition of Postmodernity* (Cambridge: Blackwell, 1989).

Harvey, D., *Justice, Nature and the Geography of Difference* (Oxford: Blackwell, 1996).

Harvey, D., *Spaces of Hope*, (Edinburgh: Edinburgh University Press, 2000).

Harvey, D., *The New Imperialsm* (Oxford: Oxford University Press, 2003).

Harvey, D., 'Neo-liberalism as Creative Destruction', *Geografiska Annaler* 88B:2 (2006a), 145–158.

Harvey, D., 'Space as a Keyword', in N. Castree, and D. Gregory (eds), *David Harvey: A Critical Reader* (Oxford: Blackwell Publishing, 2006b), pp. 270–293.

Hayes, G., 'Vulnerability and Disobedience: New Repertoires in French Environmental Protests', *Environmental Politics*, 15:5 (2006), 821–838.

Herod, A. (ed.), *Organizing the Landscape: Geographical Perspectives of Labor Unionism* (Minnesota: University of Minnesota Press, 1998).

Herod, A., *Labor Geographies* (New York: Guildford Press, 2001).

Hines, C., *Localisation: a Global Manifesto* (London: Earthscan, 2000).

Holloway, J., *Change the World Without Taking Power* (London: Pluto Press, 2005).

Holloway, J. and E. Pelaez, 'Introduction: reinventing Revolution', in J. Holloway and E. Pelaez (eds), *Zapatista! Reinventing Revolution in Mexico* (London: Pluto Press, 1998), pp. 1–18.

Holmes, B., 'The Revenge of the Concept', in E. Yuen, D. Burton-Rose, and G. Katsiaficas (eds), *Confronting Capitalism: Dispatches from a Global Movement* (New York: Soft Skull Press, 2004), pp. 347–366.

Houtart, F. and F. Polet, (eds), *The Other Davos: The Globalization of Resistance to the World Economic System* (London: Zed, 2001).

Howell, J., *New Democratic Trends in China? Reforming The All-China Federation of Trade Unions* (Brighton, Institute of Development Studies, 2006).

Huish, R., 'Logos a thing of the past? Not so fast', World Social Forum, *Antipode* 38, 1 (2006), 1–6.

ICEM, *Founding Declaration of the ICEM*. ICEM, Washington DC. Available at: www.icem.org/en/11-ICEM/1358-Founding-Declaration-of-the-ICEM, (1995), last accessed 19 June 2007.

ICEM, *Power and Counterpower: the Union Response to Global Capital* (London: Pluto, 1996).

ICEM, *Statutes* (Brussels: ICEM, 2003a).

ICEM Congress Report, *International Federation of Chemical, Energy, Mining and General Workers* (Brussels, ICEM, 2003b).

Johnston, J. and G. Laxer, 'Solidarity in the age of globalization: lessons from the anti-MAI and Zapatista struggles', *Theory and Society*, 32:1 (2003), 39–91.

Jonas, H., *The Imperative of Responsibility: In Search of an Ethics for the Technological Age* (Chicago: University of Chicago Press, 1984).

Juris, J. S., *Digital Age Activism: Anti-Corporate Globalization and the Cultural Politics of Transnational Networking* (Unpublished Ph.D. Dissertation, University of California, Berkeley, Department of Anthropology, 2004a).

Juris, J. S., 'Networked Social Movements: Global Movements for Global Justice,' in M. Castells (ed.), *The Network Society: a Cross-Cultural Perspective* (Cheltenham: Edward Elgar, 2004b), 341–362.

Juris, J. S., 'The New Digital Media and Activist Networking within anti-Corporate Globalization Movements', *The Annals of the American Academy of Political and Social Science*, 597 (2005a), 189–208.

Juris, J. S., 'Violence Performed and Imagined: Militant Action, the Black Bloc, and the Mass Media in Genoa', *Critique of Anthropology*, 25:4 (2005b), 413–432.

Juris, J. S., 'Social Forums and their Margins: Networking Logics and the Cultural Politics of Autonomous Space', *Ephemera*, 5:2 (2005c), 253–272.

Juris, J., 'Performing Politics: Image, Embodiment, and Affective Solidarity during Anti-corporate Globilization Protests', *Ethnolography*, 9:1 (2008) 61–97.

Kaldor, M., *Global Civil Society* (Cambridge: Polity Press, 2003).

Katz, C., 'On the Grounds of Globalization: A Topography for Feminist Political Engagement', *Signs*, 26:4 (2001), 1213–1229.

Keane, J., *Global Civil Society* (Cambridge: Cambridge University Press, 2003).

Keck, M. and K. Sikkink, *Activist Beyond Borders: Advocacy Networks in International Politics* (Ithaca NY: Cornell University Press, 1998).

Kennedy, J. and M. Lavalette, 'Globalisation, trade unionism and solidarity: further reflections on the Liverpool Dock Lockout', in R. Munck (ed.), *Labour and Globalisation: Results and Prospects* (Liverpool: Liverpool University Press, 2004).

King, J., 'The Packet Gang', *Metamute*, 27, www.metamute.com, site accessed June 2004.

Kirsch, S. and D. Mitchell, 'The Nature of Things: Dead Labor, Nonhuman Actors, and the Persistence of Marxism', *Antipode*, 36:4 (2004), 687–705.

Klein, N., *No Logo* (London: Flamingo, 2000).

Klein, N., *Fences and Windows* (London: Flamingo, 2002).

Larner, W., 'Theorising neo-liberalism: policy, ideology, governmentality', *Studies in Political Economy*, 63 (2000), 5–26.

Latour, B., 'On actor-network theory: A few clarifications', Centre for Social Theory and Technology, Keele University, (1992), www.keele.ac.uk/depts/stt/staff/jl/pubs-jl2.htm, site accessed May 2006.

Latour, B., *We Have Never Been Modern* (Hemel Hempstead: Harvester Wheatsheaf, 1993).

Latour, B., *Reassembling the Social* (Oxford: Oxford University Press, 2005).

Latour, B., *Changer la société – Refaire de la sociologie* (Paris: La Découverte, 2006).

Law, J., 'Notes on the theory of the Actor-Network: Ordering, Strategy and Heterogeneity', Centre for Science Studies, Lancaster University, (1992), www.comp.lancs.ac.uk/sociology/soc054jl.html, site accessed March 2006.

Law, J. and J. Urry, 'Enacting the social', *Economy and Society*, 33:3 (2004), 390–410.

Lee, E., 'Trade unions, computer communications and the new world order', in R. Muck and P. Waterman (eds), *Labour Worldwide in the Era of Globalization*. (Basingstoke: Macmillan, 1999), pp. 229–244.

Lee, E., 'Towards Global Networked Unions', in R. Munck (ed.), *Global Unions* (Liverpool: Liverpool University Press, 2004), pp. 71–82.

Levi, M. and G. Murphy, 'Coalitions of Contention: The case of the WTO protests in Seattle', Unpublished paper, University of Washington, Department of Political Science (2004).

Lipschutz, R., *Global Civil Society and Global Environmental Governance* (Albany, NY: University of New York Press, 1996).

McAdam, D., *Political Process and the Development of Black Insurgency, 1930–1970* (Chicago: University of Chicago Press, 1982).

McAdam, D., S. Tarrow and C. Tilly, *Dynamics of Contention* (Cambridge: Cambridge University Press, 2001).

McDonald, K., 'From Solidarity to Fluidarity: social movements beyond 'collective identity' – the case of globalization conflicts', *Social Movement Studies*, 1:2 (2002), 109–128.

McDonald, K., *Global Movements* (Oxford: Blackwell, 2006).

McLeish, P., 'The promise of the European Social Forum', *The Commoner*, 8 (2004), available at: www.commoner.org.uk/01–12groundzero.htm.

Maffessoli, M., *La transfiguration du politique : la tribalisation du monde postmoderne* (Paris: La Table Ronde, 1992).

Maffesoli, M., *Notes sur la postmodernité. Le lieu fait lien* (Paris: Editions du Félin, 2003).

Maitland, J., *Statement to ICEM Presidium*. Available at: www.cfmeu. asn.au. (2005) Last accessed 4 June 2007.

Mann, M., 'Has Globalisation Ended the Rise and Rise of the Nation-State', *International Review of Political Economy*, 4:3 (1997), 472–496.

Marion Young, I., *Inclusion and Democracy* (Oxford: Oxford University Press, 2001).

Martin, D., ' "Place-framing" as place-making: constituting a neighborhood for organizing and activism', *Annals of the Association of American Geographers*, 93:3 (2003), 730–750.

Massey, D., *Space, Place and Gender* (Minneapolis: University of Minnesota Press, 1994).

Massey, D., 'Imagining globalization: power-geometries of time-space', in A. Brah, M. J. Hickman and M. Mac an Ghaill (eds), *Global Futures: migration, environment and globalization* (Basingstoke: Macmillan 1999), pp. 27–44.

Massey, D., 'Geographies of Responsibility', *Geografiska Annaler*, 86B:1 (2004), 5–18.

Massey, D., *For Space* (London: Sage, 2005).

Mayo, M., *Global Citizens: Social Movements and the Challenge of Globalization* (London: Zed Books, 2005).

Melucci, A., *Challenging Codes* (London: Cambridge University Press, 1996).

Mertes, T., 'Grass-roots Globalism', *New Left Review*, 17 (2002), 101–110.

Mertes, T., *A Movement of Movements: Is Another World Really Possible?* (London: Verso, 2004).

Michels, R., *Political Parties: A Sociological Study of the Oligarchical Tendencies of Modern Democracy* (New York: Transaction, 1998).

Miller, B., *Geography and Social Movements: comparing antinuclear activism in the Boston area* (Minneapolis: University of Minnesota Press, 2000).

Miller, B. (2004) 'Spaces of mobilization: transnational social movements in a globalizing world', in C. Barnett and M. Low (eds), *Spaces of Democracy* (London: Sage Press, 2004), pp. 223–246.

Missingham, B. D., *The Assembly of the Poor in Thailand* (Chiang Mai: Silkworm Books, 2003).

Mitchell, D. and L. Staeheli, 'Permitting protest: parsing the fine geography of dissent in America', *International Journal of Urban and Regional Research*, 25 (2005), 679–699.

Mol, A., 'Ontological Politics. A Word and some questions', in J. Law and J. Hasard (eds), *Actor Network Theory and After* (Oxford: Blackwell, 1999), pp. 74–89.

Monbiot, G., *Captive State* (London: Pan, 2003).

Moody, K., *An Injury to All: The Decline of American Unionism* (New York: Verso, 1987).

Moody, K., *Workers in a Lean World* (London: Verso), 1997.

Morales, A. L., *Medicine Stories* (Boston: South End Press, 1998).

Murdoch, J., 'Inhuman/nonhuman/human: actor-network theory and the prospects for a nondualistic and symmetrical perspective on nature and society', *Environment and Planning D: Society and Space*, 15:6 (1997), 731–756.

Murdoch, J., 'The Spaces of Actor-Network Theory', *Geoforum*, 29:4 (1998), 357–374.

Nagar, R., V. Lawson, L. McDowell, *et al.*, 'Locating Globalization: Feminist (Re)readings of the Subjects and Spaces of Globalization', *Economic Geography*, 78:3 (2002), 257–284.

Nelson, D., *Fingers in the Wound* (Durham, NC: Duke University Press, 1999).

Nelson, L., 'Geographies of state power, protest, and women's political identity formation in Michoacán, Mexico', *Annals of the Association of American Geographers*, 96:2 (2006), 366–389.

Nicholls, W. J., 'The Geographies of Social Movements, *Geography Compass*, 1:3, 607–622.

Notes from Nowhere (ed.), *We are Everywhere* (London: Verso, 2003).

Olesen, T., *International Zapatismo* (London: Zed Books, 2005).

Olivers, D., 'Counter-hegemonic dispersions: the World Social Forum model', *Antipode*, 36:2 (2004), 175–182.

Ong, A., *Buddha is Hiding* (Berkeley: University of Calilfornia Press, 2003).

Osterweil, M., 'De-centering the Forum: Is another critique of the Forum possible?', in J. Sen, A. Anand, A. Escobar, *et al.* (eds), *World Social Forum: Challenging Empires* (New Delhi: The Viveka Foundation, 2004), pp. 183–190.

Passey, F., 'Political altruism and the solidarity movement, an introduction', in Guignin, M. and F. Passy (eds), *Political Altruism? Solidarity Movements in International Perspective* (Lanham, MD: Rowman & Littlefield Publishers (2001), pp. 3–26.

Peck, J. and A. Tickell, 'Neoliberalizing Space', *Antipode*, 34:3 (2002), 380–404.

Pickerill, J., *Cyberprotest: Environmental Activism Online* (Manchester: Manchester University Press, 2003).

Pile, S. and M. Keith (eds), *Geographies of Resistance* (London: Routledge, 1997).

Piven, F. F. and R. A. Cloward, *Poor People's Movements: Why They Succeed, How They Fail* (New York: Random House, 1988).

Plows, A., 'Activist Networks in the UK: Mapping the Build Up to the Anti-Globalization Movement', in J. Carter and D. Morland (eds), *Anti-Capitalist Britain* (New Clarion Press: Cheltenham, 2004), pp. 95–113.

Rai, S. M., 'Networking across borders: the South Asian Research Network on Gender, Law and Governance', *Global Networks*, 3:1 (2003), 59–74.

Ramsay, H., 'Fool's Gold? European Works Councils and Workplace Democracy', *Industrial Relations Journal*, 28 (1997), 314–322.

Ramsay, H., 'In search of international union theory', in J. Waddington (ed.), *Globilization and Patterns of Labour Resistance*, (New York: Mansell, 1999), pp. 192–220.

Raskin, P., G. Banuri, G. Gallopin, *et al.*, *The Great Transition: The Promise and the Lure of the Times Ahead.* (Boston, MA: Tellus Institute, 2002).

Reid, H. and B. Taylor, 'Embodying Ecological Citizenship: Rethinking the Politics of Grassroots Globalization in the United States', *Alternatives*, 25 (2000), 439–466.

Retort, *Afflicted Powers* (London: Verso, 2005).

Ribeiro, G. L., 'Cybercultural Politics Political Activism at a Distance in a Transnational World', in S. E. Alvarez, E. Dagni and A. Escobar, (eds), *Cultures of Politics, Politics of Cultures* (Oxford: Westview Press, 1998), 325–352.

Riles, A., *The Network Inside Out* (Michigan: University of Michigan Press: 2001).

Robinson, A. and S. Tormey (2005) 'Horizontals, Verticals and the Conflicting Logics of Transformative Politics', in C. el-Ojeili and P. Hayden (eds), *Confronting Globalization* (London: Palgrave), pp. 208–226.

Rootes, C. and C. Saunders, 'The global justice movement in Britain', in D. della Porta (ed.), *The Global Justice Movement* (Boulder, CO: Paradigm, 2007), pp. 128–156.

Routledge, P., 'Putting Politics in its Place: Baliapal, India as a Terrain of Resistance', *Political Geography*, 11:6 (1992), 588–611.

Routledge, P., *Terrains of Resistance: Nonviolent Social Movements and the Contestation of Place in India* (Westport: Praeger, 1993).

Routledge, P., 'Space, mobility, and collective action: India's Naxalite movement', *Environment and Planning A*, 9 (1997a), 2165–2189.

Routledge, P., 'A Spatiality of Resistances: Theory and Practice in Nepal's Revolution of 1990', in S. Pile and M. Keith (eds), *Geographies of Resistance* (London: Routledge, 1997b), pp. 68–86.

Routledge, P., 'The imagineering of resistance: Pollok Free State and the practice of postmodern politics', *Transactions of the Institute of British Geographers*, 22 (1997c), 359–376.

Routledge, P., 'Going Globile: Spatiality, Embodiment and Mediation in the Zapatista Insurgency', in S. Dalby and G. O'Tuathail (eds), *Rethinking Geopolitics* (London: Routledge, 1998), pp. 240–260.

Routledge, P., 'Geopoetics of Resistance: India's Baliapal Movement', *Alternatives*, 25 (2000), 375–389.

Routledge, P., 'Convergence Space: process geographies of grassroots globalisation networks', *Transactions of the Institute of British Geographers*, 28:3 (2003a), 333–349.

Routledge, P., 'Voices of the Dammed: discursive resistance amidst erasure in the Narmada Valley, India', *Political Geography*, 22:3 (2003b), 243–270.

Routledge, P., 'Reflections on the G8: An interview with General Unrest of the Clandestine Insurgent Rebel Clown Army (CIRCA)', *ACME: An International E-Journal for Critical Geography*, 3:2 (2005), 112–120.

Routledge, P., 'Acting in the Network: ANT and the Politics of generating Associations', *Environment and Planning D: Society and Space*, 25 (2008).

Routledge, P., A. Cumbers and C. Nativel, 'Entangled Logics and Grassroots Imaginaries of Global Justice Networks', *Environmental Politics*, 15:5 (2006), 839–859.

Routledge, P., A. Cumbers and C. Nativel, 'Grassrooting Network Imaginaries: relationality, power and mutual solidarity in global justice networks', *Environment and Planning A*, 39 (2007), 2575–2592.

Sadler, D., 'Trade unions, coalitions and communities: Australia's Construction, Forestry Mining and Energy Union and the international stakeholder campaign against Rio Tinto', *Geoforum*, 35 (2004), 35–46.

Sans Titre, 'Open Letter to People's Global Action', (2002), http://old.pgaconference.org/_postconference_/pp_sanstitre.htm, site accessed March 2005.

Saunders, C. and C. Rootes, 'The "Movement of Movements" as a "network of Networks": the Global Justice Movement and the "Make Poverty History" march', (2006) paper prepared for ESRC 'Social Capital and Social Movements' seminar series, University of Nottingham, 8 December 2006.

Schlosberg, D., 'Networks and Mobile Arrangements: Political Innovation in the US Environmental Justice Movement', *Environmental Politics*, 6:1 (1999), 122–148.

Schoenberger, E., 'The corporate interview as a research mehod in economic geography', *The Professional Geographer*, 43 (1991), 180–189.

Scott, J., *Weapons of the Weak: Everyday Forms of Peasant Resistance* (New Haven CN: Yale University Press, 1987).

Scott, J., *Domination and the Arts of Resistance* (New Haven CT: Yale University Press, 1992).

Sen, J., 'How Open?', in J. Sen, A. Anand, A. Escobar and P. Waterman (eds), *World Social Forum: Challenging Empires* (New Delhi: The Viveka Foundation, 2004), pp. 210–227.

Sen, J., A. Anand, A. Escobar, *et al.* (eds), *World Social Forum: Challenging Empires* (New Delhi: The Viveka Foundation, 2004).

Sharp, J., P. Routledge, C. Philo, *et al.* (eds), *Entanglements of Power Geographies of Domination/Resistance* (London: Routledge, 2000).

Sikkink, K., 'Patterns of Dynamic Multilevel Governance and the Insider-Outsider Coalition', in D. della Porta and S. Tarrow (eds), *Transnational Protest & Global Activism* (Lanham, MD: Rowman and Littlefield Publishers, 2005), pp. 151–174.

Sklair, L., 'Social Movements and Global Capitalism', *Sociology*, 29:3 (1995), 495–512.

Smith, J., 'Bridging global divides? Strategic framing and solidarity in transnational social movement organisations', *International Sociology*, 1:4 (2002), 505–528.

Smith, J., 'The World Social Forum and the challenges of global democracy', *Global Networks*. 4:4 (2004), 413–421.

Snow, D. and R. Benford 'Alternative Types of Cross-national Diffusion in the Social Movement Arena', in D. della Porta and H. Kriesi (eds), *Social Movements in a Globalising World* (New York: St Martin's, 1999), pp. 23–39.

Solnit, D. (ed.), *Globalize Liberation* (San Francisco, CA: City Lights Books, 2004).

Solnit, R., *Hope in the Dark: Untold Histories, wild possibilities* (New York: Nation Books, 2004).

Sparke, M., 'Geopolitical Fears, Geoeconomic Hopes, and the Responsibilities of Geography', *Annals of the Association of American Geographers*, 97:2 (2007), 338–349.

Sparke, M., E. Brown, D. Corva, *et al.*, 'The World Social Forum and the Lessons for Economic Geography', *Economic Geography*, 81:4 (2005), 359–380.

Sperling, V., M. M. Ferree and B. Risman, 'Constructing Global feminism: Transnational Advocacy Networks and Russian Women's Activism', *Signs: Journal of Women in Culture and Society*, 26:4 (2001), 1155–1186.

St Clair, J., 'Seattle Diary: Its a Gas Gas Gas', *New Left Review*, 23:8 (1999), 81–96.

Starr, A., *Naming the Enemy Anti-corporate movements against globalization* (London: Zed Books, 2000).

Starr, A., *Global Revolt* (London: Zed Books, 2005).

Stirling, J. and B. Tully, 'Power, Process and Practice: Communications in European Works Councils', *European Journal of Industrial Relations*, 10:1 (2004), 73–89.

Subcommandante Marcos ,'Tomorrow Begins Today: invitation to an insurrection', in Notes from Nowhere (ed.), *We are Everywhere* (London: Verso, 2003), pp. 34–37.

Sullivan, L., 'Activism, Affect and Abuse: Emotional Contexts and Consequences of the ESF 2004 Organising Process', *Ephemera*, 5:2, (2005), 344–369.

Sundberg, J., 'Reconfiguring North-South Solidarity: Critical Reflections on Experiences of Transnational Resistance', *Antipode*, 39:1 (2007), 144–166.

Sunley, P., R. Martin and C. Nativel, *Putting Workfare in Place: Local Labour Markets and the New Deal* (Oxford: Blackwell Publishing, 2005).

Tarrow, S., *The New Transnational Activism* (Cambridge: Cambridge University Press, 2005).

Tarrow, S. and D. McAdam, 'Scale Shift in Transnational Contention', in D. della Porta, and S. Tarrow (eds), *Transnational Protest and Global Activism* (Boulder CO: Rowman & Littlefield, 2005), pp. 121–150.

Teivainen, T., 'The World Social Forum and global democratisation: learning from Porto Alegre', *Third World Quarterly*, 23:4 (2002), 621–632.

Thompson, G., 'Is the world a complex network?', *Economy and Society*, 33 (2004), 411–424.

Thrift, N., 'The still point: resistance, expressive embodiment and dance', in S. Pile and M. Keith (eds), *Geographies of Resistance* (London: Routledge, 1997), pp. 124–151.

Tilly, C., *Trust and Rule* (Cambridge: Cambridge University Press, 2005).

Torgerson, D., 'Expanding the Green Public Sphere: Post-colonial Connections', *Environmental Politics*, 15:5 (2006), 713–730.

Tormey, S., *Anti-capitalism: a beginner's guide* (Oneworld: Oxford, 2004a).

Tormey, S., 'The 2003 European Social Forum: Where next for the anticapitalist movement?', *Capital & Class*, 84 (2004b), 151–160.

Tormey, S., 'After the Party's Over: The Horizontalist Critique of Representation and Majoritarian Democracy – Lessons from the Alter-Globalisation Movement (AGM)', (2005) paper presented at the European Consortium on Political Research, Granada, 2005.

Touraine, A., *La voix et le regard* (Paris: Le Seuil, 1978).

Uhlenbeck, M., A Light Within (the Heart of Empire): The 2007 US Social Forum. *ZMag* (2007) June (www.zmag.org, accessed at 2 July).

Urry, J., *Global Complexity* (London: Polity Press, 2003).

Urry, J., 'Small worlds and the new "social physics"', *Global Networks*, 4:2 (2004), 109–130.

Valins, O., *Identity, Space and Boundaries: Ultra-Orthodox Judaism in Contemporary Britain* (Unpublished Ph.D Thesis, Department of Geographical and Earth Sciences, University of Glasgow, 1999).

Vanaik, A., 'Rendezvous at Mumbai', *New Left Review*, 26 (2004), 53–65.

Vaneigem, R., *The Revolution of Everyday Life* (London: Rebel Press, 1983).

Wainwright, H., *Reclaim the State* (London, Verso, 2003).

Walby, S., 'The myth of the nation state: Theorizing society and politics in a global era', *Sociology*, 37 (2003), 529–546.

Wallerstein, I., 'New revolts against the system', *New Left Review*, 18 (2002), 11–29.

Wallerstein, I., 'The dilemmas of open space: the future of the WSF', *International Social Science Journal*, 56 (2004), 629–637.

Wallgren, T., 'Political Semantics of 'globalization': A brief note', *Development*, 41:2 (1998), 30–32.

Warren, K., 'Narrating Cultural Resurgence: genre and Self-Representation for Pan-Mayan Writers', in D. Reed-Danahay (ed.), *Auto/Ethnography: Rewriting the Self and the Social* (Oxford: Berg, 1997), pp. 21–45.

Waterman, P., *Globalization, Social Movements, and the New Internationalisms* (Washington, DC: Mansell, 1998).

Waterman, P., 'The Secret of Fire', in J. Sen, A. Anand, A. Escobar, *et al.* (eds), *World Social Forum: Challenging Empires* (New Delhi: The Viveka Foundation, 2004), pp. 148–160.

Waterman, P., *The Bamako Appeal of Samir Amin: a post-modern Janus!* CSGR Working Paper No. 212/06 (Warwick, Centre for the Study of Globalisation and Regionalisation, 2006).

WDM, *States of Unrest: Resistance to IMF Policies in Poor Countries* (London: World Development Movement, 2000).

WEA, *International Study Circles* (London: Workers Educational Association, 2000).

Webster, E., K. Lambert and A. Bezuidenhaut, *Grounding Globilization: Labour in the Age of Insecurity* (Oxford: Blackwell).

Welker, M., 'A Global Superorganic', *Antipode*, 35:1 (2003), 191–193.

Weston, S. and M. Martinez Lucio, 'Trade unions, Management and European Works Councils: Opening Pandora's Box', *International Journal of Human Resource Management*, 8 (1997), 764–770.

Whatmore, S., *Hybrid Geographies* (London: Sage, 2002).

Williams, R., *Politics and Letters* (London: New Left Books, 1979).

Williams, R., *Resources of Hope* (London: Verso, 1989).

Wills, J., 'Great expectations: Three years in the life of one EWC', *European Journal of Industrial Relations*, 6 (2000), 83–105.

Wolford, W., 'This Land Is Ours Now: Spatial Imaginaries and the Struggle for Land in Brazil', *Annals of the Association of American Geographers*, 94:2 (2004), 409–424.

Wood, L. J., 2005: 'Bridging the Chasms: The Case of People's Global Action', in J. Bandy and J. Smith (eds), *Coalitions Across Borders* (Oxford: Rowman and Littlefield, 2005), pp 95–120.

Wright, E. O., 'A Compass for the Left', *New Left Review*, 41 (2006), 93–124.

Yuen, E., D. Burton-Rose and G. Katsiaficas (eds), *Confronting Capitalism: Dispatches from a Global Movement* (New York: Soft Skull Press, 2004).

Index